Surviving Images

Surviving Images

CINEMA, WAR, AND CULTURAL MEMORY
IN THE MIDDLE EAST

Kamran Rastegar

OXFORD
UNIVERSITY PRESS

OXFORD
UNIVERSITY PRESS

Oxford University Press is a department of the University of
Oxford. It furthers the University's objective of excellence in research,
scholarship, and education by publishing worldwide.

Oxford   New York
Auckland   Cape Town   Dar es Salaam   Hong Kong   Karachi
Kuala Lumpur   Madrid   Melbourne   Mexico City   Nairobi
New Delhi   Shanghai   Taipei   Toronto

With offices in
Argentina   Austria   Brazil   Chile   Czech Republic   France   Greece
Guatemala   Hungary   Italy   Japan   Poland   Portugal   Singapore
South Korea   Switzerland   Thailand   Turkey   Ukraine   Vietnam

Oxford is a registered trademark of Oxford University Press
in the UK and certain other countries.

Published in the United States of America by
Oxford University Press
198 Madison Avenue, New York, NY 10016

© Oxford University Press 2015

Library of Congress Cataloging-in-Publication Data
Rastegar, Kamran.
Surviving images : cinema, war, and cultural memory in the Middle East / Kamran Rastegar.
pages cm
Includes bibliographical references and index.
ISBN 978-0-19-939016-8 (cloth)—ISBN 978-0-19-939017-5 (pbk.)—ISBN 978-0-19-939018-2
(updf)   1. Memory in motion pictures.   2. Psychic trauma in motion pictures.   3. Middle
East—In motion pictures.   4. War films—Middle East—History and criticism.   I. Title.
PN1995.9.M455R38 2015
791.43'653—dc23
2014035494

1 3 5 7 9 8 6 4 2
Printed in the United States of America
on acid-free paper

For Christine

{ CONTENTS }

{ ACKNOWLEDGMENTS }

The list of individuals and institutions whose support at one or another point were instrumental to the progress and completion of this book is lengthy. These acknowledgments take me back to my graduate studies, where my work with Hamid Dabashi, Richard Peña, Maura Spiegel, and a seminar taken with Andreas Huyssen first inspired me to explore the links between social trauma, cultural memory, and cinema. Later, in my first teaching position, I found support for the pursuit of this project at the University of Edinburgh, and am grateful to Yasir Suleiman, Carole Hillenbrand, and Marilyn Booth for their encouragement of my pursuit of this project. During that time, the British Council and the British Society for Middle Eastern Studies of supported my establishing a research network on the topic of "Memory and Social Trauma in the Middle East," which led to a fruitful workshop in 2008 that brought together, I believe possibly for the first time, an engaged community of scholars united by their interest in how cultural memory has shaped the societies of this region. I thank those who contributed to this workshop, including Shahab Esfandiary, Christiane Gruber, Sune Haugbolle, Tom Hill, Lina Khatib, Pedram Khosronejad, Stephan Milich, Dalia Mostafa, and Lina Tahan. Beyond the workshop, this research network cosponsored two symposia, the first on New Arab Cinemas (2007) and the second on Cultural Memory in Iraq (2008), whose many participants also influenced my thinking on these texts and topics. Collaborating with Beirut DC on the former event, which also included a film festival, was a wonderful and stimulating experience. I thank Hania Mroué, Zeina Zahreddine, and Eliane Raheb for their work on this project, as well as the filmmaker Ghassan Salhab, who visited Edinburgh for this festival to present his film *Al-Atlal*.

Additionally, this project benefitted from frequent discussions with colleagues at Edinburgh and elsewhere in the United Kingdom, in particular Martine Beugnet, Kay Dickinson, John Chalcraft, Hannah Holtschneider, Toby Kelly, and Laleh Khalili. At Edinburgh, my graduate students, among them Kifah Hanna, Maryam Ghorbankarimi, and Jokha Alharthi, made significant contributions to aspects of this work. Finally, I was supported by a grant from the British Society for the Study of the Levant, which allowed me to travel to Israel and Palestine for research, which occasioned meetings with scholars and filmmakers there, including among many others Raed Andoni, Udi Aloni, Raed Al-Helou, Annemarie Jacir, Rachel Jones, George Khleifi,

Rashid Masharawi, Avi Mograbi, and finally Juliano Mer Khamees, whose life was tragically and horrifically cut short as this book was being written.

At Tufts University I have found inestimable support from my departmental chairs Hosea Hirata and Greg Carleton, and institutional commitment in the form of a one-year fellowship at the Center for Humanities at Tufts; and my collaborations with Lisa Lowe, Kris Manjapra, and other colleagues in the Consortium on Studies of Race, Diaspora and Ethnicity have given energy to this project. Most of the writing of this book was facilitated by Tufts's generous funding of a year's research leave, during which I was resident in Lebanon. In Beirut, my work was greatly enriched by my affiliation with the English department of the American University in Beirut and exchanges with colleagues there—an affiliation made possible by David Wrisley's initiative. Additionally in Beirut, participating as an instructor in the Ashkal Alwan Homeworks Studio Program allowed me to develop ideas in this book in dialogue with a dynamic group of young international artists in residence in Beirut. For this opportunity I must thank both Emily Jacir and Christine Tohme, as well as the participant artists of the program: Mohamed Abdel Karim, Noor Abu Arafeh, Roy Dib, Maria Elena Fantoni, Sarah Farahat, Raphael Fleuriet, Saba Innab, Samar Kanafani, Mahmoud Khaled, Joe Namy, Haig Papazian, and Tamara Samerrae.

Finally, I thank the editorial staff at Oxford University Press, in particular Brendan O'Neill for his enthusiasm in shepherding the project to conclusion, and Stephen Bradley, David Joseph, and Michael Durnin for their work in the copyediting and proofing stages of the book. The anonymous reviewers of the book's first manuscript provided critical and productive suggestions that were both erudite and generous. Part of chapter 5 was published in a different form as "The Glass Agency: Iranian War Veterans As Heroes or Traitors?" in *Traitors: Suspicion, Intimacy, and the Ethics of State-Building*, edited by Sharika Thirangama and Tobias Kelly. Philadelphia: University of Pennsylvania Press, 2010, 188–199. Portions of chapter 7 appeared in an earlier form as "Sawwaru Waynkum: Human Rights and Social Trauma in Waltz With Bashir," *College Literature* 40:3 (2013), 60–80, published by Johns Hopkins University Press. I am grateful to these publishers for permission to reprint this material here.

For many things, I am indebted to Christine Bustany, to whom this book is dedicated: I hope that this modest work in a small way testifies to the transformative inspiration she has given my life.

Surviving Images

Introduction

Cinema's vaunted social power is perhaps first and best captured in a notorious comment attributed to the American president Woodrow Wilson, upon his viewing of *Birth of a Nation* (1915). Wilson has been widely reported as having said that this seminal work of narrative filmmaking was like "writing history with lightning."[1] The profundity of this quote derives no little from the recognition that the origins of the greatest art form of the twentieth century will forever be identified with racism and communal hatred (which are celebrated in *Birth of a Nation*), but also reflects upon the fact that this medium was perhaps unrivaled for the advancement of claims upon the making of history. The poesis of light and movement that the seventh art perfected with such power has therefore always borne with it the burden of this origin, a burden of *writing history*, but only if history itself is seen as a discursive elaboration of a broader field of cultural memory. *Birth of a Nation* was much more an act of revising American cultural memory of the post–Civil War period than it was a work with any significant relationship to the discipline of history. By attending to a wound on the psyche of white Americans, not a small proportion of whom viewed the promise of equality for blacks with a tribal sense of alarm, *Birth of a Nation* represents the Civil War and its aftermath as a national trauma for whites rather than as a victory (as the prevailing, Unionist, telling would have presented it). Recasting the history of the Reconstruction, *Birth of a Nation* allowed those white Americans who were drawn to this narrative to communally share in a cultural memory of this period that presented the rise of the Ku Klux Klan as a redemptive turn after the traumas of the war. This model—of social trauma that results in the production of cinema as history, cinema as cultural memory—would be repeated across the world over the next century, by putative victors and colonial overlords to begin with, but also increasingly by those who were their subjects and victims. Wilson's attributed phrase portends the role that cinema would come to assume—a screen, however contested, upon which the images that defined cultural memory would be displayed.

In the present work, I begin with the notion that cinema has increasingly contributed to the production of cultural memory relating to social conflicts—often, in turn, contributing to what will here be described as "social trauma." At times, cinema even has served to play a significant and unique role in opposing dominant appropriations of, or conversely, cultural amnesia toward, the memory of conflicts. Offering new readings of canonical films, as well as discussing the work of filmmakers who have so far not enjoyed sufficient critical attention, I here examine cultural memory production and conflict through three historical periods: the colonial age, the independence moment, and the postcolonial period. Beginning with a study of British colonial cinema on the Sudan, then exploring anticolonial cinema in Algeria, Egypt, and Tunisia, followed by case studies of films emerging from postcolonial contexts in Palestine, Iran, Lebanon, and Israel, I resituate discussions of Middle Eastern cinema both regionally and globally. In so doing, this work aims to fill a gap in the critical literature on both Middle Eastern and North African cinemas and the cultural memory of conflict.

It bears mention here that the reader will quickly discern that the term "Middle East" as utilized here is nothing more than a relatively arbitrary boundary marker for the subject under discussion. Not wishing to revisit discussions of the origins and artificiality of the term and the various presumptions its incantation often rests upon (whether as a fallacious stand-in for representations of Islam, or as a hologram-phoenix rising from the ashes of the "Orient"), the grouping of themes and questions discussed in this book only coincidentally conforms to the geography of the Middle East, and could easily have been drawn to include other contexts, and areas. Put otherwise, this is not a book about the Middle East *per se*, since in this discussion I do not presume any coherent identity to the term. When teaching, in explaining the arbitrary origins and designations of the term Middle East to my students, I often only somewhat humorously suggest that a better term may be CENTCOM (which of course maps a somewhat different if equally arbitrary global space than "Middle East" does). The benefit of a term such as "CENTCOM Studies" is at the very least to make clear the interests behind the act of naming: specifically, military-imperial interests. Nonetheless, the term Middle East does appear in the title of this book; *CENTCOM Cinemas* was simply too inelegant and would have omitted Algeria (itself only misunderstood as in the Middle East—but to add North Africa to our nomenclature here would only give each of these problematic terms further legitimacy), as well as Palestine/Israel. So, beyond a few references in the introduction, the term Middle East will not appear within the pages of this book, and a reader seeking a holistic argument about the Middle East may well be disappointed to find none presented here. However, it is hoped that students of other regionally and/or linguistically delimited cultural studies will find much in these discussions that should be reasonably familiar, whether they are students of South Asia, Latin America, Africa, or other regions. Where possible, but perhaps still insufficiently, I have attempted to gesture to such global continuities within the register of the postcolonial, which is perhaps the truer framing term that organizes this book.

In this book, each chapter addresses specific, often national, historical contexts through detailed discussions of films concerning the experiences of war, communitarian violence, and other forms of politicized discord—termed here generically as "social conflict." Each chapter respectively engages specific questions: How have the cinemas of colonial powers constructed memories of wars against anticolonial forces, as in cinematic treatments of the Mahdist revolt against British colonialism in Sudan? What is the role of cinema in the remembrance of the Algerian, Tunisian, and Egyptian anticolonial struggles? How does the cinematic medium reflect the changing dynamics of Palestinian cultural memory of 1948? How has Iranian cinema both contributed to, but also challenged, state-directed memorializations of the Iran-Iraq war? What role does cinema play in the articulation of Lebanese postwar communitarian discourse? How does cinema illustrate the use of the concept of trauma as it relates to Israeli memories of wars and occupation? These specific discussions intersect thematically and comparatively, and cover a range of social and historical contexts. Through these comparative case studies, I illustrate cinema's productive role in contributing to the changing dynamics of cultural memory of social conflicts.

I have chosen these contexts for this study because they each remain paradigmatic to concerns that remain vital to our understanding of cultural memory as it relates to colonialism, the postcolonial context, and present formations of empire and imperialism. The Algerian War of Independence presents a *longue durée* setting for exploring the links between colonialism, anticolonialism, and the postcolonial traumas that mark cultural memory of the war. Similarly, while the British adventures in Sudan in the late nineteenth century may seem now to be a minor digression within the broader histories of colonialism, I explore representations of this period primarily because it is clear that the loss of Khartoum in 1885 constituted a form of social shock or trauma to imperial Britain that offers an illustration of how colonizing societies also made use of paradigms of social trauma in forming cultural memory of their imperial period—and how these memories are reinscribed into the social imaginary in subsequent generations. The discussion of colonizing traumas is balanced by an exploration of anticolonial traumas in Egypt and Tunisia, closing out the first part of the book. The second part of the book includes discussions of Israel and Palestine, Iran, and Lebanon, which interrelate in a variety of ways, exploring the production of cultural memory both as a result of state-led initiatives, or in the face of state suppression of this memory, or indeed in the face of cultural memory formed by a stateless people.

In terms of its theoretical orientation, this book intervenes in critical discussions on cultural memory and social trauma. Following the assertion by Ussama Makdisi and Paul Silverstein (2006, 1) that "the myths and narratives that found and sustain modern national politics are situated at the intersection of competing collective memories of violence," I treat cinema as a critical arena for discerning the process of competition over cultural memory, arguing that cinema may at times reaffirm dominant readings of these memories, while at other times subjects them to critique. I use "cultural memory" quite broadly, in the manner proposed by Mieke Bal (Bal, Crewe, and Spitzer 1999, vii), as a "cultural phenomenon as well as an individual or social one," that is as much a reflection on the *present* as on the *past*. Indeed, cultural memory is a "product of collective agency rather than the result of psychic or historic accident." By linking cultural memory to the cinematic text, I also make use of Annette Kuhn's (2002) elaboration of "cinema memory," which highlights cinema's role in the development of cultural memory, as well as Janet Walker's (2005) category of "trauma films" and E. Ann Kaplan's (2005) conception of "trauma culture" as ways to describe films that participate in cultural discourse on historically or socially traumatic experiences. What emerges in my analysis is a discussion where cinematic works from the Middle East, and, in particular, those that may be termed trauma films, come to produce cinema memories of experiences of social violence. These cinema memories, in turn, I argue, contribute significantly to the development of cultural memory of these experiences.

Much of the predominant research on memory, trauma, and cinema treats the cinematic text as a screen upon which psychoanalytic theory is animated.[2] While such approaches inform *Surviving Images*, I prioritize more recent interventions made by sociocultural treatments of the concepts of both cultural memory and social trauma in studying cinematic treatments of social violence in colonial and postcolonial contexts. Methodologically, I pursue a synthesis between socially situated and close-reading approaches, disentangling the sometimes esoteric complexities of trauma theory, and breaking with the often hermetic approaches of area studies and national cinema scholarship that has defined much of the work on colonial and postcolonial cinemas such as those about and from societies of the Middle East.

This book comprises three notional sections, each performing a separate but integral role in the construction of the book's argument. First, I dedicate one chapter to using the aftermath of the Algerian struggle for independence as a portal through which the key questions at the heart of this study may be illuminated, examining theoretical and methodological debates. Next, over the course of two chapters, I lay out a historical narrative, at first examining cinematic works of the British colonial period from the perspective of the colonial metropole, and then look to films about the anticolonial liberation struggles of Egypt and Tunisia. In the subsequent four chapters, I explore thematic questions that arise from largely postcolonial contexts, illustrating each question through a close reading of selected films that address these contexts.

Chapter 1 outlines the primary concerns of *Surviving Images*—that is, how social conflict and cultural memory intersect within the cinematic text—and illustrates the book's methodological and conceptual landscape. I begin by examining the circumstances surrounding the controversy over the Cannes Film Festival premiere of Rachid Bouchareb's *Outside the Law* (*Hors-la-Loi*, 2010), which led to unprecedented public demonstrations on the edge of the festival's red carpet, and look to Bouchareb's earlier film, *Days of Glory* (*Indigénes*, 2006), as a more successful antecedent. *Outside the Law* relates the story of three Algerian brothers in France from the 1940s through the early 1960s as they respond in different ways to the call of national liberation for Algeria, while the earlier film tells the "forgotten history" of North and West African soldiers who fought for the French Free Army in the Second World War. Through a brief discussion of the films and their different receptions, I argue that *Outside the Law* and *Days of Glory* in different ways exemplify the social power of cinema to intervene upon and renarrate the cultural memory of historically traumatic or irresolute conflicts.

I treat the release of these films as a means to explore how cinema may tread into the fraught arena of trauma production, counteracting the social claims of some groups while enhancing those of others. I do so by historically reviewing the colonial presence throughout cinema's centurial history, examining the preindependence colonial film as well as the rise of the anticolonial and postindependence cinemas of the postcolonial world. Then I link colonial culture to social trauma and cultural memory, and lay out shortcomings in the perhaps dominant, psychoanalytically oriented, trends in trauma and memory studies. I next present a discussion of certain sociological approaches, which emphasize an understanding of cultural memory and social trauma as processes of social activity and performance. I conclude that *Outside the Law* and *Days of Glory* illustrate the way by which the cultural memory of colonialism lays out discursive terrains that remain contested. Consequently, I assert that these debates are crucial to the articulation of ideological formations (whether colonial or anticolonial) and to the development of various forms of identity (such as national, gender, or ethnic identity) for societies in the Middle East and the broader postcolonial world.

Chapters 2 and 3 outline a historical perspective on cinematic representations of the colonial period and independence moment. Chapter 2 focuses upon the British colonial context, beginning with an examination of the British imperial defeat in Khartoum in 1885 at the hands of Sudanese Mahdists, a defeat which the metropole termed a "traumatic" shock, one that had great repercussions on British conceptions of the colonial project. A. E. W. Mason's classic early Edwardian novel *The Four Feathers* (1902), offers a paradigmatic textual response to this traumatic shock, in that it conceives of redemption as being won through the restoration of what I term fraternal-military colonial masculinity.

With at least seven film renditions having been produced of the work between 1915 and 2002, *The Four Feathers* enjoyed an extraordinary longevity as a vessel first for colonial propaganda and later for colonial nostalgia. I here examine the three most successful film adaptations of the novel (1929, 1939, 2002). The 1929 version, by Cooper and Shoedsack, promotes a synthesis of American settler-colonial masculinity and a colonial ideology of racial supremacy. In contrast, the 1939 Korda brothers' version, released in the shadow of the Second World War, evokes a nostalgic resurrection of the novel's fraternal-military chivalry for an empire that was weakening. Perhaps most provocative is the 2002 version, directed by Shekhar Kapur, which constitutes a self-consciously "postcolonial" rethinking of the story, but one that I argue fails its stated aims due to its refusal to critique the idealization of imperial masculinity at the heart of the novel. Notwithstanding their differences, I argue that each of these versions of *The Four Feathers* illustrates a recurrent theme in colonial cinema and later of cultural memory of colonialism, one that constitutes colonial supremacy as predicated upon its projection and celebration of certain masculine ideals. In doing so, these films may be viewed as attempting to recuperate the traumatic memory of the defeat of empire by the colonized.

In chapter 3, I examine visual and cinematic representations of anticolonial independence, as they intersect with themes of cultural memory and social trauma, through their idealization of women's roles in the independence struggle. In particular, I focus on three films centered on women's experiences within the Egyptian and Tunisian anticolonial struggles, Salah Abu Sayf's *I Am Free* (*Ana hurra*, 1958), Henri Barakat's *The Open Door* (*Al-Bab al-maftuh*, 1963), and Moufida Tlatli's *The Silences of the Palace* (*Samt al-qusur*, 1992). I read these films as being motivated by a crisis of changing gender roles within the family structure of the colonized, revealing gendered discourses in the representation of anticolonial struggle. In particular, this gendering strategy sets parameters for the production of cultural memory on resistance to colonialism, and the figure of the committed woman plays a central role in framing the memory of the independence struggle.

Abu Sayf's film posits the freedom of its protagonist—and that of any committed woman—to be predicated on her submission to the political cause rather than to other social goals, such as the education of women or improvements in their roles in the workplace. Through this submission, the protagonist finally becomes free—but only when she has been imprisoned for her activism alongside her lover. In the final scene, they marry while in jail, just days before the 1952 revolution. I trace this process of gendered memorialization then to *Silences of the Palace*, which regards the anticolonial struggle as fundamentally marginal to the concerns for lower-class working women, and which presents their political engagement as subject to betrayal by the political classes in the postindependence period. In the film's structure, specifically by virtue of its framing of the story as a long flashback, memory is presented as productive to redeeming the liberatory potentials of anticolonialism for women. By illustrating the shifting registers of cultural memory (from 1950s Egypt to 1990s Tunisia) regarding the occluded place of women within the anticolonial struggle, I argue that cinema memory of the struggle betrays the ideological role of gendering within both colonial and anticolonial narratives.

Chapter 4 enters into what may be viewed as both a colonial and post-colonial context, introducing more thematic considerations that character-ize the following three chapters as well. It does so by looking at questions of cultural memory as they pertain to Palestinian cinema's reflections on the Nakba ("catastrophe") that resulted from the establishment of the Israeli state in 1948, the dispossession that most Palestinians experienced in that war, and the ongoing losses and denials to which they have been subjected. My analysis focuses upon a trilogy of feature film works by the Palestinian director Elia Suleiman—*Chronicle of a Disappearance* (1996), *Divine Intervention* (2002), and *The Time that Remains* (2009)—as they relate to the role of cultural and personal memory. I first contextualize these films by presenting an overview of Palestinian cultural memory discourse from the 1960s through the 1990s, showing how narrative treatments of the Nakba's aftermath evolve from seek-ing foreclosure upon the losses of 1948, to encountering unanswerable ques-tions, or aporias.

Introducing Elia Suleiman, I suggest that few if any Palestinian filmmakers have developed as coherent a cinematic language for exploring the aporetic dimensions of Palestinian experience as he. As I illustrate, Suleiman's cin-ematic language leads, both on the level of narrative and on the level of scene and shot, to unanswerable questions, refusing the narrative closures that characterize normative cinematic techniques. These aporias in part reflect a suspended trauma expressed as personal experience—such as through fol-lowing the illness and death of the films' protagonist's parents—that alludes to the broader predicament of Palestinian cultural memory. I argue that between the stark distinctions in visualizing Palestinian and Israeli expe-rience, Suleiman refuses the mimetic burden of documentary (associated with the Palestinian experience), but also challenges the ideological stric-tures of narrative fiction (ostensibly the privilege of the Israeli). I conclude by arguing that Suleiman's aporias broadly reflect the suspended trauma that characterizes post-1948 Palestinian experience—the irresolution of the trau-mas of the Nakba and its continuation in the form of subsequent losses and further tragedies.

Chapter 5 examines the parameters of Iranian cultural discourse on the Iran-Iraq war, looking both at officially sanctioned war and postwar cinema, as well as at works that emerge in ways that are at odds with the official discourse. I begin with an overview of what is officially termed "sacred defense" cinema, a genre promoting the Iranian state's official narrative on the war and its aftermath, showing that the genre is dynamic and even at times a venue for critique of the state ideology from within. I explore this through a discussion of Ebrahim Hatamikia's work, specifically his films *Minu's Watch Tower* (*Borj-e Minu*, 1996), which constitutes a moment of crisis for the genre, and his later work, *The Glass Agency* (*Ajanse shisheh'i*, 1997), which constitutes a further break from this official form of cultural memory, but still from within the genre. I then outline attempts to address cultural memory concerning the war arising from outside the sacred defense field. In particular, I present a reading of Bahram Beyzai's *Bashu, The Little Stranger* (*Bashu, gharibeh-ye kuchak*, 1987), arguing that this film participates in an indirect and subtle contestation of the grounds of the sacred defense field's monopoly on the cultural memory of the war. *Bashu* is a work that is marked by an urgent need to respond to the traumatic resonances of the war, by developing a language and aesthetics set outside the hermetic sphere of sacred defense culture. As a result, the film's innovative cinematic language challenges not only the normative Iranian commercial genres (including sacred defense cinema), but also more broadly those of globally dominant narrative genres. Through the broad comparison of critiques of official ideology emerging from both inside and outside the sacred defense field, I argue that the discursive limits set by this field are both fragile and permeable, and that pressure from within and without has resulted in a demand for the field to open up to other forms of cultural memory around the war.

Chapter 6 examines Lebanese representations of war, namely, the 1975–1991 Lebanese civil war and the 2006 Israeli war. In doing so, it presents a trajectory of how the war's memory is constituted in film and put to social use. Whereas early cinematic works of the civil-war generation, exemplified here through readings of the works of Mai Masri and Jean Chamoun (in particular *Under the Rubble* [*Taht al-inqadh*] 1982, and *Suspended Dreams* [*Ahlam mu'alliqa*], 1991), are motivated by witnessing and justice-seeking goals, certain later films produced at perhaps the height of Lebanese optimism vis-à-vis reconstruction are often more concerned with seeking a resolution to the war's traumas; for example, the films *West Beirut* (*Bayrut gharbi*, 1996) and *Zozo* (2005). The latter films seek, through melo dramatic narrative conventions, to produce an ameliorative "healing" of the war's divisions that accords with the broader reconstruction ideology that gained ascendancy during the postwar period.

In contrast, in other films of the reconstruction period, hints of specters and references to a liminal space between life and death seem to serve as a warning that the ghosts of the civil war have not been laid to rest—indeed, Lebanon is presented as haunted. I posit that we may find warning signs of the failure of the country's reconstruction regime in *The Last Man* (*Al-Atlal*, 2005) by Ghassan Salhab and *One Perfect Day* (*Yawm akhar*, 2005) by Joana Hadjithomas and Khalil Joreige. I argue that these films offer intriguing views of Lebanon as haunted by the irresolutions of the civil war, through films marked with an interest in monstrous presences, vampires, and the gap between life and death. I end with examining films produced in the aftermath of the 2006 war, through discussing the films *Under the Bombs* (*Taht al-qusuf*, 2007) by Philippe Aractingi and *I Want to See* (*Biddi ashuf*, 2007) by Hadjithomas and Joreige, which in different ways bring together the prior threads, with the former attempting to bear witness to the effects of the war and the latter instead recognizing the impossibility of offering sufficient testimony to the experiences of this war through visual culture, within a social context still haunted by the past.

Chapter 7 looks back to questions raised in chapter 2, concerning the traumatic claims of the colonizer, by examining the prevalence of perpetrator traumas in memory practices on recent wars. After a broad overview, discussing this question with regard to American films about the Vietnam War and the invasion of Iraq, I follow the topic through cinematic representations of the Israeli invasion of Lebanon in 1982. Via readings of a series of films about the Israeli invasion and occupation of Lebanon, in particular Ari Folman's *Waltz with Bashir* (*Valz im Bashir*, 2008), this chapter examines how cultural memory of this war risks occluding questions of responsibility by giving priority to preoccupations with the social trauma that the war produced for former fighters in the war. As trauma discourse has become more and more globalized and is translated into various local idioms, I argue that in many contexts memory practices may be viewed as competitive rather than simply constitutive or relative. In such cases, the development of social trauma discourse may work to absolve perpetrators of the ethical accounting that would be otherwise demanded by an acknowledgment of their positions within and after the war.

Folman quite poetically reflects the fragility of memory and the threat of oblivion, while also exploring the lingering irresolutions that such repression of memory may bring. On one level, Folman develops moments of provocative cross-identification with Palestinian and Lebanese victims of the war that are woven into the visual language of the film, and which also enter into the film's elaboration of a cultural memory of the war. However, despite Folman's intentional reversals of perspective, *Waltz with Bashir*'s use of personal and cultural memory eventually comes to act as a screen that forecloses on the question of responsibility. The narrative of the film is predicated upon a search for a therapeutic resolution that releases the characters from the burden of memory, without directing its investigation into difficult questions of the broader, more structural responsibility of Israel in the war. Thus, I argue that by remaining only within a memory- and trauma-based framing of the war experiences of soldiers, *Waltz with Bashir* ends by giving too great a priority to the extent to which the soldiers were in some sense victims of the war themselves.

A conclusion raises questions concerning the changing nature of memory contests in postcinematic visual cultures in the Middle East. In particular, a brief discussion identifies practices emerging in the aftermath of revolutionary social movements in the region (e.g., the Arab Spring or the Iranian Green Movement), as well as other "multitudinous" shifts that reposition the role of cinema in setting limits and boundaries for cultural memory, and invites us to view ourselves as entering a new period of postcinematic memory.

Through these varying historical, national, and social contexts I pursue a consistent set of questions pertaining to the organization and representation of history through the cultural memory of conflict, focusing specifically on the ways in which cinema has served to echo but also to challenge dominant hegemonic discursive trends in the articulation of these cultural memories. Within these discussions, the category of social trauma offers another consistent frame of reference, speaking to the ways in which experiences of conflict and loss have engendered competitive claims on the mantle of trauma. So, while the book indexes both colonial-imperial (British in Sudan, Israel in Lebanon) and oppositional (Algerian, Egyptian, Tunisian, and Palestinian) experiences as "traumas," it does so not to offer each of these an equivalent or relativistic claim to suffering and loss, but rather to show how what I term "trauma production" is a part of the field of cultural and political contestation prevalent in both colonial and postcolonial contexts. In a sense, these are different forms of social trauma, and these differences demand specific ethical questions. Put simply, this work views trauma not as a natural and anointing category which produces cultural capital, but rather as a mode of social production which organizes and gives vitality to political contestations—issues I will pick up in greater detail in chapter 1, following.

Clearly, the selection of works addressed in this book, and by extension the national contexts addressed, is not comprehensive, even to the Middle East. Chapters could have been included on other contexts in the region, primary among them perhaps being cultural memory around the issues of the Armenian genocide and the Kurdish experience in Turkey and beyond, or the cultural memory of the 1988 prison massacres in Iran, along with the broader campaign against the Left in that country in the 1980s, or Iraqi cultural memory concerning the chain of wars, sanctions, and civil strife beginning in 1980 and continuing to this writing, among others. Another area that has proven too difficult to address sufficiently is the question of reception or audience. I have made some use of critical and journalistic responses to many of the works discussed, and have cited references to audience and forms of reception of works when this data is available. However, broadly speaking, to be able to present empirical data on audiences for particular films (much less to discern how these audiences have interpreted these films) is a challenge that always haunts the scholar of cinema. I acknowledge here that my conclusions on audience reception is drawn from an uneven body of sources and I have endeavored to limit the claims I can make about, for example, the Egyptian viewers of *I Am Free* in the early 1960s. What has been included has been chosen first on the basis of a coherence that was sought through comparative approaches and resonant histories that I trust will be manifest to the reader. Furthermore, the contexts discussed very largely are ones wherein the works can make a claim to both reflect and speak to a domestic audience. In this book I have self-consciously avoided purely diasporic or exilic contexts, not for finding the latter less authentic or significant, but only for reasons of continuity and coherence. Hence, while Hiner Saleem's *Kilometer Zero* or Mohammad Daradji's *Ahlam* each are profound meditations on Iraqi (Kurdish and Arab, respectively) cultural memory of the last two decades, neither are works that have significant claims to represent or reach a domestic context, as both are works of filmmakers who have spent most of their adult lives in Europe, making films that are arguably primarily intended for external consumption. In general, the discussions included in this book address films and filmmakers working within the contexts addressed, although I recognize that there is a broad spectrum and that some of the works included—especially the cinema of Elia Suleiman—may be susceptible to being described as being at least in part exilic or diasporic. I will leave to the reader the judgment of whether I sufficiently address the ways in which Suleiman's work does reflect the quotidian realities of his domestic (even if ultimately only Nazarene) setting, and even while retaining diasporic elements, I can attest through my own travels to Israel/Palestine to the significant domestic awareness of Palestinians of the work of Suleiman. (And is this uncenteredness not true for the Palestinian experience more generally?) In the case of Suleiman, and to some degree that of the Lebanese filmmakers discussed, the transnationality of the works in question is very much part of the reflection of the domestic realities of their respective societies.

Productive Traumas

CINEMA, SOCIAL CONFLICT, CULTURAL MEMORY

Black and white newsreel footage of crowds celebrating the liberation of France in Paris on May 8, 1945, crossfade into black-and-white staged footage of what seems at first a similar parade. A title card reads, "Sétif, Algérie, le meme jour." The second parade is a demonstration for Algerian independence. French colonial troops, assisted by armed settlers, emerge to block the progress of the demonstration. The troops open fire on the demonstrators, before running through the town and killing the Arabs they encounter.

This scene (figure 1.1), the opening of French filmmaker Rachid Bouchareb's *Outside the Law* (*Hors-la-Loi*, 2010), is a flashback, establishing how the film's protagonist, an Algerian liberation militant who later lives in Paris, survived what would become known as the Sétif Massacre.

Screening at the 2010 Cannes International Film Festival, *Outside the Law* enjoyed a rather unconventional form of publicity. For perhaps the first time in the festival's history, riot police were deployed to guard against a political demonstration protesting a film selected in the competition, making its world debut at the festival. The protest on the edge of the red carpet drew approximately 1000 angry marchers. Inside the theater, the filmmaker was protected by bodyguards as he addressed the controversy in his comments to the audience: "It is for sociologists or other experts to say why in France people find it difficult to journey into the past" (Hoyle 2010). The past to which Bouchareb referred was that of the Algerian War of Independence (1954–1962), the subject of his film. While perhaps none of them had in fact seen the full film, the protestors, who included a variety of media personalities and politicians, had mobilized in reaction to the clips and synopses of the film released by the distributors. They may also have been motivated by their presumptions of what a film by a French director of Algerian origin may say about this historical period, doubting little that it would be an affront to their own memory of the war.

FIGURE 1.1 *The Sétif massacre* (Outside the Law)

Reporters described the demonstrators as being largely made up of elderly people, most of them drawn not only from among the ranks of veterans of the French-Algerian war, but also members of the *pieds-noirs* community, as well as pro-French Algerians known as *harkis*, who had fought on the side of France in the war and resettled in France after Algeria's independence in 1962. Elderly veterans festooned with medals argued angrily with the festival-goers attending the screening. Benjamin Stora, a noted French historian of the Algerian war, suggested that the controversy over the film indicated that the war "hasn't been sufficiently named, shown, come to terms with in and by collective memory" (Marquand 2010). The protestors represented themselves as the forgotten victims of the conflict, their injuries rekindled by "the herald of a one-sided and hateful reading of history" (Marquand 2010). In other accounts, Bouchareb was "accused of falsifying history" (Enjelvin and Korac-Kakabadse 2012, 170). In the intersection of these competing narratives—those offered by the protestors, the commenting media, and the film itself—it becomes clear that interpretations of the cultural memory of the War of Independence remain a major point of contention in French society. But perhaps more importantly, this encounter shows the degree to which cultural memory has come to be an instrument in the encounter between differing interpretations of histories of social conflict. What is most at stake is identifying who has the right to interpret this history, what forms of cultural memory are given legitimacy, and whether it is possible to arrive at a resolution of the putative traumas of the various claimants.

The events surrounding the Cannes premiere of *Outside the Law* are perhaps more significant, and found greater resonance in the public arena, given the festival's high profile. However, conflicts concerning cinematic works on contested historical events are neither rare nor inconsequential. Events such as these testify to the social capital that cinematic works afford, even those by *auteur* filmmakers who are institutionally outside of the commercial mainstream; they evince the manner in which cinema is often deemed to play a role in developing a consensus in the historical interpretation of socially traumatic events. The controversy that *Outside the Law* generated is emblematic of how cinema may tread into the fraught arena of what I will here term "trauma production," counteracting the cultural memory claims of some groups while enhancing those of others. In the following pages of this chapter, I intend to contextualize this phenomenon by historically reviewing the colonial presence throughout cinema's centurial history, examining the pre-independence colonial film as well as the rise of the anticolonial and postindependence cinemas of the postcolonial world. Having established the centrality of colonial themes to the rise of the cinematic medium, I argue for the need to better apply the frameworks of social trauma and cultural memory to the colonial context. I lay out shortcomings in the more dominant, psychoanalytically oriented, trends in trauma and memory studies, and show the greater applicability of more sociologically oriented approaches to the contexts which are here my focus. Through this discussion, and by returning to Bouchareb's works, I show how such debates are crucial to the articulation of ideological formations (whether colonial or anticolonial) and to the development of various forms of identity (such as national, gender, or ethnic identity) for societies in the Middle East and the broader postcolonial world.

Prior to directing *Outside the Law*, Bouchareb had already entered the fraught grounds of cultural memory as relating to French colonialism in his earlier film, *Days of Glory* (*Indigénes*, 2006) which concerns North African soldiers fighting in the Free French army in the Second World War. As one French reviewer noted, the film is highly effective in its objective of "overcoming the amnesia concerning the role of the former fighters from the French colonies, and denouncing the injustices they suffered until today" (Thénault 2007, 205, my translation). The film focuses on the discrimination North African soldiers faced while serving in the French forces, as well as systematic efforts not to afford recognition to their service after the war, including the cancelation of their military pensions in 1959. The film, which was a significant box-office hit in France, opened a public dialogue that led to an official apology issued by President Jacques Chirac and a restitution of pensions for surviving North African war veterans (Sandford 2006). Here, a cinematic work played a productive role in addressing a historically traumatic context and advancing a particular interpretation into public discourse concerning the war.[1] While drawing praise from a president of the Republic and effecting a major governmental policy change is perhaps a rare form of achievement for a cinematic work, nonetheless *Days of Glory* also serves to note the manner in which cinema memory—understood here as written into both the text and the social circumstances that qualify the reception and aftermath of a film's public screening—may fundamentally change public discourse and consciousness of a historically traumatic event, and to rework the interpretive

limits of cultural memory around that event. *Days of Glory*'s themes of sacrifice for the nation established its claims' legitimacy by using French nationalist themes as "the emotional catalyst to real political action" (Norindr 2009,
126). Given this, the film was largely immune to attack from those who would
otherwise oppose its integrative and multiculturalist aims, a politically astute
approach that was perhaps a primary reason for the direct political outcomes
that resulted. Interestingly, as Ayo Coly (2008, 154) notes, "The overwhelm-
ingly positive reception of this film in France was not echoed in Algeria,"
and given its incitement of French nationalist sentiments, the film, "does
not . . . offer a counter, Algerian memory of the event." However, as Norindr
(2009, 127) notes, "part of the movie's success can be measured by the way
it fulfilled its role as a militant film that demanded urgent action from the
government, its enduring legacy may be its ability to transform French public
perception by re-inserting these *tirailleurs* into France's collective memory
and rewriting these forgotten men into history." Thus setting aside the question of the Algerian reception of the film, important as that is, nonetheless
the work must be deemed an accomplishment as an intervention into French
cultural memory of that war, as well as of colonialism.

In contrast, *Outside the Law* treads into more sensitive territory, raising
questions that are not easily reconciled within the French nationalist imaginary, which may explain the rather different reaction to the film seen at its
premiere. French cinema representations of the Algerian war have failed
to establish what may be termed a "national" narrative on how the conflict
should be remembered. The comparison of these two works and their respective receptions illustrates the manner in which cultural memory is situated
within wider sociocultural fields and the ways in which it contributes to or is
defined by prevailing political dynamics and conditions of possibility. As this
episode illustrates, the function of cultural memory of conflict in contemporary political and ideological formations is complex, but highly significant to
setting the parameters of public discourse on disputed historical episodes.

The intersection of cultural memory and social trauma has been subject
to different methodological and theoretical treatments. While the present
study focuses on the Middle East, these questions are recurrent in many
postcolonial settings and contexts. The concept of trauma as a social force
is usually traced back to the late nineteenth century via the trenches of the
First World War, with sociopsychological phenomena of "shell shock" pulling the formerly individualistic diagnosis of trauma—"as an epidemic of
male hysteria"—into broader social understandings (Leys 1994, 623). Scholars
have suggested a similar mapping of cultural memory and conflict over the
emergence of "cultures of defeat" and an attendant phenomenon of "defeat
empathy," which dates to nineteenth-century wars such as the American
Civil War and the Franco-Prussian War of 1870–1871 (Schivelbusch 2003, 4).
Schivelbusch argues cogently that nation-states, especially in Europe and

North America, have since their inception been able to make productive use of the experience of defeat, and to harness it for their particular political ends. However, what this astute analysis leaves out is the role of similar evocations of trauma—often in the form of what were seen as "crises" or "defeats"—within the colonial imaginary. Moments of imperial crisis, such as the 1857 Rebellion in India, the Boer Wars, and the routing of Gordon in Khartoum (which is discussed further in chapter 2), appear again and again as settings for spinning the colonial tale, as do defeats such as the "last stands" of General Custer or Davy Crockett in the American context. In fact, these and many other historical episodes that similarly led an imperial or colonial force to come to terms with the experience of military defeat serve as popular backdrops for novels, poems, and films as often as any of the many triumphal victories of these colonial systems. One may say, in fact these defeats come to feature as necessary sacrifices so as to continually prove the essential merits of the colonial project.

I discuss further the relationship of defeat, shock, crisis, or trauma to the formation and evolution of the colonial imaginary later in this chapter. What I am here most interested in is the manner in which these historical moments are represented in cultural activity, and how these representations change and evolve as the colonial project evolves. In this sense, the question we are facing is: What role do cultural productions—such as cinema—play in elaborating and disseminating particular conceptions of traumatic histories and experiences? Before considering this, it will be beneficial to look back at the historical relationship of colonialism and cinema, and follow this relationship through to the postcolonial context.

Colonialism and Cinema

It is perhaps only historical coincidence that finds the origins and rise of the motion picture mapping closely the apex of colonialism and the zenith of its cultural logic. The link of cinema to colonialism is only a continuation of the already established close links between precinematic popular and mass cultural forms and the colonial project, however. Before the emergence of the technology of the moving picture, over the course of the nineteenth century, the European literary field made prodigious use of colonialism to generate a broad imaginative canvas of a world constructed by a metropolitan center connected to disparate nodes of dominated other-worlds. In these other spaces, the social restrictions and mores of an ascendant bourgeoisie were tested by empty spaces for adventure and personal transformation. As Edward Said (1993, 62) notes, "[n]early everywhere in nineteenth- and early twentieth-century British and French culture we find allusions to the facts of empire, but perhaps nowhere with more regularity and frequency than in the

British novel.". However, this assessment arguably applies more to the nine-teenth century than to the subsequent century, given the rise in significance of cinematic and other visual cultural forms—what W. J. T. Mitchell (1994, 11–35) has termed "the pictoral turn"—and the attendant changes in consumption practices and prestige given to literary forms. Over the course of the twenti-eth century, visual cultural forms—primary among them, cinema—came to adopt colonial genres from literature, and further developed these imperial narratives in a more popular and widespread manner than the novel could ever have done.

The major genres of colonial imagination, such as adventure and explora-tion stories, military narratives, and historical dramas, became fundamen-tal to the success of the cinema industry. Cinema, along with other visual forms, played a key role in communicating certain ideas about this project and defining public discourse around them. So while the project of colonial-ism evolved and found new cultural contexts for its ideological justifications, cinema eventually took on a central role in communicating these ideals.

Cinema itself began with a mythos of its own adventures, which were often colonial. The early pioneering directors, such as Cecil B. DeMille, Merian Cooper, and Raoul Walsh, often developed elaborate personae as world explorers and adventurers, conquering untamed lands with their cameras.[2] Hence the presence of two factors at the heart of the emergence of cinema as a form of mass entertainment: first, the critical role of a colonial imagi-nary in the content of narrative cinema, and second, the establishment of a wide-reaching international cinema market. The former factor was important relatively early in the development of the medium, while the latter has con-tinued to gain in importance over the course of cinema's history. As Ramón Grosfoguel (2002, 210) has noted, "We live in a world where the dominant imaginary is still colonial." These factors place colonialism and postcolonial-ism at the center of any historical assessment of cinema's origins and its con-tinued cultural role internationally.

Cinema's earliest innovators, the Lumière brothers, were quite forthright in their employment of colonial themes and settings in their short films, which screened in metropolitan centers from Paris and London to colonial cities such as Alexandria. Moving only slightly away from the motion picture's roots as a festival or circus sideshow entertainment, the cinematic technol-ogy pioneered by the Lumières and quickly duplicated and refined by others in the last decade of the nineteenth century and first decade of the twentieth often presented material shot in colonial settings—as often informational as it was spectacular—in their screenings. The link, already established in photography, between colonial ethnology and modern representational tech-nologies, only expanded with the spread of cinema.[3]

By the time of its institutionalization in the 1920s, Hollywood's "univer-sal" cinema language—what later would be termed "dominant cinema"—was developed in fictional works intimately tied with the question of colonialism. The colonial film, which has its roots in the silent era but which comes to full fruition in the 1930s, applied the spectacles of cinematic technique to the ideological and narratological roots of the adventure novel. In this period, in France the *cinéma colonial* and in Britain the "colonial film" became distinct genres on their own. As David Slavin notes, the *cinéma colonial* genre played a significant role in maintaining broad social support for the project of colonialism in North Africa.

> Colonialism contributed one of the binding agents of a social "cement" that insured working-class loyalty to the Third Republic, and film joined other forms of mass leisure and entertainment that were creating cultural cohesion. Colonial subject matter[s] in film added to its cohesive powers and made cinema inordinately influential . . . French colonialists awakened early on to cinema's potential to capture imaginations and to promote the empire by associating modern arms, machinery and medicine with white, Western supremacy.
>
> (SLAVIN *1997*, *24*)

In Britain, colonial cinema carried out a similar ideological and propagandizing function. As Chapman and Cull (2009, 3) argue, "These early films of empire need to be understood in the context of wider popular culture of imperialism during the late Victorian and Edwardian periods." Institutionally, British colonial cinema in the interwar period worked hand in hand with the efforts of bodies such as the British Empire Producers Organization, the Empire Resources Development Committee, and the Empire Marketing Board, which saw promoting cultural productions that supported colonial aims as part of their mandate (MacKenzie 1999, 216). The Hollywood colonial film, of which the American Western must be properly regarded as a subgenre, also gave evidence of the strong alliance that bonded the United States and Britain during this time. As primary allies in the two world wars, the ostensible "anti-imperialist" sympathies of Americans in the film industry were frequently sacrificed to a desire to close ranks between the declining empire of the United Kingdom and the rising global power that the US was becoming. It is true that the US maintained some ideological distance from the colonial adventures of its European allies. However, its own internal colonial histories, whether of the enslavement of Africans or of the dispossession and genocide of the indigenous population, as well as its military and colonial activity in Latin America and the Philippines, help to explain why, when viewed as whole, the film industries of the US and the UK evinced very slight differences of approach where the ideologies of colonialism are concerned.

Hollywood studios regularly hired British colonial officers as advisers on films with colonial themes, and the involvement of US government offices reinforced the ideological imperative to support Britain's colonial system as a buttress against the rise of European fascism in the interwar period (and particularly in the years of the Second World War). As Jaher and Kling (2008, 36) note, "Collaboration between England and Hollywood involved consultations between American studios and the British India Office and Board of Censors in London and the British embassy. These government organizations provided an institutional conduit for official colonial policy and recommended technical advisers, retired colonial civil servants, or British-Indian army officers." Not surprisingly, within the British film industry, the links to the colonial administrative system were only stronger. While some critics have persuasively argued that nuanced ideological differences may be found when comparing the American and the British colonial movie, the fact remains that by and large the films made in each industry worked with similar notions of racial superiority, of colonialism as a civilizing mission, and so on. Chapman and Cull (2009, 7) also note that the economics of cinema, in terms of marketing and distribution between the two markets of the United States and Britain, from the interwar period until the late 1950s dictated an interdependence between British and American film industries, as much as a "shared sense of Anglo-American values." The two film industries thus had common goals, not simply ideologically but also in economic and institutional terms. The colonial film was simply the epitome of this complex relationship.

The colonial film was also a commercially highly successful genre, and "films with an Imperial content attracted an immense public" (MacKenzie 1999, 228). The genre attracted top stars, talented directors and drew the commitment of enterprising entrepreneurs and financiers. As MacKenzie notes, "[f]ilms in the context of Empire offered their vast audiences not only escapist entertainment but also a sense of security, as well as feelings of pride and achievement. . . . They constituted the most significant evidence for the argument that the public was little infected with anti-Imperial sentiment" (229). Cinema in this way provided one of the most effective vehicles for the diffusion of colonial ideologies throughout the West in the latter years of classical colonialism, the 1930s and 1940s. While the later emergence of a more independent, auteur-oriented approach to filmmaking in the 1950s and 1960s allowed for a greater range of nuanced exploration of the presumed triumph of colonialism, nonetheless the dominant thrust of commercial filmmaking would be one of celebrating and valorizing the colonial project, in a way that marks a striking continuity from the 1920s through the 1960s.

A brief illustration of this may be traced in the works of John Ford, whose personal vision of the conquest of the American West allowed for the evocation of liberal regret where the treatment of the Indians was concerned (as in the betrayal that ends *Fort Apache*, 1948), yet never moved far from the racial logic upon which the destruction of Native American culture was predicated, even in his later and more complex works, such as *The Searchers*

(1956). It is not surprising that Ford's first talkie, *The Black Watch* (1929), celebrated British imperialism in Afghanistan and India, as did his highly popular Shirley Temple showcase, *Wee Willie Winkie* (1937), itself based upon a Rudyard Kipling short story. His *Lost Patrol* (1934) is about a British military foot patrol lost in the desert during the 1917 British colonial war in Iraq (figure 1.2). The men are trapped at a remote desert oasis as the sniping of an unseen enemy, and the eventual explosion of inner tensions within the group, leads to the death of each man, one by one. The film, while a masterful exploration of the psychological breakdown of the group, nonetheless shows no interest in exploring the motives compelling the indigenous Arabs to fight the British. The stark setting and the shadowy opponents the men face would work as well if the film were a Western, with a group of white settlers surrounded by Indians who perplexingly have no goal but to kill them off one by one. Ford's unique touch, whereby many of his films take on a humanist allegorical quality, nonetheless is grounded in the soil of the colonial ideologies of Europe and the United States. In John Ford we find a superior example of the marrying of the genius of Hollywood studio production to the colonial context of the British imperial adventure, but one which also betrays the inherent links of the colonial film to the American Western genre.

In this sense, dominant European and American commercial cinemas of the 1920s to 1960s viewed the question of colonialism through a very

FIGURE 1.2 *Looking for the enemy* (Lost Patrol)

narrow window, at times offering limited criticism of tactics or strategies, but rarely exploring the ideological structures of colonialism, much less viewing the colonial experience through the eyes of the colonized. In this expanse of time—from the coinciding emergence of cinema technologies and the ascendance of colonialism as a global political and economic order to the eventual success of national liberation struggles—motion pictures were largely utilized by colonial societies in the mirroring of their own vision of the world. Rare indeed were films that sought to represent the experiences of the colonized, and rarer still were those made by colonized peoples in opposition to the imperialist systems of which they were victims. In many colonial contexts, cinema had not been developed into an effective domestic or even regional industry. In others, where cinema industries were nascent, colonial administrators and local comprador or puppet leaders sought to censor or stifle anticolonial voices.

For example in Egypt, despite the rise of a successful film industry after the 1920s, and despite rising discontent among the Egyptian cultural elites concerning the colonial arrangement, few if any cinematic works would even attempt to hint at anticolonial views in the period before 1952, and nearly all works "avoided subjects that critically addressed the political situation" due to both censorship and self-censorship (Schochat 1983, 23). Instead, films of this period indirectly fed public discontent through focusing on class-based tensions and addressing broader themes of social injustice within an Egyptian society largely shown to be absent of colonial presence. A similar template also defined pre-independence Indian cinema, where "themes that directly dealt with the [independence] struggle were not always portrayed and much of this was due to censorship by the colonial government" (Dasgupta 2003, 368). In other colonial societies, the lack of an indigenous cinema-making capacity only further limited the possibilities of the emergence of a critical anticolonial cinema.

It was really only after the Second World War that American, British, or French filmmakers began to raise serious questions about the colonial project. The collapse of many arrangements of formal colonial rule in the mid-twentieth century necessitated new arrangements where cinematic representations of the colonial project were concerned. While colonialism was now no longer unquestioned, still the memory of colonial rule continued to provide effective material for commercial cinema, keeping alive many of the popular colonial genres, from the adventure film to war cinema. Even after the loss of major colonial holdings, both Hollywood and British filmmaking held fast to the colonial movie genre, revisiting the glories of British India in films that trafficked in a nostalgia for empire. Films like *King of the Khyber Rifles* (1956) or *Kim* (1951) revisit the primary themes of earlier colonial films, but do so with a new sense of loss and resignation. By the 1960s some shifts may be viewed in films that viewed the civilizing claims of the entire colonial project as incoherent, or as well intentioned but doomed, and by the 1970s the empire was often marked as simply folly. A sort of mourning prevailed in films such as *Lawrence of Arabia* (1962), where the supposedly more benevolent colonialism of T. E. Lawrence would fail in the face of a more malevolent colonial vision directed from the British government, or in *Zulu* (1964), where the British loss at Rorke's Drift is seen as all but inevitable, and the African attackers—while still faceless savages—are given a historical purpose lacking in prior cinematic representations. By the 1970s, colonialism was being represented as a form of comic madness, as with films like *The Man Who Would Be King* (1974).

More significant European anticolonial works would emerge from the radical fringes of the independent filmmaking world—perhaps no better example is Jean-Luc Godard's films *Le Petit Soldat* (1963) or *Ici et Ailleurs* (1976). The latter, which seeks to draw links of shared interest between Palestinian fighters in refugee camps in Jordan and a French working-class family, is exemplary of the current of anticolonial critique that is found in much of Godard's work, and that of other radical filmmakers. Werner Herzog would use colonial backdrops in *Aguirre: Wrath of God* (1972) to do more than simply critique colonial ideology as a form of insanity or folly; for Herzog, the colonial setting offered an allegorical framework for exploring the rise of German fascism. Through this oblique evocation of an ideological link between colonialism and fascism, Herzog also sought to release German cinema from the bounds of guilt in which it had found itself for many years after the end of the Third Reich and to reenter the "cultural good graces of the West" (Davidson 1999, 52). However, as Davidson argues, Herzog's project to recuperate German national culture through linking Nazi fascism to the colonial madness of Aguirre ends with the film's "re-legitimation of Western neocolonial hegemony," complicating the picture of a critical anticolonial presence in European "new" cinemas of the 1970s (104).

Perhaps of all the European responses to colonialism, none was more significant in either impact or influence than Gillo Pontecorvo's *The Battle of Algiers* (1966). Saadi Yacef, whose appears as himself in the film and whose memoir is the origin of the film's screenplay, poignantly suggests that the film itself is a reflections of his memories of the militancy of that struggle, saying, "I have substituted the camera for the machine gun. The idea of re-living those days and recalling the emotions I felt, moved me greatly, but there is no rancor in my memories" (Quoted in Reid 2005, 98). Pontecorvo's internationalist approach resonated with sympathy for the Third Cinema movement (about which more will be said shortly), and acted as a bridge between European critiques of colonialism and the emergence of an anticolonial cinema in societies recently or still under colonial control. Guy Austin argues that Algerian national cinema was itself in no small part influenced by the legacy of *The Battle of Algiers*. The question of "national trauma" is at the origin of a new national cinema: "Born out of the war for independence, Algerian cinema is possessed by history. The 'repeated possession' of the new national cinema by the national trauma begins in earnest with its most celebrated manifestation, Pontecorvo's *Battle of Algiers*" (Austin 2009, 20). Only a small number of other European or American filmmakers can be argued to have made as serious an effort to produce committed anticolonial forms of representation, and most of them shared Pontecorvo's ethic of filmmaking as an expression of internationalist leftist anti-imperialist solidarity. However most of these works rarely found wide audiences beyond those of other committed fellow-travelers or anticolonial elite groups engaged in struggles of national liberation. Nonetheless, the effect of some of these works—*The Battle of Algiers* primary among them—was significant for the development of indigenous national liberation cinemas in the colonial world.

Where the early stages of the emergence of cinema industries in the West are associated with the spread of colonial ideologies, in the postcolonial world often the development of indigenous "national" cinemas came about in the early years of the postindependence period. The global rise of anticolonial ideologies accompanied a similar set of often internationalist projects aimed at "decolonizing the mind" of the subjects of colonial rule through cultural revolutions. However, cinema first emerged as a tool for cultural development in some anticolonial liberation movements, nascent revolutionary regimes, and for those who continued revolutionary struggle against neocolonialism. Postcolonial governments such as those of the Arab world saw state sponsorship of cinema for the propagation of revolutionary principles as a high priority. Egypt's post-1952 regime coopted the major prerevolutionary cineastes, many of whom had indeed harbored anticolonial sympathies but had been frustrated by the censorship regime of the colonial system. In the early years of independence, they enthusiastically produced popular anticolonial films that would find broader audiences around the Arab world, given Egypt's reputation as the capital for Arab cinema. In this period, Armbrust (1995, 83) argues, commercial and art genres of cinema had a common language and could be "plotted onto the same ideological map." Following from this, broadly speaking commercial and art cinema sectors had a common goal in finding a place within the postrevolutionary nationalist calling, whether explicitly in the form of statist propaganda or, more often, implicitly through the diffusion of social ideals that were coded into genre works. Over the course of the 1950s and 1960s, the state took over more and more components of the film industry, including studios, labs, and schools; the cinema theaters were nationalized in Egypt in 1962 (Shafik 2007, 21).

Other Arab societies found cinema playing an active role in the articulation of new postindependence national identities. As Roy Armes (2005, 7–8) notes with regard to North Africa, "The national cinemas born in the late 1960s, in the aftermath of independence in the Maghreb, are clearly very much part of

the new sense of national identity which is seeking new forms of expression."
Aesthetically, these postrevolutionary cinemas also sought new inspirations.
Chaudhuri (2005, 56) argues that Arab films made in the wake of 1952 were
innovative in form as well as content, and, "[i]nspired by new movements
in Europe such as Italian neorealism and *cinéma-vérité*, these films departed
from both Hollywood and the region's own commercial traditions."

For several years this arrangement of critical filmmakers and a state-
sponsored cinema industry remained tenable, but increasingly filmmakers
found the interference that state sponsorship brought to be inhibiting, and
the economics of state film production also became less and less sustain-
able. The foremost inhibition, of course, was the increasingly heavy-handed
and interventionist censorship practiced by the authoritarian regimes of
the region. By the late 1960s, many Egyptian filmmakers had sought ways
to reposition themselves as critics of the postcolonial order, looking now to
other postcolonial contexts for support and inspiration, so as to introduce
a more fundamentally revolutionary approach to filmmaking, rethinking
the old pieties of cinematic aesthetics, funding, and audience. In part this
was because filmmakers could not remain immune to the regional political
transformations, and as Nouri Bouzid (1995, 247) argues, a new generation
of filmmakers emerged in the late 1960s who, buoyed by the social movements in Europe and the United States in that decade, and disappointed by
the defeat of the 1967 Six-Day War, set out to develop a "new realism," which
"destroy[ed] the old, ossified molds" and which was a more "distinctly and
intimately personal" cinema.

Bouzid's "new realism" was mirrored also by the New Arab Cinema
Collective's work, started at the 1968 Damascus Film Festival, to challenge
"the old submissive cinema . . . [and] move towards documentary realism and
women's issues" (Van de Peer 2010, 17). By 1971, the Egyptian experiment of a
public-sector cinema industry, already long in decline, was ended with Sadat's
neoliberal *infitah* policies privatizing most of the industry (Shafik 2007, 25).
Many other Arab countries had also experimented with a state-sponsored cinema industry, and in most cases had abandoned or significantly reduced state
sponsorship by the 1980s. From the 1980s onward, the trend across the Arab
world, with the partial exception of Egyptian cinema, was toward filmmaking with multinational film coproductions, usually involving European film
funds, both national and private. Given the strings that are attached to these
funds, the rise of this coproduction model has fueled the view that cinema
production in much of the Arab world is largely still conditioned by the legacy
of neocolonial relationships, because the continued presence and influence of
European cultural institutions affect the content and aesthetics of these works
in a significant manner.

However, a variety of cultural movements have attempted to eke out a
space independent of such colonial and neocolonial arrangements. The Latin

American "Third Cinema" movement was perhaps the most internationally visible of the efforts to emerge in the 1960s and 1970s to revolutionize post-colonial filmmaking.[4] Fernando Solanas and Octavio Getino's manifesto that defined the movement called for a rejection of the universal claims of dominant Hollywood cinemas and charted a path apart from that of the European national "new waves" and that of auteurist cinema. As Solanas has suggested, Third Cinema is "neither a commercial cinema nor a 'cinéma d'auteur' with all sorts of cultural intentions, conditioned by the consumer society and its political and economic structures. It's a cinema that is created within all the limitations and all the possibilities inherent in a setting loose of the revolutionary forces" (Solanas and MacBean 1970, 38). The Third Cinema movement laid out a call to rethink the content, aesthetics, means of production, and methods of distribution of film works along antineocolonial, revolutionary lines. While the movement was rooted in the neocolonial experiences of Latin America, its broader aims appealed to filmmakers in postcolonial settings all around the world. While it is debatable how ultimately influential the Third Cinema movement was, its spirit of fundamentally rethinking the aims and methods of cinema arts would find fertile ground in Africa and the Middle East, as well as among insurgent voices in European and American independent filmmaking in the 1960s and 1970s. Third Cinema coincided with and very likely inspired new cinema movements in the Middle East during this period. For example, in 1968 the "New Cinema Organization," comprising a group of young Egyptian filmmakers, published the "New Cinema Manifesto" of Egypt, which in some ways echoes the Third Cinema manifesto in proposing revolutionary changes to an understanding of both what cinema is and what the intellectual preoccupations of Egyptian cinema should be, as well as addressing new approaches to its production and distribution. Further revolutionary manifestoes issued from the Palestinian Cinema Group (1973) and the Third World Filmmakers Meeting (Algeria, 1973) (MacKenzie 2014, 273–283). While the tone of the Egyptian manifesto is less radical than that of Solanas and Getino, nonetheless its ambition to fundamentally rethink the work of cinema as well as its economy derives from a similar set of internationalist concerns about seeking freedom from the Hollywood paradigm, as much as from a domestic imitative filmmaking tradition ("Bayan al-Sinima al-Jadida fi Misr (1968)" 1994). The ambitions of this movement are visible in films such as Shadi 'Abd al-Salam's *al-Mumia* (The Mummy; released in English as *The Nights of Counting the Years*, 1969) and Youssef Chahine's *Al-Asfour* (*The Sparrow*, 1972), which eschew the didacticism that has been imputed to Third Cinema, while nonetheless performing aesthetic and formal innovations that follow the spirit of its radical call.

Despite the rising voices of postcolonial cinema theorists and practitioners, whether those of distinct movements such as Third Cinema or in more disparate forms, and despite the presence of an increasingly sustained critical

voice among commercial American and British filmmakers, nonetheless sentimental or nostalgic views of colonialism have continued to be the dominant
mode of cinema memory for commercial cinema, from the 1970s onward.
This nostalgia and sentimentality is evinced in epic dramas, comedies, and
romances that appear with regularity each year; a long list that would include
Out of Africa (1985), *The English Patient* (1996), or in the seventh remake of *The
Four Feathers* (2002), as much as a science fiction work like the ostensibly anticolonial *Avatar* (2008). The re-dressing of colonial narratives into a stream of
often ahistorical "costume" dramas no longer pursues the more urgent ideological imperatives of the colonial film during the pre-independence era, but
many of the tropes carry over and reemerge even within works that may see
themselves to be critical of colonialism. Colonialism as adventure remains
a common theme, as witnessed in the regressive nostalgia at the heart of
the *Indiana Jones* (1981–2008) and *The Mummy* (1999–2008) franchises, both
highly successful multifilm serials with spin-off series. In the Peter Jackson
remake of *King Kong* (2006), the racist caricaturing of the indigenous people
on Skull Island is only one colonial layer in a film that does not in the slightest
reflect upon the white supremacist storyline of the 1933 original, or revise it.
The echoes of colonial ideological structures remain discernible in dominant
cinemas, even while the globalization of the production and distribution of
cinemas from the postcolonial world have increased access to filmmaking
from these societies, and have at times impacted public discourse on colonialism in critical ways.

   Here, I have presented a broad overview of the history of cinema and its
colonial dimensions, and while no doubt this summary is far too cursory,
what remains clear is the persistent if changing role of the colonial imaginary in cinemas of both the colonial and the formerly colonial world, as
well as those of postcolonial societies. Returning at this time to the questions that were encountered when examining the social reception of Rachid
Bouchareb's films *Days of Glory* and *Outside the Law*, it will be necessary to
move into a different, if related, discussion, on the role of social trauma discourse in the trajectories of colonialism and anticolonialism, and in the postcolonial context.

Colonialism, Cultural Memory, and Social Trauma

The colonial projects that came to spread across the Middle East and North
Africa brought with them new formations of collective identity, which while
diverse in arrangement were nonetheless united in setting out binaries such
as colonizer and colonized, metropolitan and peripheral, developed and
underdeveloped. The formations of these distinct identity categories were
to some extent promoted through the transmission of cultural memory that

articulated social traumas. As Bernhard Giesen (2004, 113) notes, "referring to a past as a collective triumph or collective trauma transcends the contingent relationships between individual persons and forges them into a collective identity." The formation of collective identity, then, depends upon broadly shared understandings of historical events, whether as triumph or trauma, and the accumulation of a common cultural memory around these events. While colonialism is defined by the triumphal military superiority of the Western powers over much of the rest of the world, it is too simple to view the identity of colonizers during the colonial period as being defined only by triumph.

Colonizing societies projected an unmitigated belief in their own material as well as racial superiority, and also linked these to a post-Enlightenment view of their own historical destiny. These beliefs gave priority to cultural memory as a celebration of triumphs, often articulated in the form of military victories over colonial competitors or over colonized populations. Nonetheless, colonial history has its share of "traumas" for the colonizing societies; these also emerged as cultural memories of military conflicts, but those that had resulted in defeat for the colonizers. When native forces were able to successfully pose a military challenge to European domination, this often came to serve as a locus for a form of cultural memory which we may well term as traumatic for the colonizing society.

In the history of British colonialism, perhaps the earliest instantiation of an experience of historical national trauma is to be found in what is termed the Sepoy Rebellion or Indian Mutiny, but known to many Indians as the 1857 War of Independence. As Christopher Herbert (2008, 7) suggests, the events of 1857 represent "a profoundly traumatic cultural crisis" to Britain, which reverberated for generations. The year 1857 was remembered as the moment when "[f]or the first time in their hundred-year stay in India, the British faced rebellions on a scale that threw the authority of their rule into crisis" (Sharpe 1994, 227). As Jenny Sharpe recounts, the memory of the rebellion for the British crystallized into hyperbolic and fictitious claims of the mass rape of European women by marauding Indian rebels—lurid recollections of the rebellion flooded public discourse in the form of book "memorials" and purported witness texts testifying to public sexual violence followed by corporeal mutilation enacted upon English women residing in India (230–231). The anticolonial rebellion is in these memories relegated to a register of acute cultural trauma, where English force in the colonies is insufficient to protect the honor of English women. The cultural memory of 1857 is framed within this fictive narrative, which also allows the English to view themselves as victims of Indian brutality and their uncivilized, inhumane, violence. As Sharpe summarizes, "The sexual nightmare of rape and mutilation remained fixed within the British imagination throughout the nineteenth century, forming an historical memory of 1857 as the savage attack of brown-skinned fiends on defenseless women and children. It was possible by the end of the nine-teenth century, to relive the 'heroic myth' of British martyrdom by making a pilgrimage to all the major sites where Europeans had been killed" (234). The socially traumatic cultural memory of 1857, formed in part by the spread of a fiction of terror, served a productive role in the collective identity of British colonizers, one that would be as important as the cultural memory of any of the many triumphal moments of colonialism.

So, for colonial forces as well as for the colonized, traumatic memory has operated as a productive and even necessary mold for collective identity. For the British, subsequent defeats, such as the loss of Khartoum under Gordon to the Mahdists in 1885, were again coded as traumas and would further serve a similar social purpose—a topic I explore more fully in chapter 2. Further and later colonial defeats or failures, perhaps most crucially in the success of the Indian movement for national liberation, all have led to what Paul Gilroy (2004, 90) calls a "post-imperial melancholia," which is itself part of a larger phenomenon he terms as "postcolonial melancholia." This "cultural disori-entation that accompanies the collapse of empires" (113) has itself become the defining paradigm of postmodern Britishness. Gilroy suggests that melan-cholic echoes of the colonial period are at the center of contemporary debates on race and immigration in Britain, and have come to replace the concept of national identity. In other words, the traumas of the colonizer, even now when bereft of her colonies, remain productive and contribute to the shifting parameters of national identity. Gilroy argues that the "melancholic pattern" to be found in continual returns to debates and controversies over identity, race, and nationality are themselves "the mechanism that sustains the unsta-ble edifice of increasingly brittle and empty national identity" (106). The pro-cess described by Gilroy may well have its roots in the colonial period, even if the project of developing a national identity was possibly more stable then. Britain's role as the preeminent colonial power, despite being overlaid by layer after layer of a lingering triumphalist sentiment, also involved historical cri-ses of self-definition. These concerns were always about the preservation of a particular form of national identity which has long been contested, from without as well as within. In the face of these challenges, social traumas may go very far in shoring up the project of national identity formation for post-colonial societies that often lack other forms of nationally cohesive traits, be they common languages, religious or ethnic cohesion, or a shared sense of a historical destiny.

The history of anticolonial resistance, what we may term the national-liberation period, is similarly framed by the experience of wars and social conflict. While the ethical claims that adduce to trauma in the context of the colonized are, in my view, fundamentally distinct from those of the colonizer, nonetheless similar forms of cultural memory frame historical memory on both sides of this divide. As Fanon so presciently observed in

the first sentence of *The Wretched of the Earth* (Fanon [1963] 2007, 1), "decolonization is always a violent event." Indeed, the violence of decolonization
was only an expression of the violence that was woven into the fabric of the
colonial project. One problematic reflected within the work of Fanon and
picked up by later scholars is the question of how to evaluate the psychological experiences of the colonizer, as a perpetrator figure, and the extent to
which these may be also termed as traumas. This problem is well illustrated
in the responses of the former French colonial soldiers to the film *Outside the
Law*, which they found offensive or dangerous for challenging their interpretation of the Algerian War of Independence. When commentators and
scholars speak of a "national trauma" with regard to the French-Algerian
war, they must be careful so as not to elide differences in the experiences of
the colonized and the colonizers, or indeed to even give greater value to the
suffering of the colonizers. However, the disproportionately greater power
wielded by the culture industries of France does mean that narratives and
perspectives on the war will often include a richer and more complex view
of the psychological cost of colonialism for the colonizer, and less so of that
of the colonized. Even in a film as critical and nuanced as Michael Hanake's
Caché (2006), which represents the lingering guilt of the colonial encounter as a specter that threatens the peaceful lives of members of the French
bourgeois intelligentsia, the perspective on offer is decidedly that of the
colonizer's—"it is the viewpoint, then, of (colonial) guilt, betrayal, and later
repression" (Mirzoeff 2011, 259). While there is little doubt that the colonial
subject in the film is the true victim in the relationship, the film contributes
to cultural memory discourse that elaborates the psychological traumas of
colonialism as they continue to impact upon the French. An analogous tendency predominates in American representations of the Vietnam War and,
more recently, of the US invasions of Iraq and Afghanistan. Israeli films
about the 1982 invasion of Lebanon also raise broadly similar questions (as
I will discuss in chapter 7).

What these tendencies show is that for various reasons, the social traumas of colonizing nations often are subject to greater representational work,
qualitatively and quantitatively, while the traumas of the colonized suffer
from obscurity and conjecture. It is unfortunate that a similar dynamic has
also prevailed in the realm of scholarly attention to social trauma. Very generally, colonialism is not often featured in discussions of cultural memory or
social trauma, although the work of a small number of scholars—primary
among them Michael Rothberg, Stef Craps, and Ogaga Ifowodo—have
begun to "decolonize" trauma studies.[5] From the perspective of the colonized, the experience of colonialism was fundamentally disruptive and may
be termed socially traumatic. Again, Fanon presents us with some of the
earliest and most useful thinking on this matter as it relates to colonialism,
outlined in some detail in the case studies presented in his chapter "Colonial

War and Mental Disorders" in *The Wretched of the Earth*. Fanon does not rely upon the concept of trauma to articulate the effect of colonialism on the colonized, but rather theorizes the violence of decolonization as a form of catharsis to end the ravages of colonialism. The forms of cultural memory that relate to the colonial experience may be many; nostalgia, for example, is common in former colonizing societies, and may be found even in some postcolonial contexts. However, memories of social trauma, at least for those formerly colonized, must be among the most significant forms of cultural memory.

The concept of trauma both avails us of certain opportunities and presents certain problems when applied to the colonial context. In the field of trauma studies, in particular in the application of trauma theory to literary and cultural analysis, the predominant mode of interpretation draws an analogy between individual and social trauma, and applies the symptoms of individual trauma to the social context.[6] Many of the seminal theorists of "trauma theory," such as Cathy Caruth and Shoshana Felman, have developed their approaches by drawing from psychoanalysis as well as from deconstructionist trends in poststructuralism more generally (Radstone 2007, 10). Using this framework, they have often been motivated by the potency of the metaphor of individual responses to trauma when discussing social trauma. A key postulate for this approach is that social trauma is analogous to individual experience in that it is essentially beyond representation, in the same way that the trauma of the individual puts that experience psychically beyond representation. Put more simply, social trauma is treated as presenting symptoms broadly similar to individual trauma, if on a much larger scale. However, this move between individual and social overlooks the significant gaps that exist between human psychic processes and the social dynamics that motivate or delimit the interpretive parameters for traumatic experience in a broader social sense. After all, social trauma is not simply the multiplication of personal trauma as experienced by series of individuals who have all lived through the same traumatic experience. Wars are commonly described as socially traumatic, but this label often applies to large sections of a population who may never have directly experienced the horrors of war, or to those whose direct experiences may be much more limited than others from the same population. These disparate experiences—which may in many cases involve individual trauma—corporately constitute social trauma.

Contrast this notion of social trauma with the application of the term to groups who all experienced a relatively common experience of trauma: Holocaust survivors of the death camps, for example, or the citizens of Hiroshima who survived the atomic bomb. Clearly the "symptoms" of these different applications of the term "trauma" must be very different—yet too rarely have those engaged in trauma studies effectively explored the nuanced implications of these differences. Along these lines, Kansteiner argues:

> it might make sense to argue with Freud that an individual's failure to work through his or her past results in unwanted symptoms of psychological unhealth, that the self relies on a sense of continuity that makes it impossible to repress the past without having to pay a psychological price for this repression. But on a collective scale, especially on the scale of larger collectives, such assumptions are misleading. Nations *can* repress with psychological impunity; their collective memories can be changed without a "return of the repressed."
>
> (KANSTEINER 2002, 186)

As an example, this conflation of the individual and social forms of trauma is apparent in Caruth's discussion of the film *Hiroshima Mon Amor* in her seminal work of trauma theory, *Unclaimed Experience* (Caruth 1996). There Caruth does note the "controversy" relating to the comparison the film makes between the experiences of a French woman whose lover, a German soldier of the occupying army in the Second World War, is killed, and those of a Japanese man whose entire family perished in the bombing of Hiroshima. However, her response to this paralleling in the film (what may be termed a largely individual trauma with one of a broadly social trauma) is that "the question of comparison, which made [*Hiroshima Mon Amour*] so controversial—what some people felt was a reductive equation between mass catastrophe and a historically less significant individual loss—has been displaced or rethought by the film" (124n14). Thus Caruth is apparently satisfied to conclude that film operates on a psychic level where such distinctions between the individual and social may be rendered unproblematic by displacement. Through such elisions, or "rethinkings," it becomes clear that the categorical distinctions between individual and social trauma are often given less than suitable attention. Admittedly, this focus on one relatively minor dimension of Caruth's work does not suitably acknowledge the complexity of her thinking on trauma, particularly in its challenges to the representational order. The problem I am here addressing is one where these insightful treatments of trauma as an ontological or epistemological concern are not clearly distinguished from the phenomenon of social trauma. We here must pass over the entire controversy concerning trauma studies' reliance upon psychic models and theories that have long lost favor among clinicians and scientists.[7]

In an attempt to give the concept of trauma a sounder sociological basis, Jeffrey Alexander (2004, 26) has set out a distinction between two scholarly approaches to the question of what he terms cultural trauma: one that is reliant upon the "naturalistic fallacy" that cultural trauma "result[s] from the intrinsic nature of the original suffering," and another, "constructivist" approach that recognizes the importance of "imagination [in] inform[ing] trauma construction" (9). Alexander argues that often social actions that come to constitute cultural trauma—what I will be here terming social trauma—are viewed widely as being the *natural* outcome of a particular event or experience. Alexander argues that there is no reason to think that societies act in ways that are analogous to individuals in how they react to historically traumatic events. In this sense, he argues, the term "trauma" itself, when applied at a social level, is at best simply a metaphor. Alexander argues that a constructivist approach to cultural trauma would posit instead that these are outcomes of a social process requiring particular institutional and other actors (10). He further argues that the reaction to experiences such as these will always be socially determined and fundamentally defined by the interests and aspirations, and the fears or anxieties, of a particular social group. Alexander terms this the "trauma process," which, when successful, leads to a routinized engagement with the trauma, formalized in official and semiofficial memorializations, monuments, commemorations, and in state nomenclature (24). He finds that accepting the social construction of trauma, and thus bringing to light the "trauma process," only confirms that narratives of trauma present opportunities for social groups to gain solidarity or at the very least to be recognized with a kind of sympathy by their Others. To summarize, an often predominant scholarly approach to the study of trauma seems to ask: How do theories of individual trauma elucidate the communal repercussions of socially traumatic experiences? Rather, in light of the points raised above, the question may be reframed: What social value accrues to different strategies for producing cultural memory of socially traumatic experiences, and why do certain social actors engage in such a production of cultural memory?

To begin to answer these questions, it is necessary to first discuss the manner in which social trauma may be seen to be socially productive. Dominic LaCapra identifies trauma as one of the key loci for comprehending modernity, arguing that trauma discourse has come to permeate historical and cultural engagements with the experience of the modern. He notes that often modern cultural engagements with social trauma come close to sacralizing the experience of trauma, of elevating it (or representations of it) to the level of the sublime:

> Trauma and the sublime are two vanishing points of an extreme contrast that threatens to disrupt all continua and disfigure all mediation. Traumatization might be taken as another name for the perhaps terroristic excess of abjection which is tantamount to negative transcendence. Hence the temptation is great to sacralize it. The sublime may already be the ecstatic secularization of the sacred in a radically "excessive" or transcendent form,

and the question is whether any mode of materiality may only signify or be a paradoxical vehicle for it rather than "incarnate" it.

(LACAPRA 2001, 190)

It is precisely among what LaCapra (2001, 23) terms the "secularized displacements of the sacred and its paradoxes" that social trauma emerges. Modern representations relating to trauma often "[keep] faith with trauma in a manner that leads to a compulsive preoccupation with aporia, an endlessly melancholic, impossible mourning, and a resistance to working through" (23). It is also of use to consider here LaCapra's conception of "founding traumas," which he defines as "traumas that paradoxically become the valorized or intensely cathected basis of identity for an individual or a group rather than events that pose the problematic question of identity" (23). We are here concerned with his application of the term more to the group than to the individual, but in either case it would seem that the designation of a particular trauma as "foundational" is significant to understanding the social repercussions of the traumatic experience. For LaCapra, this "resistance to working through" is inherently problematic, as his work tends to subscribe to the teleological arc of the psychoanalytic diagnosis of trauma: that with "working through" trauma comes some form of healing.

LaCapra carefully hints at but does not fully engage with the variegated uses (and abuses) of trauma discourse on the social level.[8] Rather, he reinforces the idea that social actions and cultural productions are part of a process of ending or overcoming trauma, which is the natural result of working through trauma. There exists a valuative divide between cultural works that contribute to this process and those that do not—a distinction denoted by his terms "writing trauma" and "writing about trauma." To this end, he argues, "writing trauma . . . involves acting out, working over, and to some extent working through in analyzing and 'giving voice' to the past—processes of coming to terms with traumatic 'experiences,' limit events, and their symptomatic effects that achieve articulation in different combinations and hybridized forms" (LaCapra 2001, 186). Again, the prescription is one that appears well grounded as far as individual trauma may be concerned, but LaCapra does not overtly problematize the idealized application of "writing trauma" as a form of "coming to terms" with trauma to his own very useful conception of founding traumas and their often social constitution. While LaCapra rarely touches directly upon the postcolonial, the tendency he observes in modernity to elevate traumatic experience to a kind of secular sublimity has a certain purchase within postcolonial contexts, as we will discuss.[9]

To better explore this problematic associated with the rise of trauma as a framework for rendering intelligible the history of the modern period, it is necessary to still further refine and focus our definitions, especially of what I am terming "social trauma." Understandings of trauma as a social phenomenon have often been muddied by the origins of "trauma" as a diagnostic term in individual psychoanalysis. Piotr Sztompka is not the first scholar to insist upon the understanding that social trauma is simply a metaphor, drawn from the human body in psychology and psychoanalysis and then deployed upon "the *body social*" (2000, 452). In this sense, Sztompka notes that "[t]rauma, like many other social conditions, is at the same time both *objective and subjective*: it is usually based in some actual occurrences or phenomena, but it does not exist as long as they do not become visible and defined in a particular way" (456). In other words, one may confirm the factuality of events that produce trauma (e.g., the massacre at Srebrenica) but social trauma itself is a product of particular historical interpretation (e.g., UN reports on the massacre at Srebrenica, popular cultural representations, memorials by the survivors, etc.). Absent the social apparatuses that allow for these facts to become "visible and defined," social trauma will not be a factor.

Sztompka (2000, 457) continues that "[t]here is always a pre-existing pool of available meanings encoded in the shared culture of a given community or society. Individual people do not invent meanings but rather draw them selectively from their surrounding culture and apply them to the potentially traumatizing events. Hence the traumatizing event is always a cultural construction." What is difficult to appreciate, then, is the extent to which social trauma may also be produced by events that may not "objectively" be understood as psychologically traumatizing. This point is important in understanding the emergence of the dynamic of perpetrator trauma, which may extend to contexts and settings far from the site of trauma. Sztompka goes farther than LaCapra in rethinking the teleology of social trauma when he poses the difficult question, "can the traumatizing events be—objectively—positive, beneficial" (458)? This provocative query requires us to come to terms with the ways in which trauma may be productive, and thus the ways in which social institutions may deploy cultural memory to enhance or promote claims of social trauma outside the affected society, or for consolidating concepts of social trauma within the group. In this sense, social trauma itself—whether or not based on objectively traumatizing events—may be of productive use to particular social groups or ideological aims.

Here I have all too briefly outlined the parameters of some of the debates at the heart of the use of the concept of trauma, especially as they relate to the notion of social trauma. As may be clear, this summary aims to intervene in these debates by first insisting on greater clarity concerning the conception of social trauma as distinct from individual trauma, and of thinking carefully of the utility of the metaphor of trauma when applied to the experiences of communities and collectivities. In particular, the "diagnosis" and "treatment" of social trauma may not simply be based upon seeking metaphorical readings of psychoanalytical concepts relating to the individual set against a historical and social backdrop. However, this said, I would not wish to argue that such metaphorical applications of these concepts are necessarily or fundamentally invalid when discussing social phenomena. The point here is simply to insist on critical self-awareness of the problematics involved in applying psycho-analytic concepts to discussions of trauma in the move from an individual to social context.

Having examined to some extent the phenomena associated with the concepts of social trauma, certain questions remain. If, indeed, there is a productive use to terming certain social phenomena as traumatic, and if the use of the metaphor of trauma in these applications both allows for and delimits certain understandings and interpretations of these phenomena, how do we go about evaluating them? To be certain, the question is not concerning the factual circumstances around established historical events, but rather how to assess the various social narratives that form around them, and the seemingly inevitable contestations that arise over the producing a cultural memory of these events.

Cultural Memory and Trauma Production

The constellation of social values that come to define particular interpretations of specific historical experiences as traumatic may be termed *trauma production*. "Trauma production," put briefly, is meant as shorthand for the institutional and social processes involved in articulating and codifying the interpretive parameters of (and values accorded to) social trauma, quite often at the level of the nation. In this sense, trauma production does not generally refer to any and all commemorative practices relating to traumatic histories, but the term is rather limited to those efforts that "valorize" and thus perpetuate the narratives of trauma for use in the formation of national or other communal identities. Put otherwise, trauma production is not primarily concerned with the resolution of social trauma (although it often is accompanied by the discourse of "healing" and "overcoming" trauma as a mechanism for self-legitimation), but is rather more broadly linked to the circulation of founding traumas that play a productive role in ideological and political contestations—whether local or indeed global in nature. The institutions and instruments of trauma production are many and may span the entire cultural field. Not all projects of trauma production employ all or even many of these instruments, and the particular media utilized in such a project may depend upon the positionality of the social groups involved in the project and their power within the broader cultural and political fields. Paramount among these institutions is the state itself and its various organs (or, via Althusser, the state ideological apparatus). It may be possible to argue that over the course of the twentieth and now the first decade of the twenty-first century, perhaps most nation-states have at some point sought to promote trauma production, especially through cultural and educational policy.

Across the postcolonial world, the majority of formerly colonial states also give high priority to commemorative practices relating to the struggle against colonialism, wars of independence, and in some cases wars that followed independence. These commemorations often involve aspects of trauma production, revisiting and renarrating traumatic events experienced in the course of the anticolonial struggle or its aftermath. Often, these are overlaid with the commemoration of postcolonial traumas such as regional wars, famines, natural disasters, or other catastrophes, and then set within the redemptive framework of nationalism and/or other ideological formulae (socialism, communism, state populism, etc.). The prominence of such commemorations testifies to the currency and value of trauma production for the postcolonial nation. It is for this reason that we find that contestation over cultural memory serves as a framework for political claims, and that the articulation of claims of social trauma come to play a more and more central role in social, political, and ideological formations.

Even in *The Battle of Algiers* one discerns a natural concern with the issue of cultural memory. Few if any scholars have explored the tension inherent in the temporality of how the film is structured—one of flashbacks and time shifts—and the experience of immediacy and contemporaneity given by the film's cinematography and editing. *The Battle of Algiers*'s structure highlights the question of memory that at times seems at odds with its urgent realism, by organizing the film as a flashback that moves forward to the opening scene, and in its coda that flashes forward again several years, the film is structured as, and embraces the problematics of, a memory text. What this inherent tension highlights is the degree to which the question of cultural memory was always immanent to representations of colonialism and struggles of national liberation. The contestations that will arise over the codification of a memory of these struggles is indexed within the film's structure, and may be traced in various threads within the narrative as well as in the visual semiotics of the work. For example, the often discussed sequence wherein a group of Algerian women dress in European style and place bombs in various locations in the European quarters of Algiers (a narrative element) is revived in the coda of the film, which focuses on an Algerian woman dancing with the Algerian national flag in defiance of the colonial authorities (as a semiotic element). Both of these elements make strong interventions into the politics of representation around the role of women in the revolution—a debate of which Pontecorvo was well aware. In this way, the film takes a particular stand on the cultural memory of the war of national liberation, and does so self-consciously.

Returning to the case of Bouchareb's films *Days of Glory* and *Outside the Law*, we find paradigmatic conflicts over cultural memory written both into the film texts, as well as in the broader reception afforded each film. *Outside the Law* is structured in such a way as to render the Sétif massacre as a founding trauma that motivates the protagonist, Abdelkader. During the massacre, Abdelkader's father and sisters are shot, his mother loses her sanity, and he is arrested and made to walk past rows and rows of bodies of those massacred. His activism with the National Liberation Front (FLN) when living in Paris some fifteen years after the massacre and his willingness to utilize brutally violent tactics in quelling internal dissent within the Algerian community, as well as his militancy with regard to the struggle against France, are all fundamentally to be understood as being in relation to the cultural memory of Sétif and that of the broader violence used against Algerians by the French in Algeria.

While the film's story ends on the night of October 17, 1961, when hundreds of Algerian FLN supporters were massacred in Paris, an elegiac coda ends the film with newsreel footage of Algerians celebrating their national independence on July 5, 1962—bookending the opening scenes of the celebrations of the liberation of France from Nazi occupation in 1945. The film in this way juxtaposes these two nationally triumphal moments, setting each against a moment of social trauma for Algerians. The first trauma, that of Sétif, is set against the celebrations of French liberation, while the second, that of the Paris massacre, is set against the celebrations of Algerian independence just months later. In *Days of Glory*, another postscript sets the film out as a memory text, even as the film itself contributes to the recuperation of the cultural memory (termed as forgotten by many critics) of the contribution of colonial soldiers from North and West Africa to the liberation of France. The final scene of *Days of Glory* has an elderly Arab veteran walking in a war cemetery for Muslim soldiers and praying, then follows him on a bus and walking through a crowded working-class Parisian neighborhood, ending with him sitting all alone on his bed inside a modest and empty apartment—framing the events that precede this scene as a sort of memory text.

In both cases, cultural memory of the colonial past is evoked in a manner that is politically productive for the present. *Outside the Law* in particular treads into the fraught field of trauma production, counteracting the social trauma claims of some groups while enhancing those of others. In these films we can discern the way in which the cultural memory of colonialism lays out discursive terrains that remain deeply contested. This terrain is crucial to the articulation of ideological formations and to the development of various forms of identity for societies in the postcolonial world. The images that found these memories also reflect upon the cultural memory of colonialism in the formerly colonizing world, and feed into political and social debates such as immigration policy, religious pluralism, foreign policy, and national identity. Traumatic memory in these contexts has a productive role to play in determining how these histories are interpreted. Cinema has played and continues to play a significant role in the production of cultural memory, through the proliferation of screen memories of these social traumas, and in intervening upon and resetting public discourse on these memories, in a process we may term "trauma production."

Colonialism, Memory, Masculinity

THE FOUR FEATHERS AND THE REDEMPTION
OF EMPIRE

The preceding chapter addressed the questions of cinema's role in cultural memory production and the links between cinema and colonial and post-colonial traumas quite broadly. In the present chapter I intend to move back into the colonial past, beginning with the heights of British colonial rule in the 1880s. From there I will trace the legacies of a paradoxically traumatic moment in British colonial history through the reinterpretations of that period in a novel and its film adaptations over the course of the twentieth and on the cusp of the twenty-first centuries. By doing so, I intend to illustrate the degree to which contestations over cultural memory and social trauma were already central to national cultures in the colonial metropole. In subsequent chapters I will look at how these same dynamics haunt the postcolonial world, continuing to play a central role in determining national culture and identity.

The 1902 publication of A. E. W. Mason's novel *The Four Feathers* gave a popular literary gloss to British efforts over the prior two decades to pacify Sudan and to bring the territory under full colonial control. Field Marshal Kitchener's campaign of 1898–1899 quelled the anticolonial revolt of the Mahdist movement, which had presented one of the longest and most sustained challenges to British imperialism in the colonial world to that date. Mason's novel may be seen as a late culmination of the cultural ethos projected by what one critic has termed "a series of remarkably successful books published in the 1890s" in Britain on the subject of the Mahdist revolt (Nicoll 2004, xxiii). This revolt, a messianic liberation movement that coalesced around the claim of Muhammad Ahmad ibn Abd Allah (1844–1885) to the spiritual title of Mahdi, offered Britain vigorous resistance from the inception of the Anglo-Egyptian attempts—beginning in 1882 in the aftermath of the British occupation of Egypt—to bring the Sudan under imperial control. In January 1885, the Mahdists defeated the Anglo-Egyptian army, overrunning

Khartoum and killing the army's British commander, General Charles Gordon.

This episode resonated in Britain as a painful humiliation, one of the most significant and unexpected defeats meted out to a British-led colonial army during the imperial era. The defeat echoed in public discourse around the colonial project, and circulated in the form of newspaper reports and literary accounts, which stoked fear and horror for the "fanaticism" of the Mahdists. The defeated British garrison in Khartoum was described as having been defending Sudan from savage religious extremists, and came to be identified as the victim of a brutal and inhumane sect, rather than as a colonial army which had been defeated by the resistance of native defenders. The British returned to the Sudan in 1892 and eventually routed the Mahdists in 1899. Mason's novel thus was set in the prism of a conflict of very recent memory, being published only some three years after the reestablishment of imperial control over Sudan.

The fall of Khartoum may be viewed as an occasion of profound national shock, constituting a moment of social trauma for Britain. This view obtains when reviewing the newspaper reporting concerning the defeat, noting how much attention was given to the manner in which the news affected the British public. While Gordon's Khartoum defenses had been breached by the Mahdist forces on January 26, 1885, the British press was not to report this event until over a week later, on February 5. For several weeks leading up to this date, British correspondents sent back dispatches while accompanying the troops of General Stewart as they fought a pathway to Khartoum to reinforce Gordon's troops. The resistance offered by Sudanese supporters of the Mahdi was fierce, but these news reports breathlessly conveyed a sense of inevitable triumph for the British, making the news of the defeat that much more difficult to accept. The language used in the initial reports offers testimony to the extent to which the event was not only unexpected, given the general sense of confidence in the invincibility of the British military against any anticolonial resistance, but articulated a deeper emotion of despair that was conjured among the British public.

Under the headline "Too Late!" the *Pall Mall Gazette* was one of the first to break the news in its late edition, exclaiming, "We regret to have to announce that the worst has happened in the Soudan."[1] On the next day, *The Times* of London outlined the general atmosphere in the capital, reporting that, "Not surprise, but stupefaction and indignation were experienced here when the news was received of the capture of Khartoum."[2] The correspondent goes on to convey a personal interaction illustrative of the general mood: "'We can at this moment,' an important personage said to me this evening, 'think only of the grief of England, tortured by the fate of Gordon, for we participate in the grief, and we loved Gordon as if he belonged to us.'" The article again summarizes the general feeling of Londoners, saying,

"The announcement of the fall of Khartoum has occasioned a shock which few will ever forget."

The *New York Times* also focused on the mood of the public in the face of this news, dedicating a full article to the matter with the subheading "Khartoum[,] the topic that absorbs and oppresses all." Its correspondent reported that, "old Englishmen assure me that not even the news of the famous Indian mutiny [of 1857] created such universal excitement and deep feeling in London and the entire country as have the tidings of the fall of Khartoum," and that "this shock has been a cruel one," throwing the English into "an abyss of mortification and wrathful despair." The picture outside London is no different, "all reports from the country represent the same consternation, anxiety and anger."[3] The comparison to the 1857 Indian Mutiny is revealing, as it indicates that the contemporary British public viewed the anticolonial dimensions of these distinct historical events as parallel. Individuals and organizations alike responded to the news using similarly hyperbolic emotive language. The City of London Conservative Association issued a statement that the association has "learned with deep regret and bitter humiliation that Khartoum has fallen," The *Belfast News-Letter* paints a broad picture of a sweeping sentiment of grief, anxiety, and despair across England and even into Scotland, brought on by what it terms "the catastrophe":

> London, and indeed the whole country, was startled this morning by an announcement that Khartoum had fallen. The statement was so terrible in its significance that for a time the public were unwilling to accept it. . . . Rarely has any news cause such a sensation in the metropolis. The inquiries at the War Office were incessant, the clubs were crowded with members, and newspapers could not be printed fast enough to satisfy the cravings for information. . . . In Ministerial and official circles to-day the news was received with feelings akin to dismay. . . . The news of the fall of Khartoum which was received at half-past six a.m. by a *Central News* telegram, produced a profound sensation in Edinburgh, which was increased as confirmatory telegrams from the same sources continued arriving throughout the day. At Colchester the greatest excitement prevailed and the people congregated around the principal newspaper office eagerly reading the telegram. At Nottingham the dispatch produced sensation. At Aldershot the tidings were received with mingled feelings of sadness and indignation. At Woolwich the news was received with consternation.[4]

Through the next week, the news continued to be summarized in the same extraordinary terms, except now a sense of foreboding and determination also marked the coverage. On February 15, *Lloyd's Weekly Newspaper* of London viewed the events as "lamentable tidings," which "have produced a sentiment of anguish, tempered by one of stern determination, not paralleled in England in a quarter of a century." It goes on, "the sickening alternations of fear and hope have their sequel in a fixed decision to tread the path that honour and duty mark out, to press on steadily to the goal." It ends with a call to renewed steadfastness, calling the situation a "supreme crisis."[5]

What is so striking in these reports is the way they move from discussing the events in Sudan, often including copious detail of military maneuvers, formations, and strategies, to link them to the emotive atmosphere in Britain, painting a broad picture of the "sentiments" of the British public. The emotive content is outlined in extraordinary terms, with phrases like "supreme crisis," "few will ever forget," "profound grief," and "abyss of despair," signaling the unprecedented nature of the public response to this event—occurring some thousands of miles away, in a remote and little-known appendage of British colonial holdings. Indeed, the numbers of British casualties were, in terms of contemporary European warfare, relatively few, and the economic, cultural, and even ideological links that bound Britain and Sudan were relatively weak in comparison with those of other colonial possessions. So why did the fall of Khartoum occasion such despair in Britain? The emotionally charged quality of the reporting perhaps not only accurately represented the feelings of many, but likely also contributed to the spread and recirculation of feelings that this event was a unique and singular occasion with deeply shocking and profoundly unsettling repercussions. Terming the event one of a social trauma is most salient when appreciating the excessively emotive language in which the event was reported, and the degree to which the British press participated in portraying this defeat as gravely impacting upon the public.

The Four Feathers, then, needs to be read with the emotive context of 1885's defeat as a backdrop, and is best understood as a text composed so as to address the profoundly shocking and unsettling implications of the defeat in Khartoum, despite the recuperation of national prestige by Lord Kitchener's defeat of the Mahdist army some fourteen years later. After a prologue set in 1869, Mason's book opens in June 1882, when a young man from an English military family, Harry Feversham, resigns his commission as an officer just days before his regiment is to deploy to Egypt, as part of the British occupation occasioned by the 'Urabi revolution there. On the verge of marrying an Irish woman, Ethne, Harry's reasons for leaving the service are at first unclear. Having traveled to his fiancée's estate, he there receives a package containing three white feathers and the calling cards of three of his fellow officers—a symbolic insult naming him a coward. Also angered by his apparent disgrace, Ethne adds a fourth feather to the others, and ends the engagement. Harry then spends some time in London alone before determining to redeem his lost honor by traveling to the Sudan on his own. He sets out on the voyage and disappears, vowing to an acquaintance not to return until his goal is met.

The novel then follows the fate of Harry's best friend, Durrance, who although being a fellow officer is unaware of the insult Harry has suffered.

Coincidentally, Durrance is the cause of Harry's and Ethne's short-lived engagement, despite the fact that he himself has long harbored undeclared feelings for her. Durrance is a soldier's soldier and in some ways the opposite of Harry—where Harry's sentimental qualities lead him to choose romantic love over military fraternity, Durrance sees the deployment as the fulfillment of his natural role, and represses his disappointment over losing Ethne to Harry. Over the course of three or four years spent in Egypt and Sudan, Durrance is promoted to the rank of colonel, and during visits back to England learns of Harry's disappearance and begins to grow closer to Ethne. Tragically for him, a case of sunstroke in the Sudan leads to his blindness and he is sent back to England as a casualty of the campaign. Despite having waited for news of Feversham for several years, Ethne decides to accept a marriage proposal that Durrance had made shortly before he lost his sight, which he reluctantly does not rescind after the unfortunate injury. Meanwhile, rumored sightings of Feversham are reported in Britain. Harry has carried out personal missions of value to the British, as a result of which one of the three initial dispatchers of the feathers comes to decide to withdraw the insult by reclaiming his feather. The second of his accusers is killed in battle, leaving Feversham with only one of the original three men to satisfy. This leads to the climax of the story, in which Harry is imprisoned in the House of Stone prison in the Mahdist capital of Omdurman. There he spends over a year in the company of his third accuser, before devising an escape with the help of a loyal Arab, Abu Fatima. Their escape leads to the withdrawal of the third feather, and Harry returns to England with his honor among his comrades regained. After hearing of Harry's feats, Durrance ends his engagement with Ethne to allow Harry to reclaim his former place at her side, and she withdraws the fourth feather.

While Mason's novel was published a few years after Kitchener's victory, the book is set in 1882 just before and after the fall of Khartoum, when the sense of crisis brought on by the defeat still resonated deeply throughout British society. The novel attends very little to the public dimensions of this crisis, instead choosing to use as a backdrop the more "universal" themes of reclamation of honor (Feversham), and of unrequited love (Durrance). However, it seems clear that Harry himself is to no small extent meant to allegorize the nation; his own inner conflict is projected onto the British stance on the Sudan, and the book's moral view on Harry's problem echoes in stark terms the prescriptions adopted by *Lloyd's Weekly Newspaper* (see note 5) just one week after the Mahdist victory: "to tread the path that honour and duty mark out, to press on steadily to the goal." By 1902, the anxieties and doubts raised by the defeat of 1885 had been set aside and a new confidence and swagger eclipsed the questions that had appeared in press and public forums regarding the moral justifications for imperialism instigated to some extent by that defeat. However, the anxiety within British colonial society set off by the events of 1885 continued to resonate, and in many ways the transformations in the character of Feversham reflect social unease over the social trauma of this defeat, and were based upon what many considered to be necessary alterations to masculine norms so as to recover the prior dominance of Britain as a world power.

Mason's book is often billed as a paean to unquestioning service to the British Empire. While accurate to an extent, the book is also a work marked by significant ambivalence and contradictions, motivated in no small measure by the uncertainties attendant to the realm of masculine idealization within Britain at that time. Contemporary reviewers alluded to this with their recurrent interest in the question of the "psychological" dimension of the work. For example, a review in *Academy and Literature* described the book as "a study in the psychology of cowardice."[6] Shortly after, the same journal included a longer review that noted that the short story upon which the novel was based was "excellent from a psychological as well as a narrative point of view, and well worth elaborating into a novel."[7] Various reviews alluded to Harry's psychological defects, describing him as "highly strung."[8] In other passages, quasi-psychological diagnosis was used to explain the character: "The double-shock [of receiving feathers from both his comrades and his fiancée] serves but to brace up his mind and to restore it to its proper balance" (*Athenaeum*, 647). In an assessment by the *Saturday Review*, again Feversham is described as "highly strung" but also he is termed "romantic and imaginative."[9] In all of these reviews it is clear that contemporary readers clearly discerned the book's narrative to be one pitting the abject "romantic and imaginative" tendencies of Feversham, pathologized in psychological terms as part of his "highly strung" disposition, against a form of masculinity that finds its "proper balance" in prioritizing military honor over love.[10]

Through the reception of the novel we may better discern the extent to which Mason's work is at heart a project of what Joane Nagel (1998, 247) has called the "nineteenth century renaissance of manliness." This movement included an institutionalization of "'normative masculinity', which included willpower, honour, courage, discipline, competitiveness, quiet strength, stoicism, sang-froid, persistence, adventurousness, independence, sexual virility tempered with restraint, and dignity" (245). Nagel argues that this renaissance was linked to the "institutions and ideology of empire" (249). Mason and other committed imperialists located the germ of the defeat in the Sudan in a corruption and degeneration of masculinity among young men in Britain, prescribing a "return" to what I will here be terming a fraternal-military masculinity as necessary in order to redeem the traumas brought about by the defeat in the Sudan. Feversham's failings are those of initially prioritizing nonmilitary aspirations, especially those relating to marriage and love, over the national-imperial project, as well as the filial bonds of military culture. This tension is resolved through Feversham's adoption of a robustly virile manliness, perhaps even excessive in its capacity for violence or brutality.

Mason's contemporary, E. M. Forster, treated the question of masculine idealization differently, working "toward a new synthesis in which the extremes of imperial masculinity are amalgamated with 'feminine' affections to produce a new gendered basis for literary plot and character" (Matz 2007, 40). Where Forster's imperial fiction idealized a "worthy masculinity whose strength is not brutality," Mason's work demanded a return to a muscular imperialism, literally embodied by the capacity of soldiers to eschew domestic comforts for the immaterial but transcendent rewards of sacrifice for the empire (39).

The Four Feathers was first adapted for cinema in 1915, in a little-remembered silent version directed by the pioneering American filmmaker Searle Dawley. Over the course of the next seventy-five years, six further cinematic or television versions would be produced. These versions are significantly different in how they adapt the novel to screen. While Merian C. Cooper's 1929 version retains the book's frame story, the depiction of Feversham's actions in the Sudan diverge greatly from the original, and reveal a protagonist significantly at odds with the one found in the novel. The Korda brothers' 1939 version is in general more interested in retaining a degree of fidelity to the literary text, but subtly adds new dimensions to the Feversham character. The 2002 film, directed by Shekhar Kapur—an Indian director with Bollywood roots—with a screenplay co-written by an Iranian-British screenwriter, is noteworthy in self-consciously setting out to revise the imperialist and racist dimensions of the story by casting Feversham as a conscientious objector to colonialism rather than as a coward, and elevating a minor African character in the book to becoming a close friend and comrade who accompanies him in his adventures across the Sudan. This "postcolonial" version, however, does little to mitigate many of the core ideological precepts of the narrative, thus settling on a fairly uneasy synthesis that neither fully embraces the imperial origins of the narrative nor fundamentally disavows them. Here I will compare the three aforementioned film adaptations, focusing in particular on the production of an idealized masculinity through the transformations that each presents to the Feversham character. These textual dimensions will be reflected against broader contextual questions relating to the biographies of the filmmakers, the production environments, and reception of each work, exploring the status of the story as a "memory text" for understandings of the use of that period of colonial history for later British and American cultural contexts.

What this chapter will examine specifically is the manner in which Mason's novel has provided the raw materials for recurrent appropriations of the colonial topos for varied uses in different times and in different places. The films discussed are American and British in terms of their production, and emerged at distinctly different historical moments, having been directed by filmmakers with significantly different political and ideological inclinations. While the differences between the various adaptations of *The Four Feathers* are telling, they map coherently upon their social contexts, which

share in their idealization of imperial masculinity but which do so for somewhat different ends. Given the vastly different historical contexts it may be
seen as paradoxical that each of these versions of the story resonates so significantly with the others, as well as with the novel, in the fundamental issue
of its valorization of imperial masculinity. While each filmmaker may have
entertained ideas of co-opting Mason's tale for his own uses, what we find is
that over the course of the twentieth century, the various incarnations of this
story remain at heart subservient to the powerful theme of seeking social
redemption through the transformation of masculine ideals to those which
serve the interests of empire.

Cooper and Shoedsack's *Four Feathers*:
Revenge and Masculine Redemption

Merian C. Cooper represented his relationship to *The Four Feathers* as deeply
personal. Prior to assuming a career as an entrepreneur of early American
cinema, Cooper flew sorties against German forces in the First World War,
eventually being shot down and held as a prisoner of war. Later, he was again
captured while fighting, this time while serving as a volunteer for the anticommunist Polish resistance to Soviet rule. During this time, Cooper has
reported, *The Four Feathers* was one of only four novels in his possession, and
so presumably his copy was rather well worn by the time of his release, given
that it was "the book that most inspired him" (Vaz 2005, 63). In fact, beyond
these specific references to *The Four Feathers* related by Cooper in his autobiographical writing and repeated by biographers, there seems to have been
much about the book that was resonant with the director's own life story.
While in Poland, he met fellow American volunteer Ernest Shoedsack and
together they began a career in the early cinema industry. While they went
on to direct several films together, most film historians attribute to Cooper
the superior position in their collaboration; Shoedsack was the technical wiz-
ard who conjured Cooper's visionary stories and ideological commitments in
moving picture form.[11]

Like Harry Feversham, Cooper was born into a military family, and was to
disappoint his father by being expelled from naval college. Like Feversham,
Cooper went on to seek a degree of redemption through volunteering to
enlist in the military in the First World War, dispelling his past imperfections
through pursuing acts of heroism on the battlefield. Again, like Feversham,
Cooper escaped from a military prison, and fought ideological enemies of his
homeland. Finally, and again like Feversham, Cooper's transformation was
in no small part represented as being driven by his adoption of a new kind of
masculine persona. This interpellation of the character of the director with
the character of the film protagonist gives a particular resonance to Cooper's

The Four Feathers, even if this version is often overshadowed both by the 1939 Korda adaptation and by Cooper's trademark 1933 film, *King Kong*. In part the commercial failings of the 1929 *The Four Feathers*, which was a silent film, may also be due to the technological shifts in the cinematic medium, specifically the rise of the talkie at that time. Nonetheless, the film is a consummate example of Cooper's ideological exuberance for the colonial backdrop, not only for projecting and resolving his own personal anxieties and inadequacies, but also for exploring and celebrating American racist ideologies, and the narratives of colonial conquest that filled the American national imaginary over much of the twentieth century.

After his early colonial adventure films—*Grass* (1925), *Chang* (1927), *The Four Feathers* (1929), and *King Kong* (1933)—Cooper went on to a celebrated career as a powerful film producer in Hollywood, and his partnerships with John Ford were perhaps his most significant achievements in the industry. Ford, who also shared an early legacy of colonial adventure films, found his highest calling in the American Western, directing what are widely viewed as some of the greatest masterpieces of this genre—some of his best-known works, such as *The Lost Patrol* (1934), *Wagon Master* (1950), *Rio Grande* (1952), *The Searchers* (1956), were produced by Cooper. Cooper was outspoken in his embrace of white supremacy, and applied his racism equally between colonial settings and those of the colonial American West. This sentiment is well expressed in his writing, as in: "The lust for power is in us, we white men. We'll sacrifice anything for the chance to rule. And I believe that it is right that black, brown, and yellow men should be dominated by the white" (Prime 2006, 64). While Cooper's writing offers clear testimony to centrality of such racism to his convictions, his films represent the fuller elaboration of the power of white supremacy in his thought, and the forms of masculinity that he viewed as necessary for the retention of this supremacy.

Thus is it not surprising that Cooper's first work, the 1925 ficto-documentary film *Grass: A Nation's Battle for Life*, is a paean to white Aryanist theories of origin, and a stake-out in the long clash within European thought between the biblical "Hebraist" and Egyptian origin myths for Europe, and the later and ascendant Aryanist myths that were adopted by European anti-Semitic fascism and other related ideologies.[12] In 1925, John Finley, president of the American Geographical Society, commented on the film saying, "It is a story that has an epic quality and a memory of the nomadic period in *our* civilization" (emphasis added; quoted in Cooper 1925, viii). This ideological orientation of the film has rarely been commented upon by film historians, who usually have discussed it as only an exemplary early work of cinematic ethnography for its documentation of the Iranian Bakhtiari nomads during their seasonal migration in search of fertile grasslands for their herds. However, the film's framing involves a Euro-American film crew whose aim is to set out in search of the racial origins of Europe, which they presume to be in the

Caucasus and the Iranian plateau. The filmmakers encounter the Bakhtiari tribe while on this quest, and their observation of the extreme hardships the tribe encounters on its migration, and the people's steadfastness in the face of these natural obstacles, offers the film crew a view of the racial origins of Europe and the essential characteristics to legitimize European ascendancy. So, while the film includes spectacular documentary sequences which are among early cinema's most exciting explorations of the possibilities of the medium, the ideological justification of the film—and presumably the value of the project as a whole for Cooper and perhaps many in his audience—is one of establishing racial origin myths and of reaffirming the racial supremacy of Europe over the non-Aryan world.

Many of these documentary techniques are also deployed in *The Four Feathers*, the external footage for which was filmed in part in East Africa, while the scenes with actors were filmed on a sound stage in southern California. The African sequences include staged footage of native tribesmen who were compelled to act in the film by local British authorities, as well as documentary sequences of local wildlife. The scenes of a herd of hippopotamuses stampeding over a high embankment and into a river, and of a family of monkeys trapped on a small rock island in the middle of the raging river, left a significant impression upon critics and audiences alike. For Cooper, the adventure involved in shooting these apparently authentic (although fully staged) scenes bled into the film narrative's own representational adventure. After all, it was Cooper himself who oversaw the gathering of a herd of hippopotamuses and the direction of them over the embankment where his camera was positioned; it was Cooper who had the monkeys thrown onto the small rock island and filmed as they threw themselves into the raging waters in a desperate attempt to reach the shores. On location in "Africa," Cooper and Feversham became indistinguishable, and Cooper was perhaps driven by earlier failings to his assertion of supremacy not only over the natural setting, but also over the native populations of the areas in which he was shooting. As Limbrick (2009) reports, Cooper gleefully recounts his whipping of "every villager he could find," to ensure their "full compliance" during the shoot. Limbrick also convincingly argues that, for Cooper, the exchange between self-made characterization in autobiography and the development of characters within his film narratives, especially in the case of *The Four Feathers*, were all part of a common impulse, one that may be termed as "playing empire." As Limbrick cogently argues, an important aspect of this was the articulation of a "settler masculinity" that joined filmmaker and character into a single mold.

The 1929 film departs from the novel both in story terms and in its characterization of Harry Feversham. Some of these changes may be due to the exigencies of staging a silent film rendition of the book, but many are no doubt due to Cooper's own desire to identify better with Feversham's transformation. Even in its depiction of Harry in Britain, there is a significant rewriting that casts his departure to the Sudan as motivated by revenge rather than by a need to reclaim his honor. In the film, Harry's relationship with his father is much closer, so much so that the receipt of the feathers results in his father's demise. On his father's deathbed, Harry exclaims (in a title card), "I'll make you take back the feathers, every one!" (figure 2.1). Once in the Sudan, Harry's character alters course even more significantly from that of the novel. While in the novel there is little detail of Harry's adventures, and most of the action is related in stories and letters that are received and circulated in England, Cooper's script centers the narrative on Harry's exploits in the Sudan. In the film, Harry is depicted as a hard-drinking outcast, spending his days in a tavern in the Sudanese town where the British garrison is headquartered (figure 2.2). While in the novel, Harry is shown as determinedly laying out a plan for regaining his honor, immediately adopting a disguise to be able to infiltrate the Mahdist areas, in Cooper's film he seems to be biding his time sullenly for the right chance to act. His first adventure is infiltrating the prison in Omdurman and to save his former comrade Trench. This storyline is the final and climactic adventure in the novel; however, Cooper instead writes a new concluding adventure, which is set at a fort manned by mutinous Egyptian troops under the command of his friend Durrance, who

FIGURE 2.1 *Harry at his father's deathbed* (The Four Feathers, 1929)

FIGURE 2.2 *Harry in a Khartoum tavern* (The Four Feathers, *1929*)

has been gravely injured in an earlier skirmish. Shortly after arriving at the
fort, Feversham declares himself in command, donning Durrance's officer's
uniform to assert his authority, and saving his comrade from the rioting
troops as a result. He then leads the garrison into battle against the native
"Fuzzy Wuzzies," thus saving the life of the third feather-giver, Castleton.
The film ends with Feversham back in England wearing an officer's uniform,
being decorated for his valor in a military ceremony. Ethne looks on and
then rushes forward to see him, apologizing for having given him the fourth
feather.

Throughout the Cooper-Shoedsack film, Feversham is darkly loutish, brutal, and overwrought with a sense of grievance. During the Sudan adventures
he is many times framed closely and lit with a shadow over his eyes, glaring at
an adversary. His actions are driven by a sense of injustice for the loss of his
father and his fiancée as a result of the feathers sent to him by his comrades.
His final victory, that of obtaining Ethne's apology, is marked by a sense of
aggrieved triumphalism, not of requited love. The young Feversham states
at the beginning of the film, "I'm not afraid of anything or anyone—I'm just
afraid of being afraid!" By the end of the film it seems that, rather than having
been transformed from a coward into a hero, Harry has rather now succeeded

FIGURE 2.3 *Harry confronts Ethne* (The Four Feathers, 1929)

in demanding recognition for manifesting innate qualities that were earlier either hidden or misapprehended. If Cooper viewed his Feversham as a
reflection of himself, it would appear that he regarded his own story as less
one of a coward transformed into a hero than of a hero who has only now
found recognition for what he always had been. As Limbrick (2009) notes, a
concept of settler masculinity helps to better understand Cooper's worldview,
and these qualities may also adhere to his rendition of Feversham, as Mason's
character is drawn from a different genre of imperial man. The "resourceful,
canny and pioneering masculinity" of settler prototypes were important to
Cooper (and would resurface in his later production work with John Ford),
but the earlier attraction that both Cooper and Ford found in British colonial
narratives must also be accounted for. This *ressentiment* that marks Harry is
reflected perfectly in the final scenes of the film: first, when Castleton tells
him he wishes he could take back his feather, Harry replies by angrily producing it and stuffing it in his hand, saying "but it can't bring back my father, or
Ethne's love!" In the final scene, when Harry is given a medal and is reincor-
porated into the military, again his face betrays no joy, only smoldering anger
and resentment. Even when Ethne approaches him and apologizes, he at first
stares at her fiercely, before finally taking her hand (figure 2.3).

In its Cooper-Shoedsack rendition, *The Four Feathers* is a reflection upon the making of a new imperial American man, moving beyond his mythic settler origins to meeting and matching prior colonial forms of masculinity, and eventually bettering them. Cooper himself was a paragon of this invention, and he reflected this new masculinity onto his Harry Feversham; a masculinity not simply settler-colonial but also profoundly imperial, looking to British imperialism for its model but retaining a specifically American sensibility. Cooper's identification with Feversham is documented in his own writing prior to his career as a filmmaker. In 1921, while attempting a career as a columnist and memoirist for the *New York Times*, Cooper writes of the work as a constant companion, saying,

> Sometimes my courage droops. I think my hardships greater than they really are, though they are nothing to squeal about. Then out of the sack comes, "The Four Feathers" by A.E.W. Mason. I read how Harry suffers real hardship and torture. I seem him bareheaded, under a burning sun, in a dirty little Egyptian town, with parching lips and bleeding body: I see him in the smothering House of Stone fighting to stay on his feet amid a mob of howling blacks night after night.
>
> (A FORTUNATE SOLDIER 1922, 52)

In another setting, Cooper responded to an interviewer's question, "Your comparison of me to Harry and *The Four Feathers* may be a correct one—I'm not a psychologist" (Vaz 2005, 161). The fact that Cooper supposed this resemblance to be psychological is telling, even as he reinterpreted Feversham's motivations to mirror his own personal anxieties. By rendering Harry's shame as one that reflected deeply upon his masculinity, in a way even more profoundly than in the novel, Cooper betrays his own overperformance of the military-colonial man. In Cooper's hands, this form of masculinity is not simply one of resurrecting or returning to a prior positioning as a man, but rather it is a masculinity marked by a brooding sense of *ressentiment*, one struggling to overcome its shameful origins.

Nostalgia and Revival: The Korda Brothers' *Four Feathers*

The Korda brothers' 1939 screen version of *The Four Feathers* remains the standard-bearer for cinematic adaptations of the book. So strong was the perceived imperialist message of the film that some American reviewers of the work were significantly discomforted by its ideological content. For example, Vince Hall, writing in the *North American Review* in 1939, described the film as "a genuine 'tub-thumper' for British imperialism," finding little of redeemable value in a film that is based upon "the invincibility of British arms," through a story that communicates "what ungrateful and rebellious (and very

very villainous) natives might expect if they should decide to be a government unto themselves" (Hall 1939, 190). These anticolonial American sentiments were not strong enough to dissuade American audiences, as the film was to be "hugely successful" (Tabori 1959, 202). It went on to gain an Oscar nod for its cinematography, and brought in significant box-office receipts for the Korda brothers, just when their financial stability was in question (Drazin 2011, 306). Many film historians comment upon the political divide between Alexander Korda, the film's producer, and his younger brother Zoltan, who directed the work. Alexander was known as an active conservative—a close personal friend of Winston Churchill—who entertained strongly supportive views on British colonialism. By contrast, Zoltan, who was a socialist, was said to harbor ambivalences concerning the imperial project (Shail 2007, 119). Nonetheless Zoltan came to be identified closely with the colonial adventure genre, through his direction other classic colonial fare such as the *Sanders of the River* (1935), *Elephant Boy* (1937), *The Drum* (1938), and *The Jungle Book* (1942).

The Korda brothers' version of *The Four Feathers* adapts the novel's story reasonably faithfully, perhaps most successfully in illustrating the nuances of Harry Feversham's character, but it also offers several changes of plot as well as perspective. Where in 1902 presumably little need existed to offer a historical summary of the events around the book's action, in 1939 an epigraph sets the story firmly in the grounds of colonial history. A title card and a brief montage summarize the events of 1885. This text is then followed by scenes of Mahdist forces (represented as dark-skinned multitudes with torn clothing and wild hair) rushing in mobs across deserts, entering fortresses, and finally lowering the Union Jack and replacing it with a green flag with an indecipherable pseudo-Arabic text. The sequence concludes with a fictional *London News* tabloid cover headlined "Fall of Khartoum," followed by a close-up that shows smaller text of the newspaper reading "The Murder of General Gordon—Khartoum, 26 January 1885."

This montage fades out to a horse-drawn carriage entering the grounds of an idyllic English manor, the home of General Faversham.[13] The juxtaposition of Sudanese mayhem to English country life sets out a stark distinction between the mythic English country home, and the savage and barren rough scrub of the colonial frontier. Dr. Sutton, the general's "old comrade," arrives and conveys the news of Gordon's death, to which Faversham replies, "He wasn't hard enough!" The colonial defeat is attributed to a character flaw in Gordon. Shortly after, he says of his son Harry, "I don't understood the boy," because he was found reading a poetry book—"Shelley of all people!" Here the anxiety over an influence of romantic forms of masculinity are laid bare through the pernicious presence of one of the major figures of English high literary romanticism in his son's library. The weaknesses of Gordon are through this juxtaposition insinuated to be of a category similar to those of

Harry. It would appear that these claims of character defects find greater application in the context of the production of the film and may relate to the setting and context in the shadow of an ascendant fascist Germany, as well as a weakened and diminishing British Empire. In the face of these realities, the Korda film's concerns about romanticism and weak leadership have a specific purchase.

In the following scene, the boy Harry's predilection for Shelley is off-set by the stark poesis of the homosocial world of the general and his "old comrades," who gather once a year for a dinner at the general's home to commemorate the Crimean War. Canards such as "War was war in those days, and men were men, no room for weaklings" frame the conversation of the former soldiers, who tell stories of battles of days of yore. General Faversham draws a summary of the various strands of conversation by pro-claiming that he "can't stand cowardice"—a comment he addresses directly to his son. Later he develops the idea by saying, "There's no place in England for a coward." The lines of heroism and cowardice, outlined in nationalist terms, are sometimes illustrated with what is meant to be dark humor, with the former soldiers matter-of-factly recounting the bravery of those who "lost an arm," or whose heads were "blown off." Nonetheless, the scene con-tinually reiterates a normative position whereby bravery and national honor are monopolized by a colonial and fraternal-military form of masculinity that is set against alternatives that are coded as cowardly. The general's view that cowards have no place in England sets the question firmly into national terms that overlap with colonial objectives. The news that Gordon has lost Khartoum is necessarily resonant, in that the general places the blame for the defeat on the weak character of this colonial administrator. The national trauma, the loss of Khartoum, is thus understood as emerging from a strain of cowardice that is inimical to the worldview of the old soldiers. The film then departs from the novel by situating its action in 1892, aligning the story not with Gordon's defeat but with Kitchener's later victory. British soldiers drill in formation, the camera frames the impressive choreography of their bodies in motion. Among the soldiers, Harry is known as someone who, "can't take a joke, never takes a drink, mopes around all day, reads poetry all night." The portrait accords to some extent with romantic attributes, par-ticularly his seriousness, his moping, and again in his disturbing interest in poetry. His disdain for drinking may be less resonant to the romantic tem-plate, but here is meant as a sign of his disinclination toward brotherly bond-ing with his comrades in arms, an individualism that again incites portraits of romanticism.

Harry's fiancée, Ethne, is the daughter of one of General Faversham's comrades, a fellow veteran from the Crimean War who has a penchant for retelling old war stories to anyone within earshot. While these qualities are exaggerated largely for humor, Ethne's father nonetheless represents more than any other character the continuity of fraternal-military codes through generations, making clear his wish to see these transmitted to Harry in his union with Ethne. During a ball to celebrate their engagement, Ethne reports to Harry that due to her father's excitement over his anticipated deployment to Egypt, "we're having Egypt for breakfast and lunch, and the honor of the regiment for supper." After she admits that her father has difficulty in distinguishing Harry from the regiment in general, Harry then asks her if she has the same problem—she does not answer. This anxiety, of the metonymic value of Harry as a signifier for his regiment, underlies Harry's own wishes to be fully recognized as individual, aloof and apart from the fraternal circle into which he has been born. He diverges from the idealized masculinity of a colonial soldier by insisting upon his difference from the group identity of the regiment.

When the time comes to articulate the reasons for his resignation, Harry takes a decidedly anticolonial tone. He bemoans "the futility of this idiotic Egyptian adventure, the madness of it all, the ghastly waste of time that we can never have again." Harry links his disdain for the colonial project in utilitarian and even philanthropic terms, arguing somewhat cryptically that by staying he will be able to "save all those [British] people who've been neglected by my family because they preferred glory in India, glory in China, glory in Africa!" This rationale is later even deemed honorable by a sympathetic friend of his father who says, "You tell me you left the Army because your duty to your home was greater than your duty towards a crowd of African peasants? Well there's nothing dishonorable in that Harry, if that's all." However, eventually Harry accepts that this ideological attempt to explain his resignation is not "the whole truth," and that there is something more innate to his disavowal of military duty. Having to finally admit, "I am a coward," Harry's transformation begins and he decides to leave England to seek a manner by which to redeem his lost honor. The film thus sets a sharp distinction between the possible conviction that colonialism is wrong, or at least that other priorities should prevail, and the ontological condition of cowardice. The insinuation that cowardice is an innate character defect is, again, a marker that distinguishes a fraternal-military masculinity from other forms. While earlier assessments insinuate that Harry suffers as a romantic, Harry himself attempts to cloak his (poor) masculinity in the more acceptable discourse of a committed anticolonialist. Forced to face the truth, Harry himself accepts that his problem is one of innate qualities, resonating back to his father's concerns with his love of romantic poetry, and finds that the only remedy is one that involves a full personal transformation, and that rescues him of his purportedly natural inclination.

Having now accepted the need to transform himself, Harry is initiated upon his new path with an act of self-disfigurement, that of being branded upon the forehead with an iron once he arrives in Egypt, where he seeks to

FIGURE 2.4 *Harry has his forehead branded (*The Four Feathers, *1939)*

find a way to join the British Army in Sudan (figure 2.4). The branding, a form
of camouflage, is meant to disguise him as a Sudanese native and facilitates
his movement without recognition, but also signifies a ritual penance and
punishment for his innate character failings. While the "Sengali" tribe, of
whom he seeks to appear to be a member, are branded by the Mahdists in a
cruel act of subjugation, for Harry the branding is a public act of self-negation
for his failure to live up to the codes of colonial fraternal-military masculinity. He is made to bear further abject acts of self-negation in his journey
toward the British army, by being lashed while working as a slave, hauling
boats carrying war materiel down the Nile (figures 2.5 and 2.6). During the
latter scene, close-ups of his agonized face bear witness to his painful surrender to fate, while wider shots emphasize the racial abjection he bears in
becoming African, lost in the tumult of dark-skinned savages and no longer identified by the British as white. The soundtrack here, a pseudo-African
chant sung over rhythmic drumming, only completes the horror of the price
he must finally pay as tribute for reclaiming his honor.

The film parallels Harry's fate to that of his military comrades, in particular that of Durrance, who as a former friend and comrade of Harry sup-
plies the closest foil to him. The episodes concerning Durrance's loss of sight
and the battle which ends with the defeat of the company he commanded,
all affirm his natural disposition as a soldier, and his injury—drawn as a
corollary to Harry's branding—is celebrated as a sign of his heroism. Even

FIGURE 2.5 *Harry is flogged as a slave* (The Four Feathers, *1939*)

FIGURE 2.6 *Harry is captured by the British* (The Four Feathers, *1939*)

while blind, he feigns sight while commanding his troops in a battle, so as to preserve their morale. In this battle, Harry carries out the first decisive act toward his redemption, by saving Durrance from certain death at the hands of a Sudanese fighter, and afterwards leading him to safety through the desert. Harry goes through various further bouts of physical abnegation, by being beaten, flogged, or imprisoned alternately by both British and Mahdist forces. The emphasis on the physicality of the retribution he must pay is intense; through many of the scenes set in the Sudan, Harry's body is shown as bloody and cut, and close-ups show his face contorted, in thirst or pain. The immense scar on his forehead, balanced by the rough beard that covers most of his face, only reaffirm the profundity of his transformation. Yet when the moment for action comes—when he devises an escape from the Stone Prison of Omdurman—he is quickly able to recuperate his true identity, assuming the role of the British officer and taking command. His transformation is complete when, under heavy fire, he raises the Union Jack over the prison just as the Anglo-Egyptian army routs the Mahdists definitively.

The news of Kitchener's military achievement is shown as bringing about a public outpouring of jubilation and celebration in London. Harry's part in the battle is reported in the newspapers with necessary flourish, and so news of the recovery of his honor is publicly disseminated. Once back, his final act definitively sets out his trajectory of self-punishment as firmly in his past. Where in his youth he had cowered before the generals and colonels of his father's generation, Harry now takes the reins within the social setting and savors his newfound ability to dominate even the old heroes. At a dinner party hosted by Ethne's father, Harry dares to challenge the old Crimean War veteran in his thousandth retelling of his brave attack against the Russians (figure 2.7). By introducing the testimony of his late father about the battle, which betrays Ethne's father's narrative as self-aggrandizing, Harry neutralizes the legacy of the old veteran and assumes masculine primacy in the family. Ethne's father, who had nothing for contempt for Harry as a civilian, is made to recognize his son-in-law as not only his equal in military terms, but also as the new leader of the family. Not only has Harry proven his fidelity to the codes of colonial masculinity, but he has done so in a way that wins the primary male role in this military family. Once his symbolic slaying of the father (-in-law) is complete, Harry turns to Ethne, handing her back the final feather that had coded his dishonor, and brings her in for a kiss, while the screen fades to black.

The Four Feathers charts a narrative of transformation in Harry, who at the outset is marked by a dubious form of masculinity, coded romantic through his individualism and through his love his poetry. Other contextual "psychological" elements confirm an unbalanced constitution: Harry's mother has apparently been dead since his childhood, and he lacks any feminine

FIGURE 2.7 *Harry challenges Ethne's father* (The Four Feathers, 1939)

influence. Nonetheless, his mother's traces are observed within him, as Harry is told by his father's friend Dr. Sutton in an early scene. Even in the household, the servants are shown as solely men, and Harry's father keeps company only with male friends. The absence of women, even as secondary characters, lends high priority to homosocial relationships, even at the expense of heterosocial or heterosexual ones. This priority is echoed in many other colonial films of roughly the same period. For example, in George Stevens's colonial action-comedy *Gunga Din* (also released in 1939), a troika of soldiers in the northwest of India fight against a murderous cult of Indian nationalists. One of the three, Ballantine, is due to leave the service to be married, an event which is the focus of a lingering comic subplot wherein his comrades conspire to trick him into reenlisting, thus effectively ending his engagement. The triumph of this plan, which is shown eventually to have the support of even Ballantine himself, is coded as the victory of fraternal-military masculinity over the putative effeminacy of a civilian life and marriage. In both films, a certain revival of colonial masculinity is at the core of the story, and in *The Four Feathers* this revival is explicitly linked to the overcoming of colonial trauma and the redemption of the honor of the empire. This is clear in the various ways by which the trauma of Gordon's defeat is attributed to weakness—not only of Gordon himself, but of British men in general. Kitchener's campaign sets out to redeem this defeat, and the transformation of the British is allegorized in Harry's own personal change. By the end of the film, there is no lingering evidence of affected romantic inclinations, even in the reconciliation with Ethne—and Harry presumably no longer reads Shelley.

By 1939, the British imperial project was significantly on the wane. India was in the last stages of gaining her independence, and other major colonial holdings had been lost or promised self-rule in the interwar period. The conjunction of a sense of colonial losses, and the threat posed by the rise of European fascism, combined to present a profound challenge to British self-representations as a benevolent but supreme power, still great enough to assume an empire upon which the "sun never sets." Memories of the crisis brought about by the loss of Khartoum in 1885 perhaps found a useful resonance in this historical moment, when Britain was for the first time in many years facing a foe able to strike not only upon her shores, but indeed to sow terror on the streets of the imperial capital itself. The onset of a British war effort, in the face of impending colonial losses, required the conjuring of memory texts not only reaffirming British values, but also reminding British audiences that their country had prevailed in the face of other traumatic losses. The Mahdist revolt, then, provided a canvas upon which British publics could project their present anxieties, and find reassurance in the final victory and affirmation of supremacy that the long war in Sudan provided. In this context, Zoltan Korda's leftist sympathies and his brother Alexander Korda's conservative activism can be seen as finding a common ground by reviving *The Four Feathers* for use in the oncoming fight against Nazi Germany. The Kordas' Jewish Hungarian origins would give this project only an additional poignancy. It seems clear that the historical shift that the film's narrative makes, setting Harry's adventures as contemporary to Kitchener's victory rather than as several years prior (as in the novel) is seen as a necessary way to make certain the link between his personal masculine transformation and the national redemption of a traumatic defeat that the campaign of 1898 marked. This more decided triumphalism enhances the film's celebration of colonial masculinity, serving not only imperial interests, but also bolstering an uneasy British public and sending clear messages about the kind of British men who would be needed to face the challenges of a new world war, along with the increasingly fragile constitution of the colonial empire.

Postcolonial Nostalgia for Empire: Kapur's *Four Feathers*

Shekhar Kapur's 2002 version of *The Four Feathers* was widely viewed as "revisionist" (Ramachandran 2003, 48). With a screenplay co-written by the Iranian-British writer Hossein Amini and the Hollywood screenwriter Michael Schiffer, the film was represented by the filmmakers as well as the press as "anti-colonial" (Curiel 2002, 42). This impression of the film was strong enough to motivate a columnist in the conservative American journal the *Weekly Standard* to write at length criticizing the release of the film in the aftermath of the attacks of September 11, 2001, when the United States was pursuing new wars in the region. Kapur's film, shot and completed by early 2001, was deemed problematic to release in the months immediately after the attacks on September 11 of that year. Even months later, in 2002, the film was received as a text encumbered by the rupture that these attacks were said to have caused—perhaps one reason why the work was not a commercial success.

Kapur states in interviews that his intention in making *The Four Feathers* was to rethink the century-old story along anticolonial lines, "As much as I could take (a stand against British colonialism), I did" (Curiel 2002, 42). The film enacts a number of storyline changes to the original as well as to the preceding adaptations, the most significant of these being the rewriting of the character of Abu Fatma, who plays a very small role in the novel (and appears as a minor character in the 1939 film as well), but who in the Kapur film is made to be Harry's close friend and protector. While the 2002 adaptation makes some adjustments to lessen the starkly racial logic of its predecessors, it in fact amplifies the idealization of homosocial military masculinity that originates in Mason's novel. The few lines of criticism of colonialism uttered by Harry offer little by way of fundamentally rethinking the work's ideological thrust. Consequently, the film goes much farther in idealizing the transformation of Harry, by giving greater and more detailed attention to his journey of abjection, dwelling often and in detail upon his physical pain, thirst, and hunger and the corporeal marks of these deprivations upon his body. Again, as with prior versions, a Christian ethos demands that Harry's redemption must be paid for through his suffering, but here the suffering is more bloody, more corporeal, and often played in slow motion. His reentry into the society of British manhood demands his passing through a gauntlet of abjection, which here is aestheticized in a manner that transcends previous versions by many factors.

The 2002 film begins with a credit sequence of young men playing rugby on a muddy field in Britain, watched by a small crowd. The game is violent, but the camaraderie of one team results in their victory. This scene and the later early scenes of the film establish a theme of homosocial bonding, and jocular male friendship as a form of military masculinity. In juxtaposition with the earlier depictions of the British soldiers as stiffly formal in their relationships, here the men are shown first roughhousing and fighting on the rugby pitch, then later in a bathhouse joking, slapping one another, and sharing no little physical intimacy—the homosexual undertones are sublimated if impossible to ignore. Later, the group of men arrives at a ball that is to be the occasion for announcing Harry's engagement to Ethne in a tight fraternal group, swigging from a flask and joking with Harry.

However, Harry's resignation of his commission results in his being cast out of this tight network, and the film marks this expulsion in various ways, in particular in the scenes of Harry in London after his regiment has departed for Sudan. The hints of Harry's abjection begin even before his arrival in Sudan. His face is pale, cheeks sallow, and he is sapped of life. The juxtaposition with his prior state while in the army could not be more stark—the homosocial military family provided him a vitality and sustenance. Once in

FIGURES 2.8–2.10 *Harry suffers deprivation and beatings* (The Four Feathers, *2002*)

Sudan, as in the Korda brothers' production, Harry finds various ways to subject himself to bodily abuse. In various scenes he is savagely beaten by slave traders, Mahdists, and British soldiers (figures 2.8–2.10). Abu Fatma, here a paragon of physical fortitude and honor, saves him from death more than once, but does so only after Harry has suffered his beating.

The theme of physical abjection reaches a pinnacle in the final sequences of the film—first, in the scene where Harry is imprisoned in Omdurman, in which he is lost in a sea of perambulating prisoners, eventually trampled underfoot and nearly killed. He is saved by his former comrades, whom he has come to help escape. After they do escape, the film's climactic fight pits Harry against a lone Mahdist, in a hand-to-hand fight to the death. The battle, which takes on the overtones of a primeval struggle, ends with Harry brutally stabbing his foe and emitting a feral cry. This transition into nonhuman realms is the apotheosis of abjection—a crossing of the line between human and nonhuman. Here, his abjection marks Harry as outside of humanity, but also marks the final and perhaps ultimate price that is to be paid for his reentry into the realm of military fraternal society. In the final scene, Harry returns to England, and watches as Durrance speaks at a memorial event for the war's fallen:

> Those who have journeyed far to fight in foreign lands, know that the soldier's greatest comfort is to have his friends close at hand. In the heat of the battle, it ceases to be an idea, for which we fight, or a flag. Rather, we fight for the man on our left, and we fight for the man on our right. For when armies have scattered and empires fall away, all that remains is the memory of those precious moments we spent side by side.

Denuded of "an idea"—that of a commitment to the empire—here the colonial dimension is erased by the distilled priority of celebrating fraternal-military masculinity.

This ideological position, which veils the geopolitical realities of colonialism (in part by presenting this move as "postcolonial") and which instead proclaims as universal the form of masculinity celebrated in this film, is itself deeply imperialist. The framing of the narrative, where the errant and ethically compromised European man seeks and finds his redemption through his adherence to military-fraternal masculine codes in a colonial war, is imperialist, but more so in an American register than in one that would be familiar to late nineteenth-century Britain. The American imperial project stages itself in textual forms as ideologically neutral and socially individualistic and masks its geopolitical dimensions in narratives of "brotherhood," which are meant to be played out far from the center of troubling considerations of maintaining a global hegemony. What these three versions of *The Four Feathers* betray is the way in which the colonial essence of this story continues to remain productive in distinct historical moments, by directors working in very particular social and cultural contexts. What many view as universal in the story is in fact at the core of its ideological specificity as a colonial-imperial fantasy. The anxiety of what is viewed as a corruption of masculinity drives each story, and at core reflects the extent to which concerns about forms of masculinity that are not beholden to a military-fraternal idealization present challenges to colonial and imperial ideologies. The redemption in each of these stories, often borne out through the marks left upon the body of Harry Feversham, interpellates audiences, presumably primarily male, in a fantasy of gaining social honor through service to colonial-imperial ends. Even when self-consciously "postcolonial," as in Kapur's 2002 version, this universalization of military-fraternal masculinity leads only to a revalorization of and nostalgia for colonialism, even as a form of cultural memory.

The putative traumas of colonizers may now properly be viewed as forms of perpetrators' trauma—Harry's transformation into a colonial perpetrator (of the occluded traumas of the colonized Sudanese) is itself a redemption of the traumas of the colonizer. About this more will be said in chapter 7 of this book, as in the chapters that follow from here I will be turning to examine cinema's role in articulating anticolonial cultural memory of the struggle against colonialism, and from there will move to explore postcolonial traumas of war, civil conflict, and occupation. While certain terms remain constant across the colonizer-colonized divide—trauma, cultural memory—it would be incorrect to view this consistency in nomenclature as rendering these equivalent. Rather, the consistency in employing such terms is intended to signal the ways in which trauma production has come to define communal interpretations of the past on different sides of these political divides. The question therefore is not whether victim or perpetrator has a purer claim to traumatic memory (ethically, there should be no question), but rather how both employ the discourses of trauma in articulating their own cultural memories.

Freedom, then Silence

MEMORY AND THE WOMEN OF EGYPTIAN
AND TUNISIAN INDEPENDENCE

In the final long shot of *I Am Free* (*Anna hurra*, dir. Salah Abu Sayf, 1958) the protagonist, Amina, walks into the atrium of a prison, slowly ascending the stairs to her cell as the other women prisoners ululate in celebration (figure 3.1). She has just married a fellow political prisoner, an event that communicates the final, albeit ostensibly paradoxical, message of the film—that it is only in prison that Amina has found *true* freedom. The ideological framing which links Amina's political activism and commitment, and her resulting imprisonment, to her ability to view herself as free, performs a feat common in postindependence representations of women's roles in the anticolonial struggle—whether in Egypt or in other newly independent postcolonial nations. Amina's search for freedom as a woman has taken her through various life stages and social stations, but her sublimation of this personal quest to the greater social aims of the struggle against British imperialism presents the two political endeavors as finally in conflict. Where earlier in the film, Amina appears to embody the courage of Egyptian women of the mid-century who fought to transcend social restrictions to pursue education, employment, and economic independence within the family structure, in the last scenes of the film such gains are suddenly negated, and even coded as antirevolutionary.

In the 1950s and 1960s, as in other newly independent nations, Egyptian filmmakers idealized the anticolonial struggle in cinematic form, producing cultural memory of the independence struggle that is as gendered as it is ideological. These works contributed to broader cultural projects to set out the parameters of cultural memory of the revolutionary period, doing so in a way that served the exigencies of their own historical moment. In no small part, these works contribute to the distillation of a deeply gendered notion of this historical phase, one that may not have served purely historical aims, but which resonated with the predominant political interests that dictated

FIGURE 3.1 *Amina walks into the prison* (I Am Free)

a rethinking of women's roles in postcolonial societies. This move was not uncontested, but nonetheless constituted a form of memory discourse that came to be hegemonic in this period. However, within a generation or so, this predominating discourse on women's roles in the nationalist struggle came to be subject to new challenges. The accumulating failures of the postcolonial state, and new venues for the elaboration of cultural memory, produced openings in the national narrative within which the occluded memory of women in the independence moment was recoded, not in a triumphal register, but in one that is *traumatic*. While chapter 1 examined the use of—and indeed the productive nature of—trauma in the formation of cultural memory of war and conflict in colonial settings, the present discussion focuses on the anticolonial context instead. While by its own nature, the culture of anticolonialism sets out to oppose much of colonial practice, the present discussion would not be the first to focus on continuities that may be traced between the colonial and anticolonial. The productive use of the category of trauma in this context is perhaps initially less significant than other forms of cultural memory, but as I will show later in the chapter, trauma may come to provide a prism through which the cultural memory is increasingly reconfigured in subsequent generations of postcolonial societies.

This process of gendering the cultural memory of the Egyptian anticolonial struggle is staged within both *I Am Free* and *The Open Door* (*Al-Bab al-maftuh*, dir. Henri Barakat, 1963). The form of cultural memory presented by these films, a triumphal framing that subordinates the cause of women's equality to that of national liberation, is cast into question quite provocatively a generation later, as I will show through a discussion of the Tunisian director Moufida Tlatli's *The Silences of the Palace* (*Samt al-Qusur*, 1992), a film that reflexively stages the remembrance of the independence struggle as traumatic. I read the earlier Egyptian films as representing a postindependence impulse to efface the particularities of the ongoing struggle for women's rights and to code the demand for equal status as dangerous to the nationalist movement—a point that emerges through what I will here be terming the development of an "inner voice" to these characters. The inner-voice register of these films marks their "feminine" quality; a corollary register is not to be found in films on the nationalist struggle that feature men as the primary protagonists. Where women of the time often saw their work in both political arenas as congruent and by no means in conflict, the early postindependence narratives memorializing the anticolonial struggle often punished women characters who went too far in prioritizing gender equality in their political commitments, and celebrated those who sublimated this aim to their commitment to the national cause—all dynamics that are borne out in the expression of the inner voice of these characters. The turn against women's equality in the postcolonial context was often motivated by anxieties born in the changing gender roles within the family structure of the colonized, which resulted in deeply gendered representations of the anticolonial struggle. In particular, this gendering strategy sets limits for the production of cultural memory on resistance to colonialism, and the figure of the committed woman plays a central role in framing the memory of the independence struggle as triumphal when (and in part, because) she returns to the folds of the patriarchal national order. The inner voice returns in Tlatli's critical revisitation of the nationalist moment, but as the space wherein the traumatic memories of this period may be voiced.

Nationalist Anticolonialism and the Remembrance of Women

What the changes in the cultural memory of women's roles in the national liberation struggle betray is the nature of the contestations that have continued to mark the cultural memory of these events, and the productive incorporation of trauma discourse as oppositional to the triumphal nationalist narrative. In many films and novels set in the period, women characters achieve a significant presence, but in ways that continually subordinate their struggles for gender equality to the political demands of the nationalist movement. One way to state the problematic is that "in national liberation we find great potentialities for overturning gender and 'race' and other inequalities. But we may find inequalities, repressions, and injustices that are unattended to because the inequalities have been occluded by creeping common sense and practices of property. While in ideological terms there is a commitment to equality, it is waiting to be fully realized" (Bannerjee, Mojab, and Whitehead 2010, 265). As Beth Baron (2005, 4) similarly notes, "standard accounts of Egyptian nationalism paid little attention to women activists, or mentioned them only to signify the breadth of the movement." In many colonial locales, women's movements for equality coincided closely with the rise of anticolonial, nationalist, politics. As Baron further reminds us, "women's rights movements in the Middle East (and elsewhere) emerged as part of nation-building, or in reaction to it and histories of women's rights movements, nationalism, and anti-colonialism invariably became intertwined" (9). Ranjoo Sedou Herr (2003, 135) summarizes the predicament often faced by women who participated in the anticolonial struggle, saying that "Third World male nationalists always considered feminist agendas secondary, deferring their implementation until after the success of the nationalist struggle." However, more than simply deferring feminist agendas to another moment, the ascendant forms of nationalist ideology often came into direct conflict with these agendas after independence. Women's contributions to, and—not infrequently—their deep sacrifices for, the nationalist cause were often relegated to official oblivion. When not, nationalist discourse made prodigious efforts to harness narratives of women's participation as a cover for the lack of serious progress on issues of gender equality in postcolonial societies.

Having said this, across the postcolonial world experiences on this matter do vary and must be subject to careful local analysis, even if broader common features make comparison fruitful. For example, Elizabeth Thompson (2003, 62) emphasizes the "greater latitude that Nasser's regime in Egypt had in redrawing the gender boundaries of the public realm (civic order) once it had dismantled the previous colonial regime's network of patriarchal intermediaries," when compared with certain other postcolonial Arab nations. Deniz Kandiyoti (2003, 280) argues that the newly independent Turkish republic promoted a form of "state-sponsored 'feminism.'" As a result, "women's emancipation under Kemalism was part of a broader political project of nation-building and secularization . . . however the authoritarian nature of the single-party state and its attempt to harness the 'new woman' to the creation and reproduction of a uniform citizenry aborted the possibility for autonomous women's movements" (282). In the case of Algeria, Winifred Woodhall (2003, 568) notes that, "the promise of social equality for women faded after 1962, and this failure on the part of the nation that had played an exemplary role in anticolonial struggles provoked bitter disappointment." Similarly, in other contexts, local specificities chart somewhat differing trajectories, even while postcolonial women activists made use of committed internationalist approaches to emphasize commonalities across these borders.

What has become clear is that the dominant cultural memories of the struggle for independence reconstitute women's actual and historical sacrifices within these gendered readings—yet countermemories remain in circulation. The visual archive, whether photographic or cinematic, retains the stubborn traces of these sacrifices, even as the traces themselves are potentially ephemeral and subject to erasure. As Baron (2005, 97) notes, writing of Egypt's 1919 revolution, "Until 1919 photos of female nationalists rarely appeared. Thereafter, women allowed themselves to be the subjects of photojournalists and attempted to shape the making and initial publication of the images. But they could not then control how these images were copied, cut, cropped, and disseminated over time as the photographs memorialized political events and movements." So while women come to be included within the frame of the photographic archive of this revolution, when these images began to serve a memorializing function, they were literally and figuratively cropped out of the image, relegated to alterations and rearticulations within the narrative in a way over which they had little influence or control. In a sense, this willful reframing of the image of the revolution only proved the increasingly central role of the medium in contributing to cultural memory. Again, as Baron says, "photography played a central role in Egyptian political culture in the interwar years and after, and launched a revolution in ways of collectively remembering and commemorating. . . . Photographs proved crucial, and remained so, in creating a community of memory" (101). The visual archive, initially photographic, but then increasingly cinematic, contributed centrally to the cultural memory of the colonial period and the anticolonial struggle. While women's roles were part of the documented record of these events, over time they were "cut, cropped" out of the frame, and when fictive cinematic works emerged after the revolution and after independence, works that looked back at the memories of these events and recreated them, the roles of women were further subject to the contestations of ideological revisions of the past.

Cinematic representations followed from the legacy of photography in appropriating and reframing women's presence in the revolutionary struggle. Egypt's productive cinema industry quickly redirected its own efforts toward a revolutionary cinema in the years after 1952. Cultural figures—writers, filmmakers, visual artists—came to adapt the revolutionary ethos to their work, often in works that memorialized aspects of the anticolonial struggle, from the 1919 revolution, to the experiences of the Second World War and the 1948 war, culminating in the Free Officers' Coup in 1952. The 1919 revolution is featured in Hassan al-Imam's adaptation of Naguib Mahfouz's trilogy, in particular in the film *Palace Walk* (*Bayn al-qasrayn*, 1964). Youssef Chahine explores the experiences of the Second World War in *Alexandria, Why?* (*Eskandariyya layh?*, 1978), while Ahmad Badrakhan's *God Be with Us* (*Allah ma'ana*, 1955) explores the Egyptian defeat in 1948. The events leading up to and shortly after 1952 are treated in a number of films, among them Henri Barakat's *A Man in Our House* (*Fi baytna rajul*, 1961) and Ezz al-Din Zulfaqar's much celebrated *Restore My Heart* (*Rudda qalbi*, 1957).

Literature serves a similar memorializing role, often leading to adaptations for the screen. For example, the novel *The Earth* (*Al-Ardh*) by 'Abd al-Rahman Sharqawi, published in 1953, "epitomized the new mood of commitment following the Egyptian Free Officers' Revolt of 1952" (Meisami and Starkey 1998, 707). It did so through telling the story of an Egyptian Delta village's revolt in the 1930s against corrupt and brutal local rule within the colonial system. This novel's template—the politicization of a village community and the conflict between various men in the village over a beautiful young woman that takes on political dimensions—included many of the key tropes of committed nationalist literature; among them, a concept of authenticity that adheres to the rural setting, a struggle over a young woman who signifies the nation, and success (even if ephemeral) at confronting colonial rule once the unification of the village has been achieved. Appearing so soon after the end of colonialism, the novel distills many of the key precepts of the ascendant nationalist discourse and its ambivalence toward demands for gender equality. Youssef Chahine's 1969 cinematic adaptation of the novel represents a further, more nostalgic, reflection on the past struggles, recasting them anew within the context of the post-1967 crisis caused by the Egyptian defeat in the "Naksa," the Six-Day War—a context that is itself worthy of discussion but beyond the parameters of the present discussion. A generation later, through reviewing the narratives of liberation as traumatic, women's roles were recoded once again, and set out as a critical countermemory to the dominant nationalist discourse.

Egyptian Postindependence Remembrances: *I Am Free* and *The Open Door*

The protagonists of *I Am Free* and *The Open Door* are both self-consciously transgressive young women, dissatisfied with the social restrictions they face as middle-class, educated, urban Egyptian women in post–Second World War Egypt. In presenting these characters, both films were seen by Egyptian critics such as Ehsan Sa'id as exemplars of a new "women's cinema" (*al-sinima al-mar'a*) (Sa'id 2002, 58). *I Am Free*'s Amina is innately rebellious at first, standing up to the aunt and uncle who have raised her from the first scene, when she is scolded for presenting herself in public inappropriately by loitering on their apartment balcony and watching the young men passing below. This scene sympathetically represents the collisions of cultural values around social demands placed upon young women, inviting identification with the young woman who is accused of impropriety for presenting herself in a public manner, and by allowing her desires to be socially visible. As Amina stands on the balcony, she hears both a piano playing Western classical music as well as a radio playing an Egyptian popular traditional song, creating a mélange that signals the confusion of cultural values that will frame her story—not as West/modern versus Egypt/traditional, but as West/individualist versus Egypt/communalist. Upon being discovered on the balcony, she is scolded by her aunt for making a "scandalous" (*fadhiha*) spectacle of herself, and then is berated for not passively acceding to her aunt's demands to quickly prepare for school. She observes her aunt placing shoes on her uncle's feet, curling her lip with disdain—the gesture symbolically signals a generational and ideological divide, the provenance of which is unnecessary to explicate. After an argument, Amina decides to skip school as a protest and instead wanders the streets of Cairo. In these shots, director Salah Abu Sayf employs his trademark neorealist techniques in shooting his star Lubna Abdul-Aziz in a natural *mise en scène*, as she casually strolls through the streets, examining shop windows and movie theater posters, exploring the city on her own. This neorealist gesture relates Amina's first exploration of "freedom," which is a freedom from authority, from familial restrictions on movement, and from anxieties of the visible movement of women within the public sphere. Crossing a busy street, she skips with a smile on her face, the camera fluidly following her body moving through the streets as passersby move out of her way (figure 3.2). While relatively brief, this crucial scene gives a memorable introduction to Amina

FIGURE 3.2 *Amina explores the city* (I Am Free)

and the promise and danger that her character represents. The framing of Abdul-Aziz is consistently at a full body shot, emphasizing the physicality of her movement through these public spaces. Passersby, nonactors, often turn to watch her, creating a disjunctive sense where the performative and narrative elements of the film collide with the social order "outside" the film. The affective allure of the scene is one whereby the audience—and in particular women viewers—may be able to feel the liberatory signification of a young woman running freely and without inhibition on a busy public street.

In this and other similar scenes, Abu Sayf—perhaps the most celebrated of the postwar commercial filmmakers in Egypt—moves between forms of realism and the aesthetics of psychological depth, in a way that aims to incite cultural memory of the revolutionary struggle for his Egyptian audience. The film critic Muhammad Jaysh distinguishes Abu Sayf from the universalist appeal of his contemporary Youssef Chahine by arguing that Abu Sayf "speaks about Egyptian society in a way that is unique to Egypt, or rather speaks about social values, ideas or problems, or social aims in a way that makes these aims specific to Egypt alone" (Jaysh 2006, 11). The use of realist aesthetics, such as those utilized in the scene where Amina runs through the streets of Cairo, is balanced with his use of inner-voice, "psychological" techniques that speak to the tensions of cultural memory that are not sufficiently addressed or resolved by realism.

Amina's rebellion against the patriarchal family order (represented by the figures of her aunt and uncle) continues as she struggles internally to find a suitable definition of freedom for herself. She blames herself for poor judgment when she attends a house party thrown by a friend, after which the group of young people go to a remote desert location where they dance and kiss. Her late return home results in vicious gossip among the neighbors and she is nearly thrown out of her aunt and uncle's home and is reconciled only when a neighbor's son, Abbas, convinces her to go back and apologize. Abbas had also encountered Amina in an earlier scene, on the day during which she skipped school and walked around the city—in both scenes, his role is one of a sympathetic but didactic moral figure, who gently but uncompromisingly offers guidance to his neighbor. While she only partially follows his suggestions, his influence upon her is clear, an influence that does not stand in the way of her search for personal freedom, but rather that warns her against excess on this pathway. Amina herself comes to realize, in this episode, that her freedom is not defined by the ability to join in frivolous forms of rebellion, but requires a more elevated sense of purpose.

While remaining outwardly defiant in her relations with her parental figures, she determines to excel at her studies as a way to gain greater independence. After receiving impressive marks on her final exams, she comes under family pressure to marry a suitor rather than go to university. Initially contemptuous of the young man, she becomes attracted to him because of his love of literature, which she did not expect, but then finally rejects him when she finds him controlling and old-fashioned in his views on gender roles within marriage. Her aunt and uncle demand that she leave their home or reconcile with her suitor, so she moves in with her widowed father in the center of the city (ostensibly it is his lack of a wife that has resulted in her being raised by her aunt and uncle). Her father, who is shown to be liberal and cosmopolitan in ways that the aunt and uncle are not, supports her ambitions to attend university, and she graduates with top results. She goes on to a desirable position working in a petroleum company, along the way gaining the incredulous respect of her aunt and uncle, as well as the social status and independence she has always desired. But she complains to her father that she is now bored, and that her attainment of these goals has not brought her happiness.

I Am Free is fundamentally a moral narrative, inviting identification with Amina while repeatedly showing her making poor choices and having to come to terms with her mistakes. The film presents Amina as haunted by an inner voice that is represented through a repeated intervention into the narrative of a dream scene. The inner voice expressed in these scenes offers cues to viewers as to what the proper parameters for demanding freedom may be. Amina's inner voice is represented fairly didactically in the dream sequence that is repeated four times within the film. Shot in expressionist style, a door opens and casts a path of light into a dark field. A figure—Amina—enters the door from the top of the frame, and walks down the bright pathway as a male voice begins to speak. The voice, speaking in the style of a judge, interrogates Amina concerning choices she has made in previous scenes. In the first iteration, Amina defiantly refuses the criticism of the voice. In the second, the voice lectures her about her notions of freedom, while she remains silent. In the third, the voice again lectures, but this time Amina breaks down crying and falls to her knees (figure 3.3). In the final iteration, she speaks back to the voice, complaining that while she has now achieved freedom, something is still missing in her life. The voice tells her, "You must use your freedom in the pursuit of a specific goal. . . . Freedom is an instrument, not an objective [in and of itself] [*al-hurriyya wasila, mish ghaya*]." In this sense, seeking a goal of individualist autonomy is revealed to be a type of self-delusion. While the film treats Amina's desires sympathetically, it unequivocally devalues this form of modern self-actualization, and instead posits that fulfillment is to be achieved only through the communitarian self-abnegation that comes with the sacrifice of self for the larger, national, cause.

Amina's rebellion is first directed at the conservative tendencies of her urban petit-bourgeois family—the family of her aunt and uncle. Her rebellion is fundamentally based on her rejection of the gendered social roles she is expected to inhabit, but the film marks these as also the outcome of a generational conflict. This comes through in the subplot concerning her male

FIGURE 3.3 *Amina's inner voice speaks (*I Am Free*)*

cousin, 'Ali, whose dreams of becoming a violin player are crushed by his father. Later in the film, after Amina has escaped the family and has become a successful professional, 'Ali attempts suicide due to the limitations placed upon him. As social roles have come to change, former expectations—that girls remain at home, attain only secondary education, then marry and become mothers—are no longer to be suitable. 'Ali's story serves to illuminate the ways by which these changes also have effects in the lives of young men. Nonetheless, Amina represents a generation of women who came of age in post–Second World War Egypt, offered greater social opportunities than previous generations, some of whom could even envision fully rejecting the above-mentioned formula for a different set of social goals.

This change in Amina's understanding of the nature of freedom comes in the final major plot development, the growth of a romantic relationship with Abbas, which leads to her becoming a revolutionary. After finding her personal and professional success to be unsatisfying, Amina has occasion to reconnect with Abbas, who is now the editor of a politically radical anticolonial newspaper. They begin a love affair and through it she commits herself to his political activism, including printing underground pamphlets for which they are both arrested. Abbas has lost nothing of his didactic nature, while now channeling this into his developing revolutionary political philosophy. Amina happily subordinates herself to his leadership, through which she determines how to use freedom as "an instrument" for this cause—following the inner voice. After he invites her to his apartment and they first kiss, Amina offers to help Abbas choose his outfit for the evening, entering his bedroom and going through his clothes before selecting a suit, shirt, tie, and shoes, which she lays on his bed. Then, she kneels before him to put a shoe on one of his feet. He attempts to stop her but she perseveres, placing the shoe on his foot before looking up to face him. The music swells and he embraces her. The irony of the doubling of this gesture in the film, repeating the early scene when Amina views her aunt putting her uncle's shoes on his feet, is undoubtedly fully intentional: yet, the same gesture is here validated and even elevated. While it would be easy to read this as a simple reinstitution of patriarchal desires, this scene may speak to a more complex dynamic. Rather than simply placing Amina in the position of her aunt, the scene represents a notion that it is only though a certain self-abnegation or self-abjection that the "individualist" aims of mid-century calls for women's liberation may be stripped away and replaced by vaunted nationalist commitments that are communal in orientation. Through this destruction of the self and its priorities, Amina is able to achieve "true" freedom as a committed revolutionary, metaphorically treated in her symbolic initiation as an acolyte of her revolutionary beloved, Abbas.

Director Salah Abu Sayf speaks to this aim clearly when reflecting upon the film in an interview conducted in his later years. He says, "In the novel I was drawn by the discussion of the meaning of individual freedom [*al-hurriyya al-shakhsiyya*]: a woman imagines that freedom is to be able to smoke, to stay up all night, to dance, and to be friends with whom she pleases. But then, as events occur, she discovers that true freedom is found in action on the basis of a principle or belief that a person holds, even if this belief ends with one in jail" (Abu Sayf 1996, 114). Where in every other way, Amina has shown herself to be unwilling to the point of rebellion to assume traditional domestic roles, her dedication toward the revolutionary "objective," and not to purely seeking "freedom"—the film posits—leads her to embrace a subordinate position to Abbas. Rather than a retreat into traditional gender roles, however, the film stages this as a symbolic accommodation to the necessary hierarchies of the nationalist movement, where the revolutionary woman serves the struggle through subordination to men who are the movement's leadership. Amina's other revolutionary activities, including the production and dissemination of anticolonial publications, are of a like to her gesture of kneeling before Abbas. Once fully committed to this new role, Amina finds a fulfilling social purpose to her life, as well as love. This ending is predicated upon the conflation of the aims of gender equality with a pernicious individualism, coded as imperialist in origin, which is in conflict with the communitarian framing of anticolonial nationalism. This formula gives little consideration to the possibility of a collective and anticolonial feminism underlying the aspirations of the young filmgoing women that Amina is clearly meant to represent, and guide.

The didactic staging of an inner voice is most obvious in the aforementioned dream scenes, but throughout the film Amina is shown to be struggling to elaborate a self-image. Her sense of a lack or the instability in her self-image is conveyed through the deliberate representation of Amina as highly visible in her public presence, which is one of excessive and even vulgar self-confidence, set against her more fragile inner persona, when she is alone, or in contemplation. Lubna Abdul-Aziz performs Amina's conflicted inner voice with necessary flourish—Egyptian dramas of the period embraced physical and emotive acting styles—so that her inner conflict is one that becomes elaborated on her body. The camera's framing of her in medium or full-body shots during arguments with her aunt and uncle allow for the rebellious indignation she exhibits in her facial reactions to be also registered upon her body as whole. Yet in close-ups on her face, Abdul-Aziz often represents Amina in a much softer manner, misty-eyed or conflicted as to how to navigate her desires and what emerge as the ideological imperatives upon which she must act. It is only when she resolves the incessant conflict within this inner voice that her story is resolved—the celebration as she walks up the staircase in the prison allegorizes this resolution as a simultaneous ascension, one that again is marked physically and affectively in the movement of her body up the steps.

The trajectory that resolves with the eventual transformation of Amina into an assimilated vessel for revolutionary activism is one that is explored in a more complex manner in *The Open Door* (1963). Viola Shafik (2007, 201) notes that *The Open Door* was one of a series of Egyptian postrevolutionary films that "expressed . . . the need for female emancipation but often simply as a means to achieve national goals." In *The Open Door*, the protagonist, Layla, also begins as a self-confident and rebellious young woman. In the first scene, she leads a demonstration of girl students marching against colonialism, defying the school principal, who tries in vain to stop the students by telling them, "a woman's role is as a mother, her place is in the home!" Layla replies by shouting, "The imperialists didn't discriminate between men and women, and the bullets they shoot don't discriminate either!" She follows this by leading the others students into the street, held aloft by her classmates as she shouts, "Long Live Egypt!"

When she returns home after the demonstration, she is slapped by her scandalized father, who threatens to kill her if she demonstrates again. While her brother Mahmud and cousin Issam are sympathetic to her, signaling a generational divide as well as one that is essentially gender based, nonetheless Layla suffers various indignities and depression as she confronts the restrictions her parents seek to impose upon her. Her mother complains that she has "shamed [the family] before the neighbors," and even her brother Mahmud, who is politically sympathetic, suggests that she has gone too far in expecting accommodation of her activism—given that she is a girl. The traditional family hierarchies are even more radically challenged, however, when Mahmud volunteers to join guerrilla forces fighting against British troops in the eastern part of the country, ignoring his parents' demands that he not go. His departure provokes tearful pleading from his mother, while his father disowns him and refuses to see him off. Here, as in *I Am Free*, the family's presumed hierarchies and coherence within the patriarchal order are under new pressure, due as much to generational and ideological divides as to those of gender.

As in *I Am Free*, the film narrates Layla's quest for political self-actualization as framed by her prospects in love and marriage. Much of the film's plot concerns Layla's confusion in navigating relationships with her three suitors: her cousin Issam, her professor Dr. Farouk, and the revolutionary Husayn. While the film makes clear early on that her only hope for happiness is predicated upon her choosing of Husayn, her traumatic relationships with Issam and Dr. Farouk destroy her ability to follow this path. Issam, who as her cousin represents a family-sanctioned and traditional partner, wins her heart both with his claims of revolutionary commitment and by his recourse to tropes of romantic love. Yet, when the time arrives for him to leave home, along with Mahmud, to join the anticolonial guerrillas fighting the British in Port Said, he suddenly begs illness and stays behind. This decision is unequivocally feminized in a scene where Issam accompanies his mother, aunt, and Layla to a fabric store crowded by women. Confronted by Layla's dissatisfaction, he attempts to present his love as that of a passionate romantic, saying that he could not bear to be far from her, which for a while wins her back. However, he grows jealous of her friendships with other men, and attacks and nearly rapes her. Even this, however, is overcome with further excuses of his passion for her, before she eventually realizes that he is in fact having a sexual affair with a servant-girl, a disclosure that finally ends their relationship.

After rejecting Issam conclusively, Layla comes to disbelieve in romantic love altogether. When Mahmud's best friend Husayn returns from the front as a hero, he attempts to court her. Despite her reciprocal attraction to him, she half-heartedly rejects his advances, even as they and their friends are taken up by the news of the 1952 revolution. When Husayn gains a scholarship to study in Germany, she does not accept his marriage proposal and the offer to travel there with him. Instead, she pursues her own education at Cairo University, where she attracts the notice of the sternly authoritarian Professor Farouk, who eventually makes a formal marriage proposal to her family. Initially flattered by the attention of a distinguished intellectual, she comes to realize that he has no interest in her intellectual or personal development and sees her only as a traditional bride. Nonetheless, Layla seems unable to resist the inertia of her situation, going through with the wedding with little joy, as if sleepwalking. Shortly after the marriage, the 1956 Suez crisis

erupts, leading Husayn to return to Egypt to volunteer in the war effort. Layla
and her family follow Professor Farouk to Cairo's central train station so as
to depart to a city in the Nile Delta in case Cairo is attacked. Coincidentally,
Husayn is leaving at the same time to travel to Port Said to volunteer with
the Egyptian defenders fighting there. Layla seems resigned to following her
husband, but after seeing the wounded arriving from Port Said (figure 3.4),
she suddenly has a change of heart and abandons her family, running to find
Husayn's train. In a stirring and melodramatic end, Layla rushes along the
side of the moving train through throngs of people, as it pulls out of the station. She is eventually lifted onto the train by the hands of strangers. Then
she runs through the cars before finally finding Husayn, throwing herself
into his embrace.

In *The Open Door*, Layla too is invested with a pronounced and conflicted
inner voice, but one that is not literalized to the same extent as in *I Am Free*.
Very early in the film Layla withdraws into her bedroom, upset by her father's
violent reaction to her political activism. She reclines on her bed looking
toward a mirror. There is a knock at the door and she rises to answer it. The
camera tracks forward as she walks over to the door, her face coming into
clear view, before she turns and takes her initial position on the edge of the
bed. Her mother and brother enter the room to coax her out, and are positioned with the backs of their heads framing the shot (figure 3.5). Layla's face,

FIGURE 3.4 *Layla watches the injured arrive by train* (The Open Door)

FIGURE 3.5 *Layla faces a mirror as her mother and brother speak to her* (The Open Door)

seen only through the mirror, conveys her turmoil—the mirror evokes her inner voice. The scene continues with her mother leaving, and she continues an extended conversation with Mahmoud, complaining about the hypocrisy that frames the moralizing judgment meted out to girls who are constantly told that what they are doing is *'ayb* (shameful). As she grows passionate, she rises and moves around the bed, leaving Mahmoud framed in the mirror. A reverse shot captures her from his perspective. As she argues, a brief flashback shows her having argued with her mother on the same topic. Returning to the present scene, Mahmoud is now standing before her as she stands, face to face. She asks him, "I just don't understand—what is right and what is wrong?" (*ayya sah wa ayya ghalat?*), inverting his gentle claim that she was also wrong in expecting their parents' approval of her activism. As she asks the question and repeats it, his eyes drop and he looks ashamed. When he refuses to answer the question directly she asks him to leave, and as he does he whispers, "I must admit I don't know what is right and wrong. None of us do." In the framing, blocking, and dialogue of this scene Layla is first shown to be in conflict with her inner voice, the mirror representing this interiority. As Mahmoud and her mother attempt to intervene, she moves away from the inner voice and extemporizes this conflict, ending with the repeated question, "What is right, and what is wrong?" The scene then ends with her in sitting the dark, again facing her mirror—the active return of her inner voice.

FIGURE 3.6 *Layla looks up to watch jet fighters departing to the front* (The Open Door)

This inner voice is gestured to in other scenes through the film when much later in the film, Layla walks alone on city streets and observes people preparing for the war before looking to the sky to watch air force jets fly toward the front (figure 3.6). Its final voicing comes in the train station, as the camera frames her facial reactions upon viewing the wounded departing the train.

In both *I Am Free* and *The Open Door*, ambitious adolescent girls seek a fulfilling social role in a society where the traditional family structure is deeply in crisis and where larger communal callings—in particular, those of anticolonialism—present a possible alternative to ossified family-centered roles. As with *I Am Free*, but to an even greater extent, *The Open Door* sets parallels between romantic love and nationalist commitment, with the plot of the film predicated upon a woman protagonist finding suitable guidance and inspiration in the figure of a revolutionary man who is represented in triumphal and heroic terms. The secondary heroism of the woman is predicated fundamentally upon her relationship with her male counterpart.

At the time of the film's release, the Egyptian press reviews focused very much on the extent to which they viewed the film as successfully rendering the history of the anticolonial struggle, now codified in a form of cultural memory. For example, Saleh Musa writes in his review of the film in the magazine *Sabah al-khayr* (Musa 1963, 38), that "The film transports us in a clear sequence from one historical moment to another, without the viewer sensing any discontinuity, disruption or conceit in the flow of events, despite their being many such [historically significant] moments in the film." This framing of the film as a vehicle for "transportation" to the vital historical episodes of the liberation struggle values the film for its ability to contribute to the cultural memory of these events (Musa's only complaint is that some of the historical sequences are not long enough).

The book upon which the film is based also was celebrated for its conjuring of memories of the events surrounding the 1952 revolution, or *coup d'état*. As Marilyn Booth (2002, ix–x) notes, "as much as [the 1950s] was decade of struggle of disillusionment and hardship, it was also a decade of youth activism and of popular optimism about the future of a newly independent country ... the memory of the recent triumphs was still fresh, and a young generation grappling with its collective identity welcomed what was a bold and innovative literary work." The book, published in 1960 and the first novel by Latifa al-Zayyat, differs from the later film adaptation in a variety of ways, perhaps most significantly in their endings—in the novel, Layla chooses to go to Port Said independently, and reunites with Husayn only after herself volunteering to join the defense of the city from the tripartite forces. In this way, her initiative to join the nationalist struggle is not overshadowed by the romantic impetus, but rather the romantic conclusion is enabled by her own willing choice to join the fight in defense of the nation. Nonetheless, both book and novel essentially reaffirm the centrality of the patriarchal family unit, by replacing the conservative (petit) bourgeois family values with those of the "new" revolutionary one. As Samia Mehrez (2008, 124) argues, in *The Open Door*, "national resistance to the British occupier is parallel to the female protagonist's resistance to patriarchy. Her maturity into a free woman is identical to that of the nation. . . . Despite the fact that *Al-Bab al-Maftuh* [*The Open Door*] introduces the female protagonist's contestation of patriarchal power, it does not totally subvert the family icon, ending with two 'modern' family prospects." In this sense, what begins as a strongly critical and feminist critique of the irreconcilability of gender equality to national liberation, ends with the aspiring woman reassimilated into a family structure, one where the urban modern family, still governed by patriarchal codes, is replaced for the revolutionary one, where the committed woman remains in a subservient role to the self-sacrificing revolutionary man. This tension is developed in both films through the staging of an inner voice that not only sets the stage for this conflict, but which represents it as feminine.

Cultural Memory, Women, and Revolution

In postrevolutionary Egypt, the memory of the anticolonial period was subject to gendered revisions, which demanded that the cultural memory of this period be inscribed with the priority of national liberation over that of women's liberation. In the aforementioned films, productions emerging only years after independence, the memorialization of this period betrays deeply the anxieties that nationalist ideologies held with regard to women's increased presence in the public realm as political and social agents. A full generation or more after independence, representations of women's roles in the liberation setting would come to be more critical, especially of the failures of postcolonial nationalism in accommodating the aspirations of women that were motivated by the anticolonial struggle.

Memory—specifically, traumatic memory—frames Moufida Tlatali's *Silences of the Palace* (*Samt al-qusur*, 1992) which chronicles a young Tunisian woman's memories of her childhood growing up as the daughter of a servant in the palace home of an aristocratic family. *Silences of the Palace* sets out to recalibrate cultural memory around the liberatory claims for women of the anticolonial struggle, both before and after independence, in a manner deeply disturbing to the prevailing nationalist discourse. Framed in flashback, a young woman, 'Aliya, recalls her adolescent life in the palace, and through these reflections the film comments upon the failures of the postcolonial order to address the oppression of women in a meaningful manner. The film is structured on memories that are revealed as traumatic, as 'Aliya tries to come to terms with the death of her mother, and later her presumed father, who is one of the men of the aristocratic family. As with both *I Am Free* and *The Open Door*, *Silences of the Palace* adopts the perspective of an adolescent girl as she matures into womanhood, on the cusp of being called upon to satisfy the social demands and expectations that come with sexual maturity.

While the two earlier films allegorize the maturation of revolutionary potential through the coming-of-age framing, with the hopes of youth/anticolonialism being honed into the necessary commitments of adulthood/independence, the later work represents these two transformative periods (adolescence and the independence struggle) as overlaid by a trauma that grows clearer through memory. Donadey (2011, 36) argues that *Silences of the Palace* is primarily concerned with the question of "the transgenerational transmission of trauma due to secrets and silences around sexuality and sexual abuse, physical symptoms, the lack of avenues of escape, and finally, paths to possible healing." This assessment highlights the individual nature of the trauma, and sees the narrative as positing a possible resolution to this trauma through "healing." However, when viewed within the broader scope of the postcolonial failures where a feminist agenda may be concerned, this deployment of a trauma narrative finds new meanings. Slawy-Sutton (2002, 86) views the film as fundamentally acting as "an allegory . . . the journey of a specific nation through a traumatic period of its history." This allegorical approach is a common framework for analyzing the film, yet seeing the film as a simple national allegory strips it of its productive ambitions, in particular the manner by which social trauma is mobilized, which transcends the national setting. So, rather than simply exploring individual experiences of trauma as an allegory of the nation, *Silences of the Palace* seeks to produce an allegorical discourse of social trauma, to politically reanimate a critique of the failures of postcolonial regimes beyond the borders of Tunisia or even the Maghreb.

The film moves between a present set in the mid-1960s, during the first years of independence, and a past set in the mid-1950s, the period of open anticolonial struggle against France. 'Aliya, who works as a singer in weddings and social gatherings, was born in the palace to a mother who worked there as a household servant. The film, mostly set in the earlier time period, is organized as a series of episodic flashbacks of memories triggered by the death of the family patriarch, Si 'Ali, who is also almost certainly her biological father, driving what Robert Lang (2014, 125) has termed "a strikingly oedipal analysis of Tunisia's postcolonial condition." At the outset of the film (set in the later period), 'Aliya is performing 'Umm Kulthum's "Amal Hayati" before an uninterested audience of wedding-goers. Before the song's conclusion, 'Aliya suddenly stops singing, holds her head as if beset by painful memories, and then abruptly leaves the stage and the venue, meeting her companion Lutfi outside (figure 3.7). In the ride home and in their apartment, she expresses disappointment, resentment, and frustration at her life. Her headaches signify both her inability to overcome the present obstacles she faces, as much as the echoes of a traumatic past. Despite expressing love for her, Lutfi again refuses to marry her; she is pregnant but Lutfi insists that they terminate any pregnancy because they are unmarried; she feels suffocated by the pressures of being perceived as living "in sin."

FIGURE 3.7 *'Aliya ends her performance* (Silences of the Palace)

It is only Lutfi's off-handed comment to her that Si 'Ali has just died that takes 'Aliya out of the confines of her present dead-end life, transporting her into the realms of memory. These overtake her in the next scene when she visits the old palace, to pay respects for her deceased former master and presumed father. The disclosure of his death triggers a flood of memories, which form the central narrative of the film. The memories are from the beginning framed as traumatic, as when she enters the old palace, now in some disrepair, she comments in a voice-over that, "my old pains return, along with the past I thought I'd buried with my mother," memories that have returned for the first time "since that horrifying night." In *Silences of the Palace*, 'Aliya's inner voice is signified through the occasional but repeated employment of a voice-over, as well as visually (through the use of mirrors) and aurally (in her singing voice). The manifest inner voice of the voice-over articulates the traumatic memory as a narrative, while the use of mirrors and song elaborates upon this trauma as one that exceeds narrativization.

The memories that serve as the body of the film's story follow 'Aliya's life over the course of what seems to be a year or so, as she enters puberty. As the film unfolds, at first the memories are less than traumatizing, even joyful. The aristocratic household she and her mother serve comprises an aged bey, his two adult sons, and their respective spouses and children. The brothers, Si 'Ali and Si Bechir, who represent the aristocratic classes of Tunisia, are caught between the popular anticolonialism of the nationalists and the reactionary responses of the colonial regime, and are divided in terms of their sympathies. The allegorical division of the brothers suggests a complex view of the colonial power structure, and the gendering of constituencies within it. The beylical brothers represent the crumbling *ancien régime* in its last days of service to colonialism, with the household serving as a mirror to various aspects of Tunisian society.

'Aliya and her mother, Khadija, are both performers—Khadija is a skilled dancer who is asked to perform for parties in the palace, while 'Aliya grows into her role as not only a player of the 'ud, but more importantly as a singer (figure 3.8). In this way, as she matures she threatens the "silence" that is the rule in the palace (and highlighted in the title of the film). The generational divide between mother and daughter is elaborated through this paradigm: Khadija is of the silent generation (and hence dances) while 'Aliya represents a generation that is finding its voice. Where Khadija's creative expression is limited to her body, and reinscribes the silence expected of her, 'Aliya's increasingly confident singing gives testimony to her personal refusal to acquiesce to silence. Her songs are viewed by Si 'Ali as proof of her having "a soul"—and when he remarks as much to Khadija, she bitterly retorts that she herself "no longer [has] a soul." In this way, 'Aliya's voice serves to represent her inherent potential, the emergence of which coincides with the rise of the nationalist tide. Once 'Aliya is given an 'ud as a gift from her mother,

FIGURE 3.8 *'Aliya sings in the store room* (Silences of the Palace)

Si 'Ali's interest in her appears to increase, much to 'Aliya's delight. The 'ud comes to represent an ephemeral link between 'Aliya and Si 'Ali, as he also plays the instrument.

'Aliya's singing comes to signify her inner voice, that interior discourse that sets her apart from others and places her at the center of the film's story. While the traumas that are to affect her future are yet to come, her vocal abilities increasingly reflect upon and give an emotive texture to her inner voice. Her voice also marks her entry into a form of public visibility in the house, one that increasingly is dangerous for her. It is her singing that draws the attention and desire of the men in the palace. While Si 'Ali's observation about her soul denotes his benevolent interest in his presumptive daughter, for Si Bechir (and to some extent his son as well) her voice marks her as an object of desire, drawing attention to her anticipated sexual maturity. Lutfi, too, is most drawn to her for her voice. The traumatic experiences that mark 'Aliya's memories begin to accumulate after her first menstruation. As she begins to enter sexual maturity, so does she begin to come to comprehend the raw and often brutal gap not only between the upper and lower classes, but also between women and men in the palace. Both of the bey's sons employ women servants for their sexual gratification, although they do so in different ways. Si 'Ali carries on what appears to be a consensual and even caring relationship with 'Aliya's mother, Khadija—his own unhappy wife has not borne him a child, and his relationship with Khadija is shown to be much closer than his relationship with his wife. On the other hand, his brother Si Bechir shows little of the same sensitivity in his sexual relations with the servants, and exhibits a capacity for brutality that is manifested in his eventual rape of Khadija. Simultaneously with her entering adolescence, 'Aliya comes to discern the outlines of the sexual economy that lies beneath the surface of social relations within the palace, whereby the servant women find status and benefit in being known as the favored companion of one of the brothers, a situation that more than once leads to conflict and discord between the servant women. All of this has an increasingly traumatizing effect on 'Aliya, reaching an apex in the rape of Khadija by Si Bechir.

'Aliya's troubled interiority is signified in various visual terms. In a scene earlier in the film, the family gathers outside to pose for a photograph. When 'Aliya innocently joins the group, she is told to move away by the photographer. However, Si 'Ali calls her back for a personal photo along with his niece, Sara. 'Aliya is delighted and the gesture intimates the de facto recognition of her as Si 'Ali's daughter. The recording of this moment in photographic terms recalls the photography that registers the presence of women in the independence struggle, a documentation that is later subject to editing and reframing. While this recognition is important to 'Aliya, the ameliorative effects it has upon her inner conflicts are temporary, as later in the film 'Aliya finds a copy of the photograph and cuts herself out of it. Preempting outside reframings, or in anger at Si 'Ali's hesitation or impotence in failing to save her from the traumatic experiences she confronts, this visual dissociation of herself from Si 'Ali is an act of agency. In other scenes, 'Aliya spends time before a mirror—in one scene she enters Si 'Ali's wife's chambers and sits at her boudoir and looks at herself in the mirror, while applying make-up. In another scene, she finds a broken mirror in the storeroom and examines her face as reflected in the shards—a further visual referent to her inner conflicts. The scene then cuts to the present day, where the older 'Aliya stands looking in the same mirror—the same conflicts remain.

The factors around these realizations are deeply troubling to 'Aliya, causing her to often withdraw to a cluttered storage room where she seeks privacy and solace, while singing to herself. Things come to a head when Si Bechir demands that 'Aliya "serve his tea" (known by all to be a euphemism for providing sexual companionship), precipitating a crisis for Khadija, who offers herself instead and forbids 'Aliya from assenting to his order. At the last minute, Khadija too is rescued from her predicament by another servant, who is Si Bechir's favored companion and who intervenes perhaps as a result of her concern for losing her standing with him. Beyond her desire to protect her daughter, the subtext of Khadija's anxiety seems also more deeply linked to the "specter of incest" raised by the notion of 'Aliya's biological uncle employing the girl as a sexual companion for his nightly entertainment (Zayzafoon 2007, 50). Si Bechir, who is no less aware of the unspoken understanding that his brother is 'Aliya's father, continues to pursue the girl, but when further denied her, enacts his revenge by brutally raping Khadija. 'Aliya experiences the rape first-hand as she pretends to lie unconscious on the bed in the room while Khadija is attacked.

'Aliya's reaction to the rape—entering a catatonic state for some several days—is a traumatic reaction to this experience, despite the fact that Khadija simply tries to return to her normal work after the attack. While the servant women carry out traditional healing rituals to return 'Aliya to health, she begins to improve only after Si 'Ali visits her as she lies in her sick bed, paternally kissing her on the forehead (figure 3.9). Later she improves further when Si Bechir's daughter Sara comes by to play the 'ud for her. Another event coincides with her return to health, that of the arrival of Lutfi into the palace—Lutfi is introduced both as the teacher of the children of Si Bechir, but also as an active nationalist who is hiding in the palace so as to evade arrest. Immediately 'Aliya takes an interest in Lutfi, who reciprocates with subtle flirtation. As this romantic link grows, Khadija finds that she is pregnant, presumably as a result of the rape, and she decides to induce an abortion. The film climaxes as 'Aliya is asked to perform at the wedding of Sara, before an audience of the nobility as well as the Tunisian colonial elites. On stage she sings the song "Ghanili Shwayya Shwayya"—itself a playful and very popular track from a film starring 'Umm Kulthum, the historical melodrama *Sallama* (1945)—while her mother lies in her bed, bleeding to death from the botched abortion. 'Aliya sees Lutfi standing in the doorway of the room, and suddenly cuts short the 'Umm Kulthum song, switching abruptly to a nationalist anthem. As she sings, the wedding guests rise one by one and slowly depart the room in disgust, while Lutfi looks on approvingly.

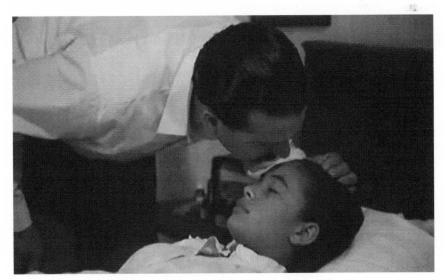

FIGURE 3.9 *Si 'Ali visits 'Aliya during her illness* (Silences of the Palace)

As she ends the song to an empty room, her mother dies, surrounded by the other servant women.

The film is laid out as a series of disclosures, cutting back and forth between the past and present, unraveling the unspoken traumas that have haunted 'Aliya through her life. The headache that cut short the song in the beginning of the film resonates with the coincidence of her performance at the end with her mother's death—both are songs by 'Umm Kulthum. 'Aliya's adoption of a nationalist song at the wedding—no doubt an act of political agency that would have brought strong condemnation from the bey's family—is shown as a brave and selfless act inspired by Lutfi, but which rings hollow from the perspective of the present day, where Lutfi is neither a courageous lover nor even a capable provider or protector for her. The former nationalist activist lives off the earnings of his unacknowledged lover, and offers her little of the freedom and independence he had promised would come with the end of colonialism. In the final scene of the film, however, 'Aliya is seen departing the palace as an adult, and a voice-over in her voice outlines her determination to not abort the child she is bearing, who she is certain is a daughter, and to name her daughter after her mother as an act of remembrance.

In some readings, the film's ending is seen as essentially one that returns agency to the character of 'Aliya. "For Alia [sic] the return to the past is a mental and emotional journey at the end of which she discovers herself, understands her mother and decides to affirm her independence" (Sherzer 2000, 52). Sherzer encounters the film as a personal, "transgenerational" auto-biography, and generally avoids allegorical readings of the narrative. She does not mention the question of 'Aliya's paternity, nor the postcolonial critique of the liberation movement that emerges through her relationship with Lutfi. Instead, Sherzer seeks ethnographic rationales for Lutfi's refusal to marry 'Aliya, and his demand that she abort their child, and overlooks entirely the film's staging of trauma, where the memories of women's aspirations in the context of the liberation struggle are concerned. Alternatively, the film may be viewed as marking out the history of the occlusion of women's roles in the nationalist struggle as being best—or, at the very least, equally—understood metaphorically, through the framing of trauma. In a text that subtly welcomes allegorical readings, tropes of trauma come to play a productive role in developing countermemorial practices to those that are prevalent. Traumatic memory, here in the form of 'Aliya's personal memories of the events that led to her mother's death, plays an allegorical role that has social implications. The social trauma that is being conjured arises from the repression of memories of women's aspirations for gender equality—the return of these memories marks a revision of this history, one that is catalyzed by the framing of these memories as a form of trauma. Again, the voice-over, as a signification of 'Aliya's inner voice, presents a path toward a resolution of the trauma, but a resolution that is contingent and uncertain. As with 'Aliya's attempts to form a coherent self-image (through looking at mirrors or at photographs) and as with her vocal performative skills to render her "soul" (an extemporization of her inner voice), the voice-over is a reflection of the traumatic core which produces the central critique of the film. Cultural memory is here rendered traumatic, but in a way that is politically productive. The film's political trajectory begins with her confusion and disappointment in the beginning of the film, through a retelling of her own past, resulting in a more coherent self-image and thus a politically self-assured subjectivity. This trajectory, of which trauma is a central part, mobilizes traumatic memory as a productive form of cultural memory.

Looking back over the two or more generations that have passed since the period of national liberation, we find a distinct shift in cultural memory of independence struggles, particularly as it relates to the position of women. The earlier triumphalist and hegemonic cultural memories represent women protagonists as heroic when they subordinate their desire for gender equality, as in films such as *I Am Free* or *The Open Door*. Postindependence regimes worked to counteract readings of trauma as central to the narrative of the struggle for independence—what traumas there were had to have been compensated for by the fulfillment of the nation. However, within one generation the memories of this history were recoded—now as traumatic. The trauma framing counters the previous triumphalist memory and gives purpose and value to an approach that seeks to recover what traces may remain, in particular of the occluded memory of women in the liberation struggle.

The Time that Is Lost

CINEMATIC APORIAS OF PALESTINE

The preceding discussion of postindependence national cinemas mobilized in the production of cultural memory traces a move from triumph to trauma in these memory formations, in particular in how the roles of women in the anticolonial struggle are represented. This discussion highlights the productive uses of cultural memory, and the turn to trauma in revisionist memories of the end of colonialism and the transition to postcolonial independence. As this chapter will explore, the Palestinian case—a case of ongoing stateless dispossession—presents neither triumph nor trauma, but rather a kind of memory purgatory.

A Palestinian *Purgatorio*

In one brief scene in his 2004 film *Notre Musique*, Jean-Luc Godard makes a presentation to a group of Bosnian students which includes two images: one of Palestinian refugees fleeing their homes by boat in 1948, the other of Jewish refugees arriving in boats to Palestine around the same time (figure 4.1). He describes the two images as corresponding to the technique of cinematic shot followed by reverse shot. He comments that in this reversal of images, Jews "walked in the water to reach the Holy Land [while] the Palestinians walked into the water to drown. Shot and reverse shot. The Jews became the stuff of fiction, the Palestinians, of documentary." *Notre Musique* is structured as a triptych, with the three parts, *Inferno, Purgatorio*, and *Paradiso*, referencing Dante's cosmology in *La Divina Commedia*. *Inferno* explores the experiences of war, and *Purgatorio* explores the aftermath of wars and their legacies on survivors, while *Paradiso* consists merely of the briefest hint of a possible redemption afterward. Thus, the Palestinian trauma of 1948 may be viewed as the reverse shot of the establishment of a Jewish state, or vice versa. Shot,

FIGURE 4.1 *Godard lectures on 1948 (*Notre Musique*)*

reverse shot. The Palestinian trauma, metaphorically, is a *purgatorio* reflected best in documentary techniques and lacking the narratological depth and completion that is "the stuff of fiction."

No doubt, the neat division of "Jews" and "Palestinians" in Godard's statement may require a degree of further nuance.[1] However, Palestinian filmmakers have indeed been preoccupied—some may say, burdened—by the documentary form, and by the perceived need to offer testimonial evidence to their communal experiences. The channeling of Palestinian experience into the mold of a cause, a just claim, has often led filmmakers to the documentary form so as to offer a witnessing of the conditions of their trauma. And even where Palestinians have engaged in narrative filmmaking, they often have resorted to semidocumentary cinematic techniques or *vérité* style, as if bound by a fidelity to the real even when exploring the imaginary. In this, fiction—or even traditional narrative form—has perhaps failed in its representation of Palestinian experiences, demanding from Palestinian filmmakers as well as from literary figures a rooting within documentary that is irreconcilable with the imaginative resolutions that emerge from the dominant fictional narrative forms. These, it may be argued, all too often lead into the dead-end of the cliché, the metaphorical (or allegorical) construction that often characterizes "political" literary efforts. As Tom Hill (2011, 88) has noted, in the Palestinian context there is a problem of works coming "dangerously close to metaphor," and that "any overly self-conscious attempt at a faithful artistic or creative rendering of Palestinian experience runs the particular risk of cliché, in its broadest sense of failure of mimesis."

Godard's use of *purgatorio* is meant as a general description of postwar experiences and the traumatic resonances of conflict. However, reading the term in a more focused way, we may arrive at a conception of it that is precisely apt for an understanding of what is unique in Palestinian cultural memory, specifying the Palestinian case against those of other conflicts—even those cited by Godard, such as the Bosnian war or the Nazi Holocaust. *Purgatorio* in all these cases connotes irresolution—and there is no doubt that for those who experienced or who live in the shadow of these historical traumas, memory often remains irresolute. However, for Palestinians, the allegory of *purgatorio* is perhaps more acute and finely drawn, given that the Palestinian catastrophe, which began in 1948, is in many ways ongoing. Amireh (2003, 751) argues that "the consensus among Palestinian historians is that Al-Nakba . . . is the most important event in solidifying a Palestinian national identity." Greenberg (2005, 110) suggests that the "continuity of trauma" among Palestinians, especially refugees and the displaced, means "the *Nakba* never ends." The phrase "al-Nakba mustamirra" ("the catastrophe continues") is commonly cited among Palestinians and scholars of Palestinian cultural memory. As Elias Khoury (2012, 265) argues, "The nakba is a continuous process. Its major event was 1948, but it never ended. It has gone through different phases and taken different shapes." A 2011 special issue of the journal *al-Dirasat al-Filistiniyya* (Palestinian Studies) is titled "al-Nakba mujaddidan" ("the Catastrophe renewed").[2] In this sense, the continuation of the catastrophe has left Palestinians in a state of suspended trauma, what we may term along with Godard as a *purgatorio*.

Where orthodox approaches in trauma studies tend to view the aftermath of trauma as resulting in one of two broad outcomes—mourning or melancholia—neither of these appears suitable to discussing the developments in Palestinian cultural memory since 1948. The work of mourning, which in conventional psychoanalytic terms is the proper or healthy resolution to an experience of grievous loss, is generally set against melancholia, which is an outcome of an unhealthy narcissism and inability to cut psychic links with the lost object. Slavoj Žižek has perceptively argued that in the last decade or so, humanities scholars have given melancholia a kind of privileged status (inverting traditional psychoanalytic judgments about the condition) and have come to view melancholia as a critical position against the normative work of mourning. He notes that, "With regard to mourning and melancholy, the predominant opinion is the following: Freud opposed normal mourning (the successful acceptance of a loss) to pathological melancholy (the subject persists in his or her narcissistic identification with the lost object). Against Freud, one should assert the conceptual and ethical primacy of melancholy" (Žižek 2000, 658). Similarly, LaCapra insists on the primacy of mourning, also opposing the trend of giving greater authority to melancholia. As he argues,

> Freud compared and contrasted melancholia with mourning. He saw melancholia as characteristic of an arrested process in which the depressed, self-berating, and traumatized self, locked in compulsive repetition, is possessed by the past, faces a future of impasses, and remains narcissistically identified with the lost object. Mourning brings the possibility of engaging trauma and achieving a reinvestment in, or recathexis of, life that allows one to begin again.
>
> (LACAPRA 1999, 713)

However, neither of these concepts effectively reflects the Palestinian context, which lends itself neither to mourning nor to melancholia, but rather is best understood as a traumatic suspension borne by the fact that the Palestinian catastrophe, an ongoing process, has not found an end point from which closure may be gained.

Godard's distinguishing of the shot reverse shot as an allegorical view on Palestinian and Israeli narratives is an act of creative provocation. Beyond his further linking of this allegory to the respective division of Palestinian and Israeli narratives into documentary and fiction, the shot reverse shot technique allegorizes a distinction between narrative completion and nonnarrative dissolution. Israeli national history effectively has come to fit within the frame of conventional fictional narrative. As an exemplary case, Leon Uris's epic novel *Exodus* "presented the story of Zionism in a popular, readily accessible form," and articulated the progressive, transformative, and heroic dimensions of the Israeli story, forming a fictional "Zionist melodrama," characteristics that were present in Otto Preminger's 1960 film adaptation of the novel (Weissbrod 1999, 129). While Palestinian nationalists have also at times attempted to produce counterbalancing dramatic or epic narratives, what remains most evocative of the Palestinian story is its frequent irreconcilability to traditional narrative forms. Hence, the most potent Palestinian writers have been either poets who have challenged normative narrative poetic forms—as in the late stage of Mahmud Darwish's work, for example—or fictional authors whose works explored fragmentation, self-abnegation, disappearances, and voids, rather than constructing coherent and progressive national narratives (one thinks of Mourid Barghouti or Adania Shibli, to name but two). What these Palestinian authors have frequently led us to are questions can have no answer: aporias. In terming these as aporias, I borrow a term from philosophical discourse in order to articulate an act of signification which seems at or beyond the limits of interpretation, and which at its extremes maps upon Derrida's citation of aporia as being that which is "beyond the limits of truth" (Derrida 1993, 1).

Consider the following set of images: a static long shot from a distance frames an empty lot behind a stone house. A woman walks across the lot, carrying a bucket of what appears to be refuse. She empties the box and piles the garbage into a small mound, then walks around the lot for a while, collecting sticks and bits of trash which she adds to the pile. The scene repeats several minutes later, this time shot from a higher angle; now the woman is continuing to gather trash from around the lot, including a small pile of dried leaves. The scene repeats yet again, several minutes later, and is again shot at a different angle, high but from the right. The angle of the light and the length of the shadows also connote that the action is taking place at a different time of day. The pile is now alight, the woman continues collecting more items to put onto the fire. On their own, the scenes, which all occur in the first half of Elia Suleiman's film *Divine Intervention*, defy simple interpretation. They occur within a cycle of other scenes with more or less repetitive actions: a man sitting at a kitchen table opening up his mail, a man emerging from his house to toss a bag of garbage into a neighboring yard, and so on. What are we to make of these scenes, and in particular that of the woman cleaning the yard? Is it an elaborate allegory, of "cleaning house," or of some other motif? Is it "documentary," in the sense of capturing a quotidian action, perhaps ethnographic or sociological? As the scenes repeat there can be no way that these frameworks will yield an answer. As with other repeated motifs in this film, the scene offers no answers—in fact, these repetitions point to only one end, the impossibility of producing a commonly accessed meaning, a breakdown of the community of interpretation.

In the realm of cinema, few Palestinian filmmakers if any have developed as coherent and self-sustaining a cinematic language for exploring the aporetic dimensions of Palestinian experience as Elia Suleiman. As I will illustrate, Suleiman's cinematic language leads both on the level of narrative, as well as on the level of scene and shot, to unanswerable ends, refusing the usual narrative closures that characterize normative cinematic techniques. Recalling Godard's framing, these aporias are in a sense a reflection of the *purgatorio* we find expressed both as personal experience in his films and as allegorical reflections into broader Palestinian contexts. Within the stark distinction of the shot reverse shot of Israeli and Palestinian experience, Suleiman resists the burden of documentary, but also challenges the ideological strictures of being "the stuff of fiction." In this sense, Suleiman's *purgatorio* broadly reflects the traumatic suspension that characterizes post-1948 Palestinian experience, the irresolution of the traumas of the Nakba, and, its perpetuation in the form of continuing losses and further dispossession. Suleiman addresses the *purgatorio* of Palestine through his recurring and increasing obsession with death, which is elaborated through his focus upon the death of his parents. By the end of his trilogy, as I will discuss below, Suleiman views himself as symbolically dead as well, but this death is only the reflection of the *purgatorio* that denies so many Palestinians the actualization of living.

The Narrative Frames of Palestinian Cultural Memory

First, however, we must briefly here consider more broadly the question of cultural memory in Palestinian cultural production, to better understand the location of Suleiman's work within this context. As a point of departure, we may revisit Edward Said's (2000, 184) argument that "perhaps the greatest battle Palestinians have waged as a people has been over the right to a remembered presence and, with that presence, the right to possess and reclaim a collective historical reality." Yet Said also argues that Palestinians had until the time of his writing, just before the outbreak of the second intifada in 2000, failed to come to terms with the significance of mounting a resistance within the field of memory: "What we never understood was the power of a narrative history to mobilize people around a common goal" (2000, 184). Nonetheless, the development of a coherent national-memory project found its place in the aftermath of the rise of an infrastructure for a national liberation movement,

> With the rise of the PLO, first in Jordan, then after September 1970 in Beirut, a new Palestinian interest arose in the past, as embodied in such disparate activities as organized historical research and the production of poetry and fiction based upon a sense of recovered history, formerly blotted out but now reclaimed in the poetry of Zayyat, Darwish, Hussein, and al-Qassem, in the fiction of Kanafani and Jabra, as well as in painting, sculpture, and historical writing.
>
> (SAID 2000, 189)

Scholars of Palestinian cultural productions have often found difficult the endeavor of matching the textual materials produced by Palestinians, which often relate closely to the traumatic histories of modern Palestine, to theories of trauma, given that "the Nakba is not over yet" and is thus "unlike the historical experiences discussed in the literature on trauma" (Sa'di and Abu Lughod 2007, 10). It would appear that at least some Palestinian artists had by the 1980s begun to ask whether the project of constructing "a narrative history to mobilize people around a common goal" was either possible or, perhaps more provocatively, even desirable. So while Said is correct to note that projects of commemoration clearly found significance alongside the development of a national liberation struggle, and while there is no question that interventions into the field of history are central to any Palestinian project of resistance to Zionism, it is possible to discern a second cultural current, perhaps developing over the course of the 1990s through the present day, that seeks to highlight and give expression to those aspects of Palestinian experience which are irreconcilable to such a project of codifying a national narrative. This cultural current embraces the conflicted temporality that Jenny Edkins (2003, 16) has termed "trauma time," which "is [both] inherent in and disrupts any production of linearity." While cognizant of the power of linear histories, these artists explored the limitations of narrative, and sought to develop what may be termed an aporetic history of modern Palestine.

Beyond the traumatic suspension that characterizes the residues of 1948, we find the problematics of nationalist historiographies, primarily Zionist but also those of Palestinian liberation groups, which have endeavored to affix a more closed interpretation upon this history. The predominant Zionist narrative closures by definition foreclose upon the Palestinian claims around the event, denying the loss incurred and refusing the responsibility that flows down, from official governmental policy within settings of political negotiation through to more public arenas, including those of Israeli popular culture such as popular cinema. In all these contexts the Nakba is rarely acknowledged, although after the generation of "new Israeli historians" presented evidence to support the research that their Palestinian colleagues had produced a generation or more before, some small but important changes to Israeli Jewish public discourse around 1948 and its aftermath have occurred.[3] For example, working from the margins to influence Israeli cultural memory, the Israeli Jewish group Zochrot pursues a mission to "tell Israeli Jews about the history and geography of the Palestinian *nakba*," through actions that include opening an art gallery dedicated to work "dealing with the *nakba*," and publishing a journal in Hebrew, *Sedek*, dedicated to the issue (Shah 2007, 34).

However, on the Palestinian side, and especially within the discourse of Palestinian national liberation groups, 1948 has played a dual and in some ways inconsistent role. On one hand the Nakba is widely subject to commemoration, yet on the other hand it is sometimes represented having been redeemed, if only in part, by the emergence of resistance organizations from the mid-1960s onwards. As Diana Allan (2005, 49) notes, "while 1948 has remained crucial to collective memory and identity, as the quintessential symbol of collective dispossession, exile and the moment of national loss, its relevance as a political and cultural tool has changed over time—alternately employed to signify victimisation and political resistance." The first generation of Palestinian *fida'in*, members of the militant national liberation organizations who emerged from within the refugee camps, were for the most part the children of those who had themselves been expelled and dispossessed, and they viewed the losses of 1948 as markers of national weakness or a shameful legacy that they endeavored to surmount.

The literary and cultural figures associated with this moment, the intellectual and cultural wing of the Palestinian national liberation movement, were engaged in developing a cultural memory of the Nakba, but one that was productive to the aims of their political commitment. Ghassan Kanafani, the Palestinian author and activist who was the spokesman of the Popular Front for the Liberation of Palestine before his assassination in 1972—all but certainly at the hands of the Mossad—exemplifies this approach very well (*Journal of Palestine Studies* 1972, 149). In Ghassan Kanafani's *Returning to Haifa*, the protagonist Said and his wife, Safiya, who were made refugees from Haifa in 1948, return to their former home after the Israeli conquest of the West Bank in 1967. There, they meet Miriam, a Holocaust survivor who has been settled in their home since their departure. They discover that Miriam has also adopted the son that they lost in the war, Khaldun, renaming him as Dov, who is now an Israeli soldier. The novella ends with Said finally embracing the choice of his remaining son Khalid to join the *fida'in*. He does so as a consequence of having to come to terms with the trauma of 1948 and in particular his own personal losses—specifically, the discovery that Khaldun is now an Israeli soldier, having been raised as an Israeli Jew—as a form of necessary closure upon these events.

Kanafani's work opens with the question of an acute traumatic memory that haunts the central characters of Said and his wife, Safiya, but ends ultimately with a gesture toward closure of this memory, a combination that characterizes much of what could be termed as committed Palestinian cultural productions. While Said and Safiya are unable even to discuss with one another their memories of the Nakba and the loss of their son Khaldun, then, at the end of the story, Khalid's decision to join the *fida'in* constitutes a redemptive turn that implies a closure of the past's traumas. Beyond the novella's fascinating staging of a developed face-to-face dialogue between a Holocaust survivor who has come to occupy the former home of Palestinian refugees and those Palestinians who have returned to visit their lost home for the first time in nearly twenty years, the work ends by firmly indicating that the book of Nakba memory is now meant to be closed. Said (if not Safiya; a gendering of cultural memory that I cannot address here)[4] comes to view the *fida'in* as the necessary recuperative force to overcome the tragic losses of 1948. There is no move toward mourning, nor is there melancholia—the novella definitively ends with a renewed commitment to national liberation.

There are significant divergences among scholars in their interpretation of the novella. Barbara Harlow views the novella as exemplifying Kanafani's "commitment to the necessity of popular armed struggle," which he viewed as a struggle "being carried out on the basis of a larger solidarity, one whose affiliations transcended the ties of family, clan, race, ethnic, and religious identity" (Kanafani 2000, 20). More broadly, Harlow argues, the complex family drama that is drawn between the parents and the two sons, and its intersection with the possible cross-identification of Holocaust survivor and Nakba refugees, is reflection that the novella "is less an attempt to restore, or even invent, a historical legitimacy to the Palestinians' claim to their homeland, than it is the elaboration of a political vision of a 'democratic solution'" to the conflict (21). Contra Harlow's more ideologically oriented reading, Ian Campbell (2001) finds that the novella's "argumentative rhetoric" (i.e., the support for militant resistance) is "undermined by the story in which Kanafani cloaks it." By "story," Campbell here largely means the subtextual dimensions of the narrative. This argument has some merit, by exploring textual complexities that Harlow's political reading may not have illuminated: Campbell posits that the work is fraught with an unresolved tension that exists between the psychological repercussions of the irreconcilable losses of the Nakba, and the political and ideological imperatives of the work, which conclude with an embrace of militant resistance. However, Campbell's summation that "the use of trauma theory has led us to the conclusion that any Palestinian who took the advice of the novel could thus be said to be acting under a delusional structure" (72), is ultimately unconvincing, as it prioritizes the psychological as a truth (or a signification of the Real) that reigns over the political and finds any dissonance between the two as signifying the latter as "delusional." In fact, this tension is precisely what I have termed the productive nature of social trauma, arising from the dialectical interplay between the psychological portrait of loss and the political imperatives of militancy. It would be an error to limit our reading of the work to a priority that must be offered to the psychological over the political, since social trauma draws upon both dimensions equally. In this sense, *Returning to Haifa* works productively as a text set at the intersection of social trauma discourse, cultural memory of the Nakba, and the militant political commitment of internationalist leftist currents in the 1960s and 1970s.

Kanafani's reflection of social trauma finds its analogues in the arena of cinematic production as well. It is significant that one of the first full-length Palestinian narrative films is Qasim Hawl's production of *Returning to Haifa*, produced in Lebanon by the Popular Front for the Liberation of Palestine in 1981.[5] The film opens with scenes of refugees fleeing Haifa in 1948—Hawl staged the scene with extras drawn from the Palestinian refugee camps, many of them were people who had experienced the exodus from Haifa and other coastal cities first hand (al-Zubaydi 2006, 68). Nonetheless, after Hawl's staging of the exodus of Palestinians in this, the first shot of what may be considered the first Palestinian feature narrative film, few Palestinian filmmakers have approached the topic of 1948 directly. As Masalha (2008, 142) notes, "for many years the topic of the Nakba was hardly broached in Palestinian film-making—a memory too painful to evoke."

Hawl's film adaptation is a product of the establishment of the PLO film units, which were developed alongside other institutions of the national liberation groups based primarily in Jordan in the late 1960s, later moving to Lebanon after Black September in 1971 (Massad 2006, 37). Most of the works of these units were documentary in nature. Godard's observation that "the

Palestinians became a documentary" is perhaps based in part on his own collaboration with members of the PLO film units in his 1976 work *Ici et ailleurs*, which was filmed in part in the refugee camps and training camps in Jordan shortly before Black September (Ginsberg and Lippard 2010, 321). The production crew of this work included Mustafa Abu 'Ali, who went on to become a leading figure in the committed cinema of the Palestinian resistance, making documentary-essay films such as *Laysa lahum wujud* (*They Do Not Exist*, 1974) and *'Ala tariq al-nasr* (*On the Road to Victory*, 1975). Yet, the works of this period largely engage in a didactic form of cultural memory that treats 1948 as a tragic origin for Palestinian experience, but one that is subject to ongoing if incomplete recuperation through the formation of a militant resistance to Zionism, a resistance for whom the concept of the right of return for the Palestinian refugees is sacrosanct.

Elia Suleiman's Aporetic Memory

In the wake of the PLO defeat in Beirut in 1982, and the political moves toward the Oslo accords over the next decade or so, changes to Palestinian cultural memory allowed a greater engagement with the Nakba and its aftermath, but did so in ways that were fragmentary and often unformed. In this period, the rise of an auteurist Palestinian cinema, pioneered by Michel Khleifi in the first instance, opened new ways of engaging questions of cultural memory and social trauma. As May Telmissany (2010, 83) notes in her discussion of Michel Khleifi's cinema, "Khleifi strives to reconstruct, in a stunningly original way, the Palestinian collective memory, using stories, tales, photography, poetry, and theater. He makes extraordinary use of cinema as a medium of remembrance, as the archival site of threatened *lieux de mémoires* (realms of memory)." Khleifi's work was pioneering not only in terms of its relative autonomy from the ideological imperatives of the national liberation project, as exemplified in the work of Abu 'Ali and others of the PLO film units. As Nurith Gertz (2002, 181) suggests, his most celebrated film, *Wedding in Galilee* (*Urs fi Jalil*, 1987), "presents an inchoate Palestinian nationhood gaining definition through continuous and contentious encounter with the Israelis." Its perspective is "very much the stuff of Palestinian national narrative, and yet it is one riddled throughout with multiple voices and perspective—blurring boundaries, juxtaposing and intertwining incompatible social topographies, and carrying always the mood of the hybrid, the ambivalent, the open-ended" (176).

Elia Suleiman, whose earliest works include short films and an experimental feature documentary dating back to the early 1990s, followed upon the fluid semiotics of Khleifi, but took this strategy to a more aesthetically distinct and original place. Through developing this individual cinematic language, he has come to most fully represent the aporetic trend within the broader landscape of Palestinian auteur filmmaking. In his first work, *Introduction to the End of an Argument* (1990), Suleiman and codirector Jayce Salloum use montages of found footage in a collage that "laments the impossibility of speaking as an Arab, particularly when one is so utterly spoken for in Western contexts" (Marks 2000, 58). In *Homage by Assassination* (1992), Suleiman represents questions of Palestinian identity and exile open-endedly. In this short film, the director spends quiet hours at home in his New York City apartment during the first Gulf War. He listens to the radio, watches lovers bicker on the sidewalk outside, looks at photos, and stands on a scale. These scenes alternate with references to the Gulf War. When he is called by a radio host for an interview about the war, the phone does not connect. He remains silent throughout the film, as if unable to find a mode of presence, as if lacking a determined subjectivity. These two early films, while aesthetically distinct, are both concerned with the question of how to speak, and whether in the face of constant appropriation and ideological overdetermination, silence itself may not be the most effective strategy. These concerns would carry through to Suleiman's later trilogy, where his protagonist in all three films never speaks.

After these earlier experiments, Suleiman moved to directing feature-length works which are significantly autobiographical and which rely upon natural setting, often nonprofessional actors (largely family members playing themselves), and elliptical storylines. Taken as a whole, Elia Suleiman's quasi-autobiographical trilogy constitutes a personal history of not only his alter ego, ES, but also those of his parents, from 1948 through the "present" (the third film ends in 2009). This historical span is not covered chronologically, but rather unravels from an ever-shifting present. The first film, *Chronicle of a Disappearance*, is set in the time of its making, 1996: the second, *Divine Intervention*, covers the period after the second intifada in the early 2000s: while the third, *The Time that Remains*, comprises four different periods: 1948, 1970, 1980, and 2009. The films are loosely narrative, but elude conventional narrative expectations as well.

In the first of Suleiman's feature narrative works, *Chronicle of a Disappearance*, ES returns to his hometown of Nazareth after some period in "self-imposed" exile. ES is, like Suleiman, a filmmaker who has lived for some time in New York City (Suleiman was compelled to leave Israel in 1980, and lived in New York for about ten years). A second protagonist, a young Palestinian woman by the name of Adan, seeks housing in Jerusalem, but as an independent single woman she fails to find a place either in East Jerusalem or as a Palestinian living in West Jerusalem. She ends up living in a theater. ES moves to Jerusalem "to be closer to the airport," impassively observing the neighborhood through his window as he works on a writing project (the screenplay for the film itself). He undertakes travels to Tiberias to speak to a priest there, and then goes to Jericho, the first city "liberated" under the

Oslo accords. Eventually he stumbles upon the theater where Adan has been living, and leaves behind a police walkie-talkie which he had found on a sidewalk. At night, Adan uses the walkie-talkie to order the police to "withdraw" from Jerusalem, causing chaos for them. The police then come to the theater to arrest her, but she disappears mysteriously—they take away a mannequin of a Palestinian woman dressed in a faux-folk costume, instead of her. In the final scenes, ES returns to Nazareth and to his parents, and the film ends with him watching his parents fall asleep in front of the TV, as the Israeli national anthem ends the day's broadcast.

Chronicle's threads weave a poetic examination of the condition of being a Palestinian, and in particular a Palestinian citizen of Israel, at the heights of the Oslo period of 1993–2000, from the point of view of an individual returning after many years away. The Oslo period's lofty idealism, that a resolution to conflict was to be achieved through the establishment of a Palestinian state in the West Bank and Gaza, is set against a quotidian reality of small frustrations, tensions, and indignities. Beneath the veneer of optimism that defined the public aura of Oslo, Suleiman explores unsettled questions about the roles for and identities of Palestinians inside Israel within the context of the two-state solution (no less, those in the Occupied Territories, or those in the diaspora), and the resulting losses of identity that arise from attendant political projects, whether defined as Israeli or Palestinian. The film enacts an exploration of a denationalized national space, and as Gertz and Khleifi (2011, 194) note, in the film "[t]hese spaces are congested and threatened, always shot through a car window, but it is possible to reside there, even if life is fraught with violence." Put otherwise, the film follows ES on a search for a homeland between a country (Israel) that does not recognize him, and a "country" (Palestine) whose presence is withheld and occluded. The small moments that constitute this search are held together by a comic irony and a fixation upon absurdity that offer nothing by way of a formed narrative or constituted ideology, but rather serve to undo efforts at such completion. As Jacqueline Rose (2011, 179) notes, the comic in Suleiman's films is itself "a form of unsolicited memory. . . bringing something to the surface to the point of eruption before, momentarily, calming it back down." Along similar lines, Hamid Dabashi (2006, 135) argues, in Suleiman's cinema, "absurdity remembers the dark dread at the heart of its own memory of the terror, it must and cannot but, remember." The thread that both Rose and Dabashi draw between comedy and memory in Suleiman's work is convincing, in that the ironic or absurd in the film consistently serves as disruptions to the façade of a fully formed subjectivity, interjections that bear hints of the unsettled and uncanny nature of an unresolved traumatic memory.

In the second film of the trilogy, *Divine Intervention*, Suleiman focuses again on his Nazarene origins, offering a portrait of intracommunal tensions in the city, set against the eventual death of ES's father. Offsetting this story, Suleiman allegorizes the imposed rupture between West Bank and Israeli Palestinians through a love story that unfolds largely with the use of a different cinematic language than that of the quotidian scenarios set in Nazareth. Contra the placid air that oppresses the city in *Chronicle of a Disappearance*, here repetitive scenes show a community rife with internal tensions and subject to flashes of sometimes absurd violence, both real and symbolic. While ES is not present for the first thirty minutes or so of the film, when he appears we learn that he lives in Jerusalem and visits his parents from time to time. ES also carries out a hopeless affair with a woman living in Ramallah. Because she is prohibited from entering Jerusalem, they must rendez vous in the parking lot of a checkpoint, a liminal zone where they are able to meet, but in which they are passive witnesses to the humiliations and violence that mark this "border." Eventually his beloved stops coming to meet him, possibly disappearing, and ES is left alone. However she continues on in fantasy sequences, where she appears to take on supernatural qualities: walking through the militarized checkpoint and causing the collapse of the watchtower, and serving as a clarion warning to ES's neighbor, a collaborator with Israeli security services. These fantasies culminate in her metamorphosis into a ninja who combats Israeli police on a shooting range. Between these scenes, ES's father suffers first bankruptcy and then a heart attack, and ES visits him in the hospital. In the final scenes, ES's father dies, and—in a final, self-aware gesture to allegory—the last shot frames ES and his mother alone, sitting in the family kitchen, watching a pressure cooker as it whistles and shakes, as if about to explode.

In *Divine Intervention*, the effects of the second intifada, which all but brought to an end the claims of the Oslo accords, are now felt in the form of a heightened security state and division between the West Bank and Gaza, and Israel, as well as in further hopelessness and marginalization for Palestinian citizens of Israel. *Divine Intervention* follows *Chronicle of a Disappearance* in focusing on the alienation felt by ES upon returning to Nazareth, and on the more existential questions relating to identity that frame the experiences of many Palestinian citizens of Israel, but adds to these the aforementioned eruptions of fantasy. While the core concerns are similar, as are the aesthetic strategies and cinematic language, what is different is the context, which has significantly changed in the eight or so years between the two films. As Gertz and Khleifi (2011, 194) argue, "The difference between [the first two films] best illustrates what transpired in Palestinian society and its cinema between the peace accords and the outbreak of the second Intifadah." In the earlier work, Suleiman works to recover the losses for Palestinians (and especially those who are in Israel) that are latently obscured by the official optimism of the Oslo process, while in the second film the intensification of violence and the increasing expansion of settlements and checkpoints give the work a much more bleak and political resonance.

Both films give priority to the exploration of space over time, in that they are founded upon the relationship of place, identity, and belonging: from Nazareth to Jerusalem and further into the West Bank. The films map a Palestinian imaginative geography of the terrain that includes territories both of Israel and the West Bank (Gaza is not featured in either work), counterposing this to the predominant mappings of the nation-state of Israel: Tel Aviv, Haifa, Jerusalem. The question of space comes into further relief with the eventual return, in both films, to the familial home, the interior if claustrophobic world of a Palestinian family, that which still remains just beyond the boundaries of the Israeli state.[6] Both films inhabit a suspended temporality, peculiar to Palestinian cultural memory, where the past is obscured, and the future is a blank space. In other words, neither film explores the past or anticipates a future. Refqa Abu-Remaileh (2008, 14) has suggested that in these films there is an "unsustainable merging of tenses into a Palestinian present where the past and future have sought refuge. The idea of 'return' that most Palestinian refugees hold on to dearly creates a sense of cyclical time as opposed to linear time." In this way, the films give priority to the spatial politics of the region as they relate to question of identity, history, and memory.

Suleiman's third film pursues a more temporally oriented approach, in episodically exploring ES's family history from 1948 until the present. *The Time that Remains* threads together elements of the earlier films, using the same film language, but by moving across time as well as space, it presents partial and incomplete interventions on several of the themes raised in the earlier films—and again, doing so in a way that remains often irresolute. Here, Suleiman deploys time—evoking historical memory—in his exploration of the question of Palestinian identity through his family's vantage as Nazarenes who were to become Palestinian citizens of Israel. Geography and place are less central here: what gives the film its breadth is its multiple settings within time. Most of the film's action in fact takes place within the walls of ES's family home. The film begins, once again, with ES arriving from abroad (as he does explicitly in *Chronicle of a Disappearance*, and perhaps implicitly in *Divine Intervention*), and taking a taxi from the airport to Nazareth. Along the way, a heavy rainstorm stops the taxi in a no-man's-land, an existential limbo, a visual *purgatorio* (more on this scene later). The film then flashes back in time to 1948, where the story of ES's parents—in particular his father, Fu'ad—in that critical year is explored. In 1948, Fu'ad first acted as a fighter against the Zionist militias and then continued as an activist against Israeli military control of the town in the years of military administration (1948–1966). The film also follows ES as he grows up, first as a young boy in an Arab school in Israel, then as a teenager who is eventually warned by police to leave the country or face imprisonment. Parallel to their son's maturation, the film follows the stories of Fu'ad and his wife as they age through the 1960s, '70s, and '80s. The film then returns to the present, to ES's arrival from the airport, and from there on charts the last period of the life of his mother—ending with her hospitalization and death. The film concludes with ES sitting in the hospital courtyard, now all alone.

Beyond the broad narratives of each film, what is at stake here is how Suleiman presents the experiences of his characters, how these presentations relate to the question of personal history, and furthermore, how they map on to a broader understanding of Palestinian experience post-1948. In these works, Suleiman has forged a coherent and hermetic cinematic language that is singular and challenging, yet is not so experimental or self-contained as to be incomprehensible to audiences accustomed only to traditional cinematic language. What emerges in these works is a system of signification and meaning production that repeatedly leads to incompletion, question, and irresolution, in ways that are often framed as humorous or absurd.

Where the dominant film language and narrative structure aim at suturing and at offering completion of meaning in their organization of recurrent forms of signification, Suleiman's cinematic language nearly always aims at confounding such expectations, or at the very least plays with them in a way that undermines expectations. Suleiman himself testifies to this, saying,

> Palestinians have always been ghettoized in a way, geographically and historically. To translate this metaphor requires nonlinear cinematographic narrative structure—there is a parallelism between the decentralization of the narrative and of the film's structure. Opting for nonlinearity in the film's narrative mode fits in a perfect synchronization with my intention to challenge the linearity of the story of Palestine. Of course, I didn't create this non-linearity, it existed on its own.
>
> (SULEIMAN 2000, 97)

It is important to recall that Palestinian and other postcolonial filmmakers set out in the 1960s and onwards to challenge normative Hollywood style and cinematic language; the Third Cinema movement came to represent this goal most comprehensively. Yet, adherents to the Third Cinema and other related movements of the international anti-imperialist left were not inaccurately accused of producing a didactic cinema, a cinema of definitive and closed systems of meaning. Suleiman's work thus rubs against what had been the predominant tendencies of the earlier generations of Palestinian cinema work by staking out a new but less definitively positioned grounding. Suleiman, following in the footsteps of Michel Khleifi and other Palestinian auteurs of the 1980s, pursues a mode of what we may term a postcolonial second cinema—a mode of cinema that is individuated, aesthetically challenging, yet rooted in some way in the soil of colonial and postcolonial experiences. While this

framing may be viewed as lacking in political commitment—though what
emerges over the course of Suleiman's three films is in fact a deeply political
set of engagements, even if unresolved—in fact, what is most political about
them is precisely their discomfort with resolution.

To better understand how the aporetic dimension is staged in Suleiman's
cinema, it is necessary to examine his film language through discussing cinematic techniques and themes that are recurrent through the three films.
Through this, the irresolute qualities of his visual language, at the level of
both technique and motif, will emerge, allowing us to draw conclusions that
will link this positioning to the broader field of Palestinian cultural memory.

Repetition and Traumatic Suspension

In all three of Suleiman's films, a recurring cinematic motif is that of a long
static shot of what at first glance appears an unremarkably quotidian scene,
often with characters who seem to be waiting for something that never happens, or with characters carrying out a repetitive action which they appear
to be pursuing with no end. For example, in *Chronicle of a Disappearance*, in
one recurring shot, ES sits with his cousin in front of his cousin's souvenir
shop. In two takes of the scene, interruptions occur—in the first, a tourist
group passes across the frame, with one tourist pausing to click a photo of
the men, while in the second a book falls from the sky, prompting one of the
men to note impassively, "It's raining culture"—but the men remain more or
less in their same posture. In another repeated scene, different cars screech to
a halt in front of a shop, usually leading to an argument between the driver
and a passenger (figures 4.2–4.4). Passersby coax the two to end their argument and then push them into the car, which drives off. In the final iteration,
a car stops, but instead of arguing, the driver and passenger merely change
seats. In *Divine Intervention*, a man stands beside a bus stop that is no longer in service, driving to distraction a man who lives near the bus stop who
keeps coming out of his home to angrily say, "There's no bus!" In *The Time
that Remains*, a neighbor repeatedly threatens to self-immolate after pouring
gasoline over his head, but is each time stopped by ES's father. It is through
these, and many other similarly constituted scenes that punctuate the three
films, that Suleiman stages *purgatorio*—the suspended state within which his
Palestinian characters are trapped. At times this suspension allows the character to act as a marginal witness to actions that occur just before him. At several points in *Divine Intervention* we encounter ES as he sits passively inside
his car at the edge of a checkpoint parking lot, waiting for his beloved to
meet him. While there, he observes the militarized rituals of the checkpoint's
administration just across the parking lot. In one iteration of this scene, three
soldiers emerge from a jeep to carry out a choreographed, almost ritualized,

FIGURES 4.2–4.4 *Repeated scenes* (Chronicle of a Disappearance)

cleaning of the mud on their boots. In another, a soldier runs amok among the waiting cars of Palestinians, moving occupants from one car to another, shouting through a bullhorn at various cars, and ending his performance by attempting to enjoin the Palestinian drivers to sing along with his rendition of a popular Zionist song. Yet, despite these changes in the external action, ES remains impassive inside his car, unable to break the repetition of his unemotive observance of these events.

Suleiman's use of repetition also has temporal and historical reflections. Where his first two films are situated in a static present, *The Time that Remains* is structured around memories of the past and explores the locus of trauma, the events of 1948, as they resonate through the lives of the primary characters of all three films: primarily ES, his parents, and a few extended family members. In this third film, the *purgatorio* that defines this history is revealed as originating in the experiences of 1948, through recurring scenes that mark the passing of time with no resolution of this traumatic past. For example, ES's mother sits on the balcony of her home, looking out or reading letters from her sister who had fled to Jordan. Time passes, she ages, but the action and setting remain the same. The cross-temporal repetitions of *The Time that Remains* are even more powerful than those in earlier films, in that they present the characters as frozen in these patterns over a much longer period of time, for nearly all of their lives. Suleiman uses virtually identical framings and sequences in, for example, the scenes of ES's mother sitting on the balcony, whether in 1980 or in 2009, and a similar consistency in other cross-temporal shots conveys the immutable fixity of this *purgatorio* (figures 4.5–4.7).

Through these repeating scenes in each film, Suleiman has constructed a thread of narrative. However, as the story unfolds, the nearly unbearable repetition of these recurring scenes—repetition that is the antithesis of narrative itself—counteracts the ideology of transformation that is at the heart of all narrative forms. What does narrative transformation mean to a society in traumatic suspension, living in *purgatorio*? This may well return us to Godard's images, the shot and countershot—narrative fiction and documentary realism. However, instead of succumbing to documentary in a failing recuperation of Palestinian trauma, Suleiman's countershot is a narrative that refuses to offer the completions so often expected of dominant narrative forms.

Screens and Subjectivity

Suleiman continually choreographs his protagonist ES as standing within doorways, or behind windows, looking through onto an action that is occurring just beyond him. His perception is mediated through literal and symbolic

FIGURES 4.5–4.7 *Repeated scenes* (The Time that Remains)

screens. In *Divine Intervention*, at several points we view him sitting passively in a car, looking ahead through the windshield (figure 4.8). In *The Time that Remains*, he adopts a similar position of a passive observer as he stands in the window, looking out at his mother sitting on the balcony (figure 4.9). A scene near the end of *Chronicle of a Disappearance*, where ES seems to stand outside a cafe while watching his father arm-wrestle, captures the essence of this technique. At first it may not occur to the viewer to perceive the shot as a point-of-view framing, as it lacks the usual devices to indicate subjective perspective, such as the motion of a hand-held camera, or a countershot establishing the character's position while looking. However, as the long shot is held, it

FIGURE 4.8 *ES looks through the windshield* (Divine Intervention)

FIGURE 4.9 *ES looks through the window* (The Time that Remains)

is the absence of ES from the scene that is impossible to ignore. The distance of the camera and ES to the action and the window that frames and screens the action set out an implacable distance between the viewer and action. Other iterations of this framing are found throughout all three films, as the camera takes ES's point of view while framing his parents in the kitchen, sitting on the balcony, or napping in their bedroom. In many cases, the shots initially appear objective or neutral camera positions, but through their accumulation, and through intratextual hints, it becomes apparent that they have been point-of-view shots. The audience is invited to view the action as ES perhaps has been viewing it, through a doorway, through a window, or at a distance. As Livia Alexander (2002, 163) notes, "Framing his film through doors and windows or gazing into spaces, Suleiman conveys his position as an eternal outsider." These various screening techniques set ES at a position of estrangement from his surroundings. When ES moves to Jerusalem, a long shot overlaid with a soundtrack moves down a hillside road toward the iconic gold dome of al-Haram al-Sharif: a subjective shot through a car windshield. The car stops before a camel, and the camera centers on the beast, decentering the golden dome and its sacred claim. When he travels to Jericho, another shot from the car window conveys the landscape. Rather than intimating familiarity, the shots betray a certain ambivalence about how to relate to the landscape, both of city and of countryside—the sacredness of the al-Haram al-Sharif dissipates in the poor framing of the golden dome, and in the abrupt appearance of the camel in the middle of the road; the charge of the landscape transforms to a wistful sense of loss in the effect of a Fayruz song on the road to Jericho.

In *The Time that Remains*, these screening scenes are given what may termed a founding moment, originating shortly after the first hospitalization of ES's father. The teenaged ES picks up his father from the hospital and takes him to pick up medicine from a pharmacy. While ES enters the pharmacy, the camera remains outside, framing both his father in the car, and ES inside the store. As he turns to come out, his father has begun to listen to a cassette of old Arabic songs. ES exits the pharmacy and stands outside the car, looking at his father, who is framed through the car window. Then ES enters the car, but his father is asleep or lost in thoughts. Slumped forward, eyes closed, perhaps lost in reveries triggered by the song, he appears dead (figures 4.10, 4.11). This moment signifies their separation to come, and is the moment when ES first comes to comprehend his father's mortality. The sense of desire for his parents, but also his alienation from them, is profoundly felt in the distances marked out by these screens, and in particular the eventuality of death is inscribed deeply in these moments. The loss is much more significant than simply that of his loss of his parents—for they represent his only link to the past, and are his "final homeland" (as his epigraphic dedication in *Chronicle of a Disappearance* terms it).

What changes, fundamentally, is the individual as he or she ages—Suleiman's works, from the first shot of *Chronicle of a Disappearance* to the

FIGURES 4.10 AND 4.11 *Father slips away* (The Time that Remains)

final shot of *The Time that Remains*, are marked by an irresolute reflection on the process of aging, and of death and loss within the family. The former film is bookended by shots of his parents sleeping. The film opens with a shot that is an indistinct close-up of an object that is slowly revealed to be the clenched fist of a sleeping old man, propping up his head. The camera turns slowly until we finally see the man's face, ES's father. As his father's sleeping body breathes, it creates a subtle rhythm, deep and resonant as if a primal echo in the firmament of the universe. The framing and lighting emphasize this nearly metaphysical quality; the backdrop is dark, so that at first the image seems disembodied, lost in space. This first shot is echoed at the end of the film, where a wider shot in the living room of ES's family home frames his mother and father asleep before a television. The national television channel is ending the daily broadcast with a prayer from the Torah, followed by the Israeli national anthem, *HaTikvah*. Behind them, in the shadows, the silhouette of ES may be discerned in a doorway. Again, he is caught and separated from them, behind a symbolic screen. The melancholic reflection that this scene intimates is fully realized only when the biographies of his parents are later explored in *The Time that Remains*. The same Fu'ad who had refused to disarm in 1948 and who had faced the threat of execution fearlessly is now aged and physically broken, dozing with his wife before the television. In 1996, when *Chronicle of a Disappearance* was released, many read the final scene as a defeatist gesture, a surrender of Palestinian identity. After the release of *The Time that Remains*, the scene may better be understood as a profound rumination on the Nakba, as a scene symbolically as violent as any depiction of the fighting in 1948 may be. Far from a retreat of Palestinian claims in the face of an overwhelming victory by Zionism, the final scene of *Chronicle of a Disappearance* may be reread not only as a defiant statement of Palestinian resistance, but also as a document of all that has been done in the ongoing dispossessions of an open-ended catastrophe.

In these ways, screens and frames are an aesthetic cornerstone of Suleiman's cinematic language, conveying an often alienated subjective view on the action within each scene. Suleiman's camera infrequently adopts what is most common in normative cinematic language, that is, an objective or disinterested position. Instead, the camera is often revealed to be deeply subjective, and scenes are frequently dependent upon action that occurs outside the frame. These techniques frustrate the viewer from assuming a presumptive position of mastering or knowing, generating exegetical aporias that prevent the satisfaction of achieving narrative closure.

Disappearance and Desire

The Time that Remains opens with a short, self-contained sequence, set in a taxi driving from Ben Gurion airport, presumably to Nazareth. The scene is largely composed from three camera positions: the most frequent of which frames the driver of the taxi in a side profile from the passenger seat. This angle is occasionally intercut by a shot from a second angle, through the windshield from the front of the car. This second angle shows ES in the back seat; however, the frame does not use deep focus, so all that may be perceived is his dark silhouette. The third and least frequent position is a point-of-view shot from the back seat, showing the driver in the rear-view mirror. Other shots show the road and surrounding landscape, spaces devoid of any human presence. The driver begins the journey by radioing his dispatcher, telling him that he will be out of range for a while and so will "disappear." This reference evokes Suleiman's first film, *Chronicle of a Disappearance*, the title of which may apply to ES's absence as a Palestinian within Israel (and, perhaps as a Palestinian-Israeli within a two-state solution). As Haim Bresheeth (2007, 176) reads the film, "Suleiman is gradually and painfully disappearing—a simile of the disappearance of Palestine, and of the Palestinians." In *The Time that Remains*, Suleiman now conjures the Israeli Jew as his own double, as also predicting his own disappearance; a point that ironically brings the driver and ES together in a shared suspension, a common *purgatorio*. The Jewish driver's name is Elie, and he bears a family resemblance to his passenger, ES (Elia). As he drives, a rainstorm brings a deluge that first slows and finally stops the taxi's progress, and eventually they pull over to await the end of the storm.

In the scene at times allegorical aspects are invoked, for example when the driver, Elie, asks "Did I take a wrong turn?"—but the scene is pregnant with aporias. It is unclear if this journey is spatial or temporal; to a mythical (or prophesized?) future. After stopping, the driver peers into the darkness, asking, "Where are the kibbutzim, the collective farms, did the earth swallow them up?" As he sits behind his wheel he looks physically spent, bereft of physical presence. He half-heartedly asks, "What is this place? . . . Where do I go? . . . How do I go home? . . . Where am I?" The questions are, in a sense, rhetorical, as ES is not the intended interlocutor for the driver (the driver hardly acknowledges him, and ES, typically, does not speak). Instead, ES remains a silent shadow in the back seat, potentially threatening, or possibly simply an observer (figure 4.12). But these questions are open-ended. Where is home for the driver, or for his passenger? Indeed, *where* is he? *What* is this place? The dark overtones of the scene tie into the nearly apocalyptic *mise en scène*, that of a rainstorm with biblical resonances, on a road that is empty,

FIGURE 4.12 *Driving in an apocalyptic storm (*The Time that Remains*)*

that seems to go nowhere. A passenger who is nearly invisible, but who is your charge and your double, perhaps your replacement if you were to disappear, or perhaps a signifier of what you will become once you disappear.

Beyond its reference in the title of Suleiman's first film, disappearance and absence are recurring motifs throughout his works. The disappearance that is chronicled in his first film is one that is never fully disclosed. Adan's disappearance at the moment of her arrest may seem to be the most likely referent within the narrative, just as in *Divine Intervention*, the disappearance of ES's beloved also frames the story. But the theme of disappearance is treated in much more nuanced ways as well, throughout all three films. Just as ES and his driver "disappear" into the storm at the outset of *The Time that Remains*, so other disappearances occur. Suleiman returns to this scene in the last minutes of the film. Directly after the one fantasy sequence (an echo from *Divine Intervention*) in which ES pole-vaults over the separation wall, the film revisits the first scene in the taxi. Now, the storm is ending with final echoes of thunder in the distance. Elie the driver is slumped over the wheel, breathing heavily as if asleep. A close up of ES shows him awake and alert, looking out the window as if watching the rain dissipate. Now Elie is absent (he is only shot from behind) and ES is present. In this and other moments in all three films, the staging and restaging of disappearances, from the level of plot to that of the visual language employed, activate an engagement with the broader notions of presence and absence that all three films explore: the disappearance of one society, its history and cultural memory, under the weight of another society, whose own narratives and histories cannot accommodate them, and the haunting of the new society by the ghosts of the old.

Death and the Unanswered Question

An aporetic reflection on aging and loss suffuses the text of all three films by Suleiman, punctuated by the deaths, first of ES's father, then of his mother. Where *Chronicle of a Disappearance* reflects upon the aging of ES's parents, *Divine Intervention* is in large part a narrative centered on the demise of his father, whose death concludes of the film. *The Time that Remains* ends the trilogy with the passing of his mother. In *Chronicle of a Disappearance*, ES is first made to contend with his parents' mortality when his father suffers his first heart attack. ES visits his father in the hospital, which is full of characters who are familiar from various Nazareth sequences in the film. The hospital is a purgatorial zone; all there are awaiting their eventual death. In one scene, patients one by one leave their beds, rolling their IV stands, and assemble in a hallway with the doctors. They all begin to smoke there, walking up and down the short hall. The hospital becomes a space where all—patients, nurses and doctors alike—are arbitrarily gathered while awaiting their inevitable ends.

In *Divine Intervention*, the death of ES's father is foretold first in other losses, most particularly the bankruptcy of his metalwork business, and the impounding of his equipment by debt collectors. Shortly afterward, his father collapses at home and, after being moved to the hospital, eventually passes away. In several scenes, ES visits his father in the hospital and watches him in his bed. One shot frames a close-up of two hands caught in a firm clasp, an echo of the arm-wrestling scene from *Chronicle of a Disappearance*. The close-up of the hands of father and son initially reads as a moment of intimacy between father and son. However, a wider shot then confounds these expectations: ES is in fact simply helping his father sit up in his bed. As he rises, both father and son stare ahead at crossing angles, their eyes never meeting. Here, Suleiman provokes an anticipated reading from a close-up shot, only to negate the initial reading through a wider shot of the same action. The first shot on its own relays a possible interpretation that the wider framing then undoes. Again, what is evoked is an exegetical alienation that haunts ES in both his observations and his actions.

The *Time that Remains* relegates Fu'ad to the "historical" dimension of the film, the past, since he has already died. The scenes in the film where Suleiman plays ES (other actors play his childhood and adolescent selves) pertain only to the narrative of his return to Nazareth to attend to his mother in her final days. She suffers from illness and spends her time in silence, staring into the distance. Her only apparent joy, raiding the freezer at night for a Popsicle, brings chidings the next day when her maid tests her blood sugar levels for her diabetes. Even the spectacle of fireworks in the night sky for Israel's Independence Day provokes no reaction from her, as she sits on the balcony with a disaffected look; the scene resonates with the last scene of *Chronicle of a Disappearance*, where she sleeps while the Israeli national anthem plays on television. Israeli Independence Day is the same day that Palestinians commemorate the Nakba, and as Jonathan Greenberg (2005, 99) notes, "Nakba Day is a day of sorrow, lament, and anger, of mourning and memory: the bitter image of Israel's *Yom Ha'atzmaut*." But we come to realize she is, as with the characters in the hospital in *Chronicle of a Disappearance*, trapped in her *purgatorio*, suspended before death, unable to even mourn the Nakba that is evoked by Israel's celebrations. Sitting on the porch, she stares determinedly at a photograph—revealed in the final scene of the film to be of her departed husband in his youth. The film suggests that ES is no less caught in a purgatorial march toward his own demise. Where in the earlier films ES traveled around Israel/Palestine and engaged in a love affair, in *The Time that Remains*, apart from one unexplained visit to Ramallah, ES stays largely within the family house. The film represents his world as being much narrower, and what is shown of the outside world is marked much more by darkness than by humor.

Eventually his mother is hospitalized. In the final scenes of the film, ES waits in the hospital as she dies. In the last scene between them, as she lies in the hospital bed he notices that she is holding a photograph in her hand. He takes it and sees that it is a photo of a young Fu'ad sitting on the same balcony where she has spent so much of her own life. As he looks into the distance in the photo, his pose conveys resolute hope—a sentiment long ago lost within the family. He realizes that her only wish now is to be able to join him in death. Through the personal and intimate loss that conjures her desire for death, the crushing weight of the post-Nakba losses of Palestine are opened. The young Fu'ad, whose youth was marked by vigor, pride, and bravery, was reduced to a life circumscribed and drawn dry by his identity as a Palestinian inside Israel. ES's mother also lost incalculably in the aftermath of 1948, the hints of which emerge in the correspondence she maintains with her sister, who was made a refugee and who lived in Jordan apart from her family. ES pauses while looking at the photo of his father, and then slides it back into his mother's hand as she looks at him meaningfully. She reaches up and removes the breathing tube in her nose. ES tries to put it back, but she grabs it again and removes it defiantly, perhaps for the last time (figure 4.13).

The film ends with ES sitting in a courtyard of the hospital. As he stares ahead, the camera assumes his perspective in a point-of-view shot that makes up the final shot. A woman walks by, speaking Arabic on a phone. Two men walk by, both wearing casts. Doctors wheel a patient on a stretcher, a man stops the doctor for medical advice. Another man tells a friend on the phone about the fight that has sent him to the hospital. Three young Arab men dressed in hip-hop style clothing sit on a bench across from ES. One of their friends comes into frame, handcuffed to a much smaller man, an Israeli police officer. Seemingly unconcerned about his captor, the young man walks over to his friends, dragging the policeman with him. He stops and takes a

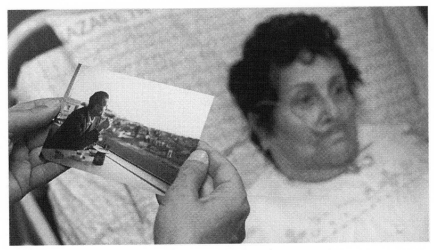

FIGURE 4.13 *ES holds a photo of his father (*The Time that Remains*)*

cigarette from one, while the policeman tries to pull his prisoner away, but in vain. Eventually the young man goes along with the policeman, but not before stopping to give his friends a peace sign—a gesture that cues the final song, a remix of the BeeGees' hit "Staying Alive." The credits roll. Through this irresolute ending scene, *The Time that Remains* hints at a resilient and possibly hopeful future, one that appears more plausible through its mirroring with the traumas of the past, through the film's representation of the Nakba. Returning from this point to the last scene of *Chronicle of a Disappearance*, we may see how ES viewed his parents then in the shadow of their defeat, but that the significance of this defeat gains fuller resonance through our understanding not only of what happens later, but also of what had happened in the past. In *Divine Intervention*'s ending, ES's father has died, and he and his mother are left alone inside the family home. The loss of his father is overlaid by a foreboding for the future. In *The Time that Remains*, ES's mother dies, and he is all alone. But as he watches the strangers in the courtyard, not only does he see life continuing, but also he sees the youth of his city—now dressed in a way totally foreign to him—continuing to resist, staying alive in the shadow of death. And yet, the liminal space between life and death is the fullest signification of the Nakba, even for those who survived, and no narrative can adequately offer a resolution to this. As Samera Esmeir (2003, 25) notes,

> One of the difficulties in discussing violence against Palestinians during the 1948 war is that "Palestine," the site of the violence, both persists and has ceased to exist. Its simultaneous presence and erasure occurs in part through the survival of Palestinians from the 1948 war in what has ceased to be Palestine. Their scattered yet persistent presence constitutes a thread with which one can return to that moment when Palestine was ruined. They embody the survival of Palestine, yet also stand for its death. This death continues both to impede their memory of what happened in 1948 and to structure it.

The specter of death that haunts Suleiman's trilogy, in particular the second and third films, is a signification of "simultaneous presence and erasure," the persistence of Palestinian life despite the death of Palestine, "embody[ing] the survival of Palestine, yet also stand[ing] for its death." We can discern neither mourning nor melancholia in the look of ES as he sits alone in the hospital courtyard, for even here he is only a witness to the ongoing and unresolved traumas of the open-ended catastrophe. The Nakba continues; its trauma is suspended, purgatorial, but not without some hope.

It is perhaps not surprising that Suleiman does not attempt a representation of the Nakba until the third film in this series. From a social perspective, treatments of the Nakba are necessarily fraught and often overdetermined—for many Palestinians and their supporters, they are often subject to a form of sacralization. This memory is signified most often through the icon of an old steel key, which recurs in visual representations within Palestinian refugee societies (such as in paintings, murals, and political posters, as well as in cinema), which has come to assume an understandably boundaried signification, that of the lost homes to which hundreds of thousands of refugees and their descendants still demand a right to return. Suleiman's cinema does not dilute the emotional significance of such signs, but his refusal to allow the Nakba narrative to be assimilated into more conventional heroic-tragic forms leads to an irresolution that may generate discomfort to those for whom the idea of al-'awda (the return) is sacred or set outside of political contestation. As Ilan Pappé (2011, 220) suggests of Suleiman's works, they "challenge the collective memory and its obedience to a nationalized space or present." But by refusing to accord collective memory to a presentist project to appropriate the past for nationalist recuperation, Suleiman leaves the signification of this past uninterpreted, aporetic.

Suleiman's use of the Nakba is a gesture that raises open-ended questions that themselves conjure nondelimited interpretive fields. The story of the Nakba is therefore set against the episodes of further eras where a continuity is formed. The questions remain unanswerable. Once again, the Nakba continues; *al-Nakba mustamirra*. Instead of rooting the Palestinian catastrophe in the historical violence of 1948, Suleiman detemporalizes the Nakba so that it may be seen as an ongoing process, present at different levels in various times over the course of modern Palestinian history. We find through his juxtaposition of different eras a continuing *purgatorio* for ES and his family, where they are subject to persistent forms of refusal and absence. Suleiman's films move between semiotically coherent and delimited social references, exploring the lives of its characters as, perhaps, representative of Palestinian and Palestinian-Israeli identity and experience, to references that are impossible to foreclose upon, that produce open and ambiguous areas of meaning, that frustrate interpretations that are politically or socially delimited.

As Jacqueline Rose (2011, 181) suggests, these films are an act of reappropriation, of the past and of memory, "Suleiman has to seize his own history back from the foreign detritus with which it is packaged every day." The aporias of Suleiman's cinema effectively frustrate any attempt to "place" his work as simply evoking or signifying a particular and foreclosed-upon mode of political representation or meaning, whether as cultural memory or as a form of mimetic experience. In many ways, his works evoke the sentiments of Edward Said (2001, 567) in his inclination to seek solace within the impermanence of being a lost cause, "Better a lost cause than a triumphant one, more satisfying a sense of the provisional and contingent . . . than the proprietary solidity of permanent ownership." Suleiman's three films embrace the provisional and the contingent while caught in the suspended trauma of an ongoing catastrophe, dwelling on what remains in the face of a lost cause, and seeking signs of hope within moments of impossibility.

Sacred Defenses

TREACHEROUS MEMORY IN POSTWAR IRAN

A mother holds a newborn baby in her arms as she looks through a glass pane into a hospital clean-room. Inside, a man, a chemotherapy patient, looks back at her—she is his wife, the child is the daughter whom he has never yet held. He sits up on the bed to look at the child, and then begins to cough convulsively. The scene then intercuts with flashbacks showing soldiers lost in the yellow mist of a chemical gas attack, on the frontline of the Iran-Iraq war. A surreal figure stands on the battlefield, beating upon a large drum. The colors of the war footage are oversaturated, the soundtrack is rhythmic, punctuated by chords sung by an angelic choir. One of the soldiers falls; he is not wearing a gas mask. His comrade stops to help him, removing his own gas mask and placing it over the fallen soldier's face, before taking a rocket-propelled grenade launcher and looking around, as if lost. The soundtrack's choral music climaxes (figure 5.1).

The scene described above, set near the end of Ebrahim Hatamikia's *From the Karkhe to the Rhine* (*Az Karkhe ta Rhine*, 1993), is emblematic of both the aesthetics and the cultural tropes at the heart of Iran's "sacred defense" cinema. The setting of the scene is the Iran-Iraq war, which lasted for eight years (1980–1988) and cost an estimated one million lives. The war, launched by Iraq to settle long-standing border disputes with Iran during a time of perceived Iranian weakness (in the year after the Iranian revolution and during the domestic chaos that followed), evolved into an existential struggle between the dominant parties in each country: the Iraqi Ba'ath regime, and the Iranian postrevolutionary Islamic Republican experiment. The longevity of the war and the devastation it wrought led to the consolidation of cultural and social control in Iran along ideological lines that reflected the values of the ascendant religious regime, represented in the figure of Ayatollah Khomeini. While the war had originally been termed by the Iranian government as *jang-i tahmili* (the imposed war), this came to be overtaken by the concept of *defa-ye moghaddas*, or sacred

FIGURE 5.1 *Flashback to the front, Sa'id during a chemical attack* (From the Karkhe to
the Rhine)

defense. The latter term retroactively encompassed all cultural activities that
were ideologically sanctioned by the Iranian government, and came to also
describe further cultural work to memorialize the war in the years after its
end. As Ghamari-Tabrizi (2009, 112) notes, "Not only did the eight-year-long
'sacred defense' play a constitutive role in the emergence of the postrevolutionary regime but its legacy also continues to inform the political strategy of competing factions." The concept of sacred defense then came to be applied more
broadly, not only to work exploring the aftermath of the war, but even to projects that promoted what were considered to be the ideological aims of the war,
even if these had little direct bearing on the war and postwar setting.

   In *From the Karkhe to the Rhine*, sacred defense tropes permeate the film's
text. The film follows the story of Sa'id, a blind veteran of the war, who has
traveled to Germany with a group of other chemical-attack victims for specialized treatment. There his estranged sister, who has married a German
man, contacts him. While at first their relationship is fraught with tension,
eventually she and Sa'id reconcile, each slowly coming to a better understanding of the other's perspectives and experiences. However, shortly after
he successfully regains his vision from his treatment, he is diagnosed with
leukemia and given only a short time to live. In the scene described above,
Sa'id's wife has finally traveled from Iran to see him and to introduce him
to their daughter. His silent wife and newborn child signify the home-front
ideals of sacred defense, fulfilling the trope of the patiently suffering woman,
and the newborn child who redeems the death of the father for a new generation. It is in this scene that the film reveals that Sa'id's injuries are due to a
selfless act in which he had removed his gas mask in order to save his comrade

Nozar. This disclosure fits perfectly the melodramatic arc that so commonly frames the narrative of Iranian war cinema. In these stories, it is precisely the act of sacrifice that drives the melodramatic structure, satisfying viewers through its cathartic resolution, giving a transcendent meaning to a death among so many thousands of other deaths in that war.

The last shot in this sequence, in which Sa'id rises in slow motion in the yellow mist—holding the rocket-propelled grenade launcher while looking around in the surreal haze—itself captures the ethos of sacred defense, reflecting both its dislocated nature and metaphysical charge. In fact, this is the very last image of Sa'id in the film, as in the next and final scene he has now died. This journey back in time, or the revisiting of memory in the fragile present, is also a link between Sa'id's life and his death. In this last scene with Sa'id, it is as if for him the front lines of sacred defense are everywhere, as if he has realized that his life was entirely a journey upon the path of this sacred defense. Despite regaining his sight in Germany, thereby softening his anti-Western views, and despite coming to terms with his sister's choice to abandon Iran and marry a German man, when faced with death he cloaks himself within the mantle of the sacred defense.

The melodramatic arc of the film tracks a radical course from hardened ideologue to cosmopolitan humanist, with a sharp return back to origins just before dying. Sa'id's initial transformation is so profound that, when regaining his sight for the first time, he tells his German doctor, "In this world, I've opened my eyes twice: once in my homeland and once in Germany. I don't remember what I saw the first time, but this time I'll remember what I've seen for as long as I live" (figure 5.2). Despite this transformative ability to

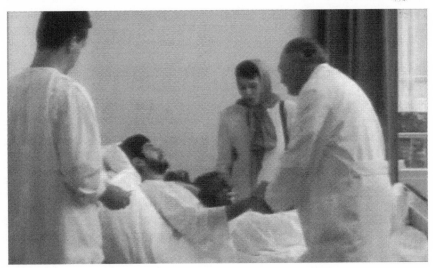

FIGURE 5.2 *Sa'id speaks to his German doctor after regaining his sight* (From the Karkhe to the Rhine)

see himself beyond the religious-nationalist limitations of the sacred defense imagination, Sa'id's reconciliation is short-lived and his reversion to the role of a martyrdom-bound Basij fighter is marked by the return of memories from the front. The intrusion of memory in the form of flashbacks and the marking of memory upon the body—in the form of Sai'd terminal illness, and the traumatic nature of his memories—are central features of sacred defense narratives. Here, the withholding of this memory until a late moment in the film signals both the cathartic possibilities of memory, but also its treachery. This is because Sa'id's sacrifice—to save Nozar—has already been shown to have been futile, as Nozar has just told Sa'id of his intentions of seeking asylum in Germany, thus treacherously betraying the central values of sacred defense in pursuit of personal gain. The emotive heart of this melodramatic twist is doubled—the first fighter (Sa'id) is lost to his war wounds (and thus martyred) while the second fighter (Nozar) is lost to the diaspora/West (and is thus, however ambivalently it is treated, a traitor).

In postrevolutionary Iran, the onset of the Iran-Iraq war allowed for the articulation of new if shifting parameters for ideological commitment and heroism, as well as treachery or cowardice. Many in the government "viewed the war not just as a struggle for the territorial integrity of the Iranian state but instead as an opportunity to further consolidate and institutionalize the revolution, purging it of known and potential opponents" (Wehrey et al. 2009, 24–25). The evolution of the "sacred defense" concept allowed for the most articulate elaboration of key binaries (enemy/friend, revolutionary/anti-revolutionary, hero/traitor, etc.), and wartime and postwar cultural producers, bureaucrats, and theorists have all contributed to the definition of their conceptual boundaries. This project did not wane after the end of the war, for as Pedram Khosronejad (2013, 7) notes, "after the end of war many governmental institutions and military organizations, which also worked on different aspects of war propaganda and the mobilization of youth during the war, tried to celebrate war achievements, important martyrs, significant attacks, etc., through the creation of martyrdom museums as well as Sacred Defense festivals and ceremonies."

In the postwar context, sacred defense also bore the burden of accommodating the necessary work of mourning for the losses of the war. With hundreds of thousands dead, families from every social background, ethnicity, and location were affected by the war's ravages. Sacred defense cinema came to set out the terms for legitimate mourning work, even though by doing so it only reopened the wounds of loss that so many had experienced. As Michaël Abecassis (2011, 394) argues, "Cinematic images can only offer the illusion of presence. They cannot bring back the dead, nor bury them, and they continue to haunt us to the point where we incorporate their own image; otherwise they spectralize onto the screen until the "vanishing point" of no return. The process of mourning is never complete and keeps reverberating in post-war Iranian cinema." Beyond the diminishing effect of its ideological propagation of the Islamic Republic's values, the sacred defense cinema genre has come to be marked with just such a spectral haunting, where its attempts to lead the way in mourning the war's dead have served only as a return to the starting point of loss.

This chapter examines the shifting discourse on sacred defense cinema, first by exploring how the genre is to be defined, as well as examining its perceived successes and failures. After, I explore the limits of the sacred defense discourse, by presenting readings of two further films by Hatamikia—*Minu's Watch Tower* (*Borj-e Minu*, 1996) and *The Glass Agency* (*Ajans-e shisheh-i*, 1997)—which I argue lay out a trajectory that begins firmly at the core of sacred defense themes exemplified in *From the Karkhe to the Rhine*, but that ends, by the third film, with a profound ambivalence about the continued relevance of sacred defense ideology for postwar Iran. Finally, I turn to Bahram Beyzai's *Bashu, The Little Stranger* (1987), by way of exploring war cinema that falls outside of the sacred defense field, showing how Iranian filmmakers who were not committed to the revolutionary system sought ways to engage with the war's traumas in ways that were firmly and intentionally at odds with the sacred defense mantra.

Defining the Sacred Defense Field

All Iranian war and postwar cultural enunciations must be viewed as being fundamentally defined by the discourse of sacred defense. These enunciations are either legitimated within this project, or are set outside of it and are thus coded as treacherous to it. Defining the term sacred defense is a fraught endeavor, even for those who work within the field. Generically, the term has come to be applied by many as pertaining to any cultural works relating to the Iran-Iraq war and its aftermath (usually in the form of narratives about veterans of the war). However, many who play roles within sacred defense institutions insist upon a more ideologically refined definition, distinguishing between "war cinema" and "sacred defense cinema," for example.

Here I will first focus upon the constitution of the *sacred defense field*, to describe the ideological ethos that surrounded the war. In this sense, the sacred defense field is the dominant expression of cultural memory of the Iran-Iraq war in the postwar Iranian context. The field is subject to ongoing contestation, not only from without but also from within, which means that the field has shown remarkable dynamism and a capacity for transformation. However, despite this, it is also true that for many years after the end of the war this project has remained essentially coherent in its core ideological orientations. The sacred defense field thus serves as a singular, and dominating, field of representational and memorializing activity regarding the war, although it is not the only one. And again, the sacred defense field is not static, but rather is marked by intense conflict and redefinition within itself.[1] Peter

Chelkowski (2002, 135) argues that in particular, visual cultural activity was central to the origins of the sacred defense project, saying that "never in the history of propaganda have the graphic arts systematically played such an important role as they did in Iran in the years 1980–88 . . . a veritable army of artists labored ceaselessly to produce art that would encourage and inspire soldiers and civilians alike." Here, Chelkowski's use of the metaphor of an army has merits in that through the Iran-Iraq war, cultural mobilization and military mobilization became entwined to an extent that distinguishing between them was often futile.

In postwar Iran, state intervention into both the representation of the war and its aftermath has led cultural producers to adopt very different strategies, largely relating to their own political commitments and subjective identification within the parameters of postrevolutionary ideology. State sponsorship of film production about the war, led by the Anjoman-e Sinama-ye Defa-ye Moghaddas (Council of Sacred Defense Cinema), has promoted work that follows state imperatives for interpretations of the war.[2] This council has carried out myriad activities since the war's end, including organizing film festivals of sacred defense cinema, providing production support to selected film projects, training filmmakers and screenwriters, among other activities. Perhaps the greatest impact of sacred defense cinema institutions was felt in the early and mid-1990s, when the genre produced many of the most popular films in Iran and attracted a wide range of talented filmmakers to contribute to the sacred defense project. For example, in 1993, *From the Karkhe to the Rhine* was the highest-grossing Iranian domestic film, and its director, Ebrahim Hatamikia, whose works are "considered some of the best ever made in the genre of war cinema," produced a string of highly popular and critically acclaimed films on sacred defense themes throughout the 1990s and 2000s (Abecassis 2011, 392).

When Iranian filmmakers elected to treat the war with a measure of ambivalence, as, for example, in Amir Naderi's two documentary films titled *The Search* I and II (*Jostejoo 1*, 1981, and *Jostejoo 2*, 1982), the films were repressed or censored.[3] Both parts of *The Search* were commissioned by state television in the early years of the war, but were not shown and were then embargoed, ostensibly for focusing on the question of losses brought about by the war, rather than promoting sacred defense themes. In this way, the various cultural agencies of the Iranian state apparatus, including film and television censors, film production funds, training facilities, festival curators, and many others, all have contributed to the formation of the sacred defense field. To be a cultural producer during the war and in the years just after it was to be continually reminded of the relative prestige and favor afforded to sacred defense themes, which was joined with a strong project of denying or delegitimizing engagements with war that fell outside of these authorized themes. For stepping outside of the sacred defense field, a high price could be paid in the form of preproduction obstacles, such as denial of funding or script censorship. Perhaps even worse, barriers could be raised after the film's completion, from complete banning to simply a lack of distribution or broadcasting opportunities being made available to it. Thus it is not surprising that very few films have been made that address the war in a way that does not participate in engaging with, and thus reproducing, sacred defense themes, tropes, and forms of legitimation. However, counterinterpretations of the war experience have also circulated in Iranian cultural productions, and cinema works have reflected, often in oblique fashion, these alternative approaches. While ideologically committed filmmakers began to explore the war largely through narrative fictional means, quickly developing a language and repertoire for sacred defense cinema that became enclosed, self-referential, and self-reifying, those for whom participation in sacred defense culture was socially impossible or politically unacceptable sought to find other outlets for exploring the traumatic cultural memory of the war.

To better illuminate the contours of this paradigm, we may compare the Iranian context to another setting where war and postwar cultural productions have played a significant social role, that of Lebanon. When juxtaposed with the Iranian, state-sponsored project of predetermining the interpretive parameters for war traumas, the Lebanese civil war discourse (see chapter 7) offers what may be a nearly diametrically opposing context, wherein official discourse on the war is limited only to what Sune Haugbolle (2005, 193) calls "state-sponsored amnesia," against which a preponderance of memorial projects may be viewed as potentially threatening to the political status quo and national unity. Narratives on the Lebanese civil war range broadly, but as in Iran find themselves delimited by certain discursive and institutional boundaries. In Lebanon these boundaries are set not only by a weak state's disinclination and inability to tackle difficult war questions, but also by the demands and interests of the funders of these films—most often European national cultural funds which promote memory discourse that occasions nonsectarian views of the war, but the support of which also leads to complaints of a fetishization of the spectacle and trauma of war.[4]

What a comparison of these two national contexts illuminates is their congruences and distinctions as to how traumatic memory may be harnessed for productive social ends. In Lebanon, the state has relinquished the grounds of cultural memory of the war, which have in turn been occupied by cultural productions that use memory discourses to animate critical questions about postwar Lebanon's failures, and to militate against the terms of official amnesia. In Iran, the state's aim to monopolize the terms of war-related cultural memory has led some filmmakers to cede the grounds of representing war memory to the sacred defense project, while others have entered the state-delimited grounds, but have had to stake out dissenting views largely through works that emerge from within the sacred defense field, and which made use of its claims to legitimacy in articulating alterative representations of the social traumas of the war. Still others animate counterimaginaries of the war in more oblique terms.

To better understand the sacred defense field, we must begin by addressing how its institutions have collaborated in articulating a discourse of social trauma that is productive to the state's ideological aims. Historically, the sacred defense field had roots in the war effort itself. Initially, for a period after the beginning of hostilities, the cultural response to the war was poorly defined and lacked coordination or direction. Nonetheless, within months of the initial Iraqi invasion in September 1980, the revolutionary state had begun to develop key elements of what would become the sacred defense project, although sacred defense cinema only emerged somewhat later as part of its repertoire. This process may be noted quite clearly in comparing the first examples of cinematic responses to the war, such as the 1984 film *Eagles* ('*Uqabha*, dir. Samuel Khachigian), to later, more developed sacred defense works (largely produced in the last years of the war or in the postwar period). Although a film made to support the war effort, *Eagles* is fundamentally a conventional war action film with Iranian soldiers set as national heroes in the fight against a villainous Iraqi enemy, and lacks any use of the conventions and tropes that would later define sacred defense productions. So as to improve upon the ideologically insufficient if patriotic responses of filmmakers such as Khachigian, the state began to develop institutions to formulate more ideologically sound means by which to represent the war and to formulate cultural memory around it. One Iranian critic, a supporter and theorist of sacred defense cinema, describes the qualities that characterize this earlier form of war film, which generate

> sympathy based on Western forms of fantastical and exaggerated heroism on one side, and place on the other side a group that is stupid, cowardly, criminal and doomed to defeat. . . . The works of those years [i.e., the first years of the war] were also characterized by use of exaggerated film techniques. Disconcerting zooms, unnecessary camera movements in various directions, overwrought music, long close-ups for effect on the faces of famous actors, chase scenes and drawn-out and bloody fighting that result in victory for the heroes of the film.
>
> (MOSTEGHASI 1380 [2001], 147)

Sacred defense filmmaking is based on a rejection of these aesthetic formulae, and seeks to harness cinematic technique to more exalted ends. The aesthetics of sacred defense move away from fantasies of military heroism derived from action film genres, and emphasize what are seen as the transcendent aims of the war, both personal and communal. In this conception, the sacred defense encompasses human activities of a wide variety beyond their battlefield conduct, and the front lines of the war provide what may be seen as only the most opportune and distilled manifestations of a struggle that precedes the conflict with Iraq, and which will no doubt find its resolution only at the end of time. As Partovi (2008, 519) suggests, what distinguishes the ideological subtext of sacred defense cinema from that of more common national war cinemas is that, "It is not out of legal obligation or national pride or family honor but rather out of love for God that one goes to the front. The ultimate victory is not the vanquishing of the enemy but the spiritual fulfillment and eternal life gained through freedom from the bonds of flesh." Roxanne Varzi (2006, 79) echoes some of the same themes in her discussion of sacred defense cinema: "The film images of the sacred defense were also used as metaphors or examples for how a young man might commence on the path to God."

These aims cast the Iranian articulation of a war culture in terms that are rather distinct from those of many other modern international wars, which have tended to rely upon nationalist conceptions of the homeland, and sacrifice for the national body, to legitimize the losses brought about in war. So it is perhaps to be expected that practitioners of sacred defense culture, and cinema in particular, conceiving of their work as at odds with predominant, often Western, narrative or aesthetic conventions, have "employed images of martyrdom and self-sacrifice" that fit into the broader visual repertoire of the postrevolutionary ideological project (Lotfalian 2009, 165). And yet, despite these aims, most Iranian sacred defense films adopt a decidedly conventional narrative structure, that of the melodrama, with the sacrifice of the protagonist serving as an emotively cathartic point within a "family" drama involving either biological families or those involving the "brotherhood" of soldiers. Yet, in distinction to the secular sublimity of a patriot's death in defense of his nation, the sacred defense martyr is celebrated for his achievement of a transcendent status in defense of religion, of the oppressed, and fundamentally of humanity.

Working from the material of this ideological framework, a new genre developed. The elaboration of its aesthetic and formal conventions was significantly complemented by the emergence of a wide variety of institutions supporting such filmmaking. During the war, training programs were instituted by the state television broadcasting service through its office, TelFilm, so as to bring to the fore a new generation of filmmakers and documentarians to provide wartime materials for both television and cinema (Partovi 2008, 519). Other filmmakers were given support and training opportunities through the Hozeh-ye Honari-Islami (Islamic Cultural Center), a quasi-independent ideologically committed Islamic cultural organization which began to offer funding for sacred defense films during the war (Zeydabadi-Nejad 2009, 38). Some of these filmmakers, who initially began as volunteers, came to establish successful careers for themselves over the course of the war and the first postwar years, deriving support from the state as well as gaining

large audiences for their works. A number of Iran's most commercially successful postrevolutionary filmmakers rose through these ranks: Ebrahim
Hatamikia, Jafar Panahi, Mohsen Makhmalbaf, and Kamal Tabrizi, to name
a few. The emergence of the national Farabi Film Foundation in 1983 also
sets out another institutional basis for the development of the sacred defense
field, with its War Films Bureau, which was established to promulgate the
ideological aims of sacred defense. This project was further developed in
the postwar period during the Rafsanjani presidency of 1990–1997, through
further institutionalization. Most of these projects found affiliation with,
or support from, the cultural organs of the state, in particular the Ministry
of Culture and Guidance, while enjoying the support of other ministries
as well (Varzi 2006, 98). Independent foundations and organizations have
also arisen, including the Bonyad-e Hefze Arzeshha-ye Defa-ye Moqaddas
(Foundation for Preservation and Propagation of the Values of the Sacred
Defense), which "maintains memoires, notes, articles, lists of commanders,
and lists of Iranian victims of chemical weapons during the Iran-Iraq War"
(Wehrey et al. 2009, 101).

However, despite the rigid terms and ideological focus adopted by the
founding institutions of the sacred defense field, the contestation present
within the field has consistently led to the rearticulation of these terms. This
phenomenon may be traced not only in the shift in tone visible in the works
of sacred defense filmmakers, but also in the position of politicians and other
public figures toward the hegemony of the sacred defense project in the cultural memory of the war. There is no better illustration of this than the failed
impeachment of Ataollah Mohajerani, the minister of culture under President
Mohammad Khatami (who was in office from 1997 to 2005), by principalist
and ultraconservative parliamentarians in 1999. The articles of impeachment
give evidence to the fact that the parliamentary committee viewed the perpetuation of the sacred defense field to be a key responsibility of the minister of culture, one alleged to have been abrogated by Mohajerani—during
Mohajerani's administration, the privileged position of sacred defense cinema was seen to have begun to erode. This is noted in plain language in the
following charges in the articles of impeachment: "Lack of attention to Sacred
Defense filmmakers, which has resulted in the drastic decrease in the number of the[se] films. Stopping the subsidies for this sort of cinema (which is
one of the main incentives for the spread and propagation of the values of
the eight years of Sacred Defense and its transfer to the next generation)"
(Zeydabadi-Nejad 2009, 52).

In the case of the Mohajerani impeachment effort, we clearly see the conflicts that lie at the heart of state projects of defining cultural memory of the
war. The legitimating terms of social trauma are here harnessed by the state,
but this control is fragile and subject to threat. The sacred defense field, which
is given legitimacy by its production of social trauma discourse, acquired a

new configuration through the changes that producers in the field began to demand of it. In the early years of the millennium, a number of events signaled a profound crisis in sacred defense cinema, as even a former high-profile practitioner such as Ebrahim Hatamikia became one of the "many filmmakers who previously made Sacred Defence films [who] abandoned the genre," and as new films in the genre have commanded smaller and smaller audiences (Zeydabadi-Nejad 2009, 167n29).

During the first years of the Khatami administration, there was already official acknowledgement that the genre was in crisis, as a study funded by the ministry of culture found that in 1999, only "3.6% of the general public liked Sacred Defence films" (Zeydabadi-Nejad 2009, 50). One sacred defense filmmaker, Abulqasim Talebani, sees the genre as having become degraded by opportunism, saying, "sacred defense cinema today has taken on the appearance of commerce and trade. Now those who want to make films just grow beards [i.e., affect religiosity] and then enter the profession. This person makes his first film on the war and the sacred defense. No one remembers it, but after making this first film he enters the Iranian commercial cinema and pursues other topics" (Rahmani [Azar 1387] 2008, 45). Despite the fact that institutional support has invited opportunism among neophytes, many of whom are too young to have participated in or possibly even to remember the war, the foundations of sacred defense are increasingly seen as being weak, and even the annual Sacred Defense Film Festival was cancelled several times in the 2000s. As a solution to this crisis, the Sacred Defense Film Festival of 2010 incorporated a wide range of international films under the rubric of "resistance, revolution, and sacred defense." This seems to have been a formula to rejuvenate sacred defense as participating in broader international currents. However, this decision was not uncontroversial, as some filmmakers protested the internationalization of the festival as deviating from the core concerns of the sacred defense (Khaza'i 2011).

During and in the aftermath of the war, the Islamic Republic successfully developed cultural policies to exert control over the boundaries within which the Iran-Iraq war could be represented and later memorialized. While not unique in this effort—modern nation-states have frequently endeavored to control the cultural representation of wars in which they are involved—what is particular in the Iranian case is the manner in which the sacred defense themes extended from specifically valorizing the war effort, to defining postwar ideology and culture in arenas far from war themes, long after the end of the war. However, despite the state's efforts to continue to promulgate sacred defense ideals long after the war's end, the genre has faced growing apathy among viewers and has come under pressure even from within to change or to be dismantled all together. As Shahla Talebi (2013) argues, the more the state has attempted to hold onto sacred defense values—for example through monopolizing memorialization activity concerning the war's martyrs—the more public interest in these values has diminished.

> As the distance between the Iran–Iraq war and the so-called reconstruction era lengthened, the need of the state to use martyrs to maintain the faith of the people in the state increased. Yet the more martyrs are utilized for political agendas, the more disillusionment sets in towards them. The greater the crack of "unity" among the state supporters, the more diverse and inconsistent the role and the messages of the state martyrs. The proliferation of jokes about martyrs, war veterans, and all that is related to the war, speaks to this reality, as do the protests against state policies of burying martyrs among the living.
>
> (TALEBI 2013, 136)

While Talebi is describing the slow erosion of the hegemony of the sacred defense project over the course of the 1990s, a sense of crisis within the field may be traced back as far as the first year or two after the war's end. In sacred defense work such as Mohsen Makhmalbaf's *The Marriage of the Blessed* (*Arusi-ye khuban*, 1989) we may observe the beginnings of a critical reflection upon the purported aims of war and the realization by formerly ideologically committed cultural figures that the postrevolutionary regime's devotion to these aims was overstated. In this film, a war veteran, called only by the honorific title Haji, emerges from the hospital to a postwar world in which he is expected to fulfill his marriage engagement to Mehri, the daughter of a wealthy businessman. In preparation for this new life, Haji takes on employment as a photographer for a newspaper. His fixation upon images of destitute poverty, drug addiction, and other social ills causes problems with his editors, who want him to take more anodyne photos, reflecting the positive official discourse of the reconstruction period. Instead, his photographs come to more and more reflect the inner turmoil he constantly experiences as a consequence of his memories of the war. His pursuit of images of social inequity and injustice is a natural emanation from his prior commitment to the war's aims, and he cannot accept the admonitions of those around him that he needs to forget these and to reintegrate into postwar civilian life. Instead, Haji begins to spiral into psychosis, obsessively viewing videos of starvation in Africa and of war, but not before he is able to cause a near riot at his own wedding by accusing his future father-in-law of corruption, and singing religiously themed songs about martyrdom. The film ends with Haji institutionalized in a mental asylum—postwar society is not able to tolerate his relentless dedication to what he saw as the core aims of the war, ending injustice around the world.

Marriage of the Blessed comes early in the trajectory of sacred defense cinema, and yet it gives evidence of the internal social and political critiques that the sacred defense field allowed. Over the course of the next decade such criticism became even more profound and trenchant, eventually leading to the dissociation of formerly committed cultural figures from the field altogether. To better illustrate this transition in the sacred defense field, from being a strong and vital cultural force to becoming rent by internal as well as external dissention and questioning, let us look at two further films by Ebrahim Hatamikia—whose early works such as *From the Karkhe to the Rhine* are considered by many to be among the best examples of sacred defense cinema—illustrating the increasing ambivalence within his work toward the core values of the sacred defense field.

From *Minu's Watch Tower* to *The Glass Agency*

The tower referenced in the title of Ebrahim Hatamikia's film *Minu's Watch Tower* (*Borj-e Minu*, 1996) is a spotting tower constructed by Iranian troops at the war's front lines, in order to direct mortar batteries in their targeting of Iraqi forces across the Arvand/Shatt al-Arab river. But as with so many of the central elements found in Iranian sacred defense films, the tower is more than a material construction, it is a multifaceted allegorical object and space. The tower is a site of traumatic memory for Musa, the veteran who is the protagonist of the film, and is also significant for Minu, his new bride, since she is the sister of his closest war comrade, Mansur, who was killed during the war while inside the tower. It is also a symbol of the sacrifice and selflessness that characterize the fraternal relations of the soldiers who fought in the war. Ultimately, Musa and Minu are themselves largely vessels for the elaboration of the social trauma arising from the war, Musa, representing the front-line fighter, is a veteran who lived through the horrors and losses of the war, while Minu, as the sister of a war martyr, represents the home front's experiences. The central tension of the film is predicated on the idea that these two domains—the front lines and the home front—have different and not entirely reconcilable memories of the war, and thus make different uses of the war in their present lives. The film's aim, then, is to imagine a reconciliation between these two arenas, to produce a single and more coherent field of cultural memory around the war.

To do so, the film begins in the hours immediately after the wedding of Musa and Minu. The couple prepares for their honeymoon trip to Isfahan as they clean up after the guests depart their apartment. That evening, after being visited by a mysterious woman who hands him a scroll, Musa's cheerful disposition changes and he grows anxious and argumentative. Minu wishes to know more about the scroll and their visitor, but Musa refuses to speak about the matter. Later, they embark on their honeymoon trip, intending to drive from Tehran to Isfahan, but argue in the car over the matter of the scroll. Eventually Musa falls asleep in the passenger seat and Minu furtively examines the scroll while she drives. After seeing what is written on the scroll, she changes course and drives them to southwestern Iran, near the former front. Musa awakens as they arrive, and, realizing what has happened, is compelled to discuss the scroll, which contains a vow written and signed by all the members of his unit. The unit had collectively built a spotting tower along the front lines, and the vow is that whoever survives the war will dismantle the tower after the war's completion. However, as yet this has not been accomplished, and with all the other members of the unit now dead, the responsibility falls to Musa—a responsibility he is no longer interested in honoring.

The second half of the film takes place at the tower, where Musa is overtaken by his memories of the war. Between flashbacks to the war and memories of the building of the tower—an enterprise that claimed many lives in and of itself—Musa climbs up into the tower, refusing Minu's entreaties to come down. In the tower he is overtaken by further flashbacks to the war and in particular to times spent with his mentor and friend, Mansur. Minu eventually climbs up the tower and also enters the hallucinatory space into which Musa has been lost, thus coming to understand the circumstances behind her brother Mansur's death. The two then ritually "bury" Mansur metaphysically. As they lower a specter of Mansur's body (as if it were still there) from the tower, Minu falls from the tower and is injured. After awakening in the hospital some time later, she escapes while covered in bandages, returns to and reenters the tower, where Musa is finally at the last stages of working out his traumatic memories. They eat a meal in the tower, and then begin the work of dismantling the tower, together, returning to the earth at the end.

The film posits Musa as suffering from the repression of his traumatic war memories, and in particular the trauma of the death of Mansur. In the first scene of the film, Musa wears a colorful shirt, and his apartment is filled with works of modern, abstract art. When the mysterious visitor arrives as his door, she comments disparagingly on his appearance and on the decor in his apartment. Handing him the scroll, she says, "I had thought it was my turn, but luckily you are still here. So then it's your responsibility to finish the work," but he refuses to acknowledge the purpose of her visit and glibly bids her goodbye. When Minu then asks him about the visitor, Musa changes the subject with a joke. In these first scenes we discern that Musa has surrounded himself with objects that semiotically separate him from his memories of the war or his prior ideological commitments as a soldier. The abstract paintings on his walls and the bright pop-art motif on his shirt act as screens to obstruct the return of cultural memories of the war. However, this repressed memory interjects itself when least expected, on the very night of his wedding. The agent of its return is charged with a signification that is in direct opposition to that of Musa's new life. Minu, on the other hand, seems less willfully intent upon avoiding her own memories of the war. For example, after the visitor's departure, Musa finds his wife in the bedroom, hanging a portrait of her dead brother over their nuptial bed. He jokes with her, "That picture over the bed?" to which she replies, "That's nothing new for me. I can't sleep without Mansur above my head." The two allegorize divergent responses to the haunting memories of the war—willful forgetfulness, to the point of denial, or literally suspending the memories above one's head, as Minu insists upon doing with the portrait of her dead brother.

When Musa finally agrees to speak to Minu about the scroll and the vow, he is still unwilling to accept the responsibility that it entails. However, as he explains the matter to her, memory interjects and he is forced to face his past. In a montage sequence Musa recollects the building of the tower. The construction is represented in a mythical light—in particular through the use of slow motion, dramatic musical scoring, and saturated lighting and other visual stylistics of the scene. The tower rises slowly, even as individual soldiers working on it are shot and die—their bodies are simply brought down and the work continues. The labor is depicted as methodical but purposeful, fearless in the face of death. The aesthetics of the scene imply not a mimetic representation of the past but an overdetermined representation of a memory of the past—aesthetics that are restaged over and over in sacred defense films, such in the battlefield scene, already discussed, at the end of *From the Karkhe to the Rhine*.

Once Musa is ensconced in the tower, memories of the past overtake him and the narrative. Musa's hallucinations initially separate him from Minu, illustrating the qualitatively different memories each has of the war, which have led them to different ways of relating to the legacy of the conflict. Minu is frustrated by the experiential gap this opens between them—physically denoted by Musa's position high in the tower, while she is left on the ground. This distinction also illustrates the relational differences between the cultural value of the memories of each, as the sacred defense field valorizes the transcendent sacrifices that fill Musa's memories, while giving less priority to those of the home front, which are the memories of the war that most Iranian women have.

By staging Minu's ascent into the tower, the film idealizes a break in these distinctions, allowing the couple to share in what had been an experience exclusive to Musa and to his war comrades. Since the trauma of the death of his close friend Mansur, Musa has tried to repress or avoid the memories of the war, while Minu, who did not directly experience the death or the war, has sought any hints that would avail her of a better understanding of it. For both, the return through memory to the traumatic setting and to the moment of Mansur's death avails them of an opportunity to integrate this memory productively into their lives. Rather than finding it a burden or as "unassimilable," Musa is able to share these memories with Minu in ways he had been unable to do before. For Minu, the experience is also cathartic, and allows her to come to terms not only with her brother's death, but also to engage with the ethos of sacred defense in a way that had been unavailable to her, in particular as a woman, before. However, memory alone does not suffice: through Minu's fall from the tower, and her return to the site covered in bandages, the film intimates that she must pay a price for entering this sacred domain. Where the men who fought the war presented their bodies as sacrificial canvases for the art of martyrdom, she in turn is made to corporeally inhabit the wounds of war as a result of entering the fraternal cultural memory of the war experience that has been previously limited to the male veterans of the fighting.

What is particularly noteworthy is how the catharsis of the climactic scenes of *Minu's Watch Tower* follow a common trope in trauma narratives more broadly. The paradigmatic trauma narrative follows the repression of memory that then requires a form of catharsis to be resolved and assimilated into normal psychic functions. In the case of sacred defense memory discourse around the war in Iran, *Minu's Watch Tower* follows a national imperative to imagine a path out of the troubling forest of repression and ambivalence around the war, positing that with catharsis, the nation may seek a resolution to the trauma of war.

The framing of this problem within a story of newlyweds situates this imperative within the family and offers a role to women as well as to the men who personally experienced the fighting. This is precisely what marks the film as somewhat subversive within the pieties of sacred defense discourse—the title of the film posits the tower as Minu's, not Musa's, and the film ends by staging her incorporation into the sacred fraternal order that had been limited only to the men who had fought in the war. As Zahir Tavakoli has noted, "we should accept that one of the reasons for the failure of what we see in our present society regarding the Sacred Defense is based on the real social fact that those who were at the rear of the war (*posht-e jang*) couldn't communicate well with those who were on the fronts (*adamha-ye jang*)" (Khosronejad 2013, 7). To address this failure, Hatamikia posits that the feminized home front needs to be given access to the metaphysical and sacred charge of the war experience, rather than remaining outside its circle. By so doing, the nation will find consensus on the cultural memory of the war, and will indeed relieve the burden of the surviving war veterans from the necessary repression of their traumatic memories within postwar society.

Hatamikia continued to make films on the subject of postwar trauma, and would later significantly revise the relatively optimistic ending of *Minu's Watch Tower*—a resolution of the troubled memories of the war through a cathartic act that leads to all members of society together working to "dismantle" the legacy of the war for a new future. In his later works, there is neither the transcendent martyr's death that ends *From the Karkhe to the Rhine*, nor a redemptive ending that allegorizes the resolution of war trauma for a nation consolidated around sacred defense values. This shift in tone emerges distinctly in his next film, *The Glass Agency* (*Ajans-e shisheh-i*, 1997), which posits the role of veterans in postwar Iran in a much more ambivalent manner, raising questions that may even lead to their being viewed as acting treacherously toward the government. Later films continue in this same trajectory, with *The Dead Wave* (*Moj-e mordeh*, 2001) exploring an intergenerational conflict between a military commander and war veteran, and his son, who attempts to emigrate to the West. The pessimism continues with *Low Heights* (*Ertefa-ye past*, 2002), about a hijacking carried out by an aggrieved war veteran that ends with the airplane crashing into surreal a no-man's-land, where nothing is certain—have they died or have they finally found a place for themselves on earth?

The Glass Agency follows the story of a taxi driver, Kazem, who happens upon his old war comrade Abbas on a traffic-clogged street in Tehran. Abbas and his wife, Nargess, have traveled to the city from their rural farm to find medical treatment for a wartime wound that has afflicted him since his time in the trenches, but which has now rendered him disabled. After visiting a doctor in Tehran they find that Abbas needs immediate surgery and must travel to London for specialized care. Kazem takes on Abbas's plight and together they visit various government offices that offer services to war veterans, but are confronted by red tape and indifference. To make matters worse, it is the eve of the Persian New Year and many offices are closing. Now desperate, Kazem arranges to sell his taxi and reserves two tickets on the next flight. Once at the travel agency, the taxi's buyer is late, and the agency threatens to sell the tickets to another buyer. A confrontation ensues in which Kazem strips a security guard of his gun and holds all people in the agency as hostages, demanding that he and Abbas be allowed onto the flight. A standoff with police ensues, with two negotiators—Ahmad and Salahshur—representing two different responses to the situation. Ahmad, a veteran who knows the two men from their war days, shows sympathy for them, while Salahshur is aggressive toward the men, and dismissive of their grievances. An agreement is forged that the next morning the men will be taken to the airport and allowed to fly to London if they release the hostages. In the morning the men leave the agency to be transported to the airport, but find themselves entrapped by Salahshur, who has deceived them. However, just as he is arresting them, a helicopter lands and Ahmad emerges, bearing a letter (presumably from the Supreme Leader) that allows them to be released. They board the flight with Ahmad chaperoning them. Yet, as the captain announces that they are leaving Iranian airspace, Kazem turns to speak to Abbas and finds that he has quietly died in his seat.

The problems that the veterans encounter at the outset of the film are representative of a theme common in many postwar films both in Iran and elsewhere, which present a critique of the limitations that exist in the services governments provide for those who have previously sacrificed themselves for the nation. These initial scenes display other tropes generally familiar to the postwar film genre—the camaraderie of the former fighters despite the passing of years, the withering disregard of official institutions toward their predicament, and the increasing apathy of the general society toward their dedication and sacrifices. Here these general themes are given an Iranian particularity through references to the ideological aims of the war, but interestingly, in the first sequences of the film, these references are very subtle. Neither Kazem nor Abbas directly invokes their ideological commitment, yet there are still many references to the fact that their wartime duty was not only to the nation but also to the universalist ideological struggle claimed by the sacred defense.

However, after first offering a sympathetic portrayal of the men and their grievances, after the hostage-taking, the film then opens their ideological commitment to various forms of criticism. At one point, one of the hostages attempts to bribe Abbas to let him and his wife leave the agency. He offers to "pay my portion" to be released, and pleads that his wife needs medicine that she doesn't have with her. When Abbas hesitates to free them, the woman becomes angry, and shouts, "What more do you want from us, you're given jobs, given places in the universities, and now you hold us here?" She refers to legal and social programs that ensure that war veterans are given preferential treatment in employment and in gaining admission to highly competitive placement in university. Her response presents a view of the legacy of the war veterans as something other than heroic. The woman's accusations give voice to postwar concerns over the priority given to the men who fought in the war where the distribution of meager social services is concerned. Rather than being rightful claimants to an advantaged position in the dispersal of social assistance, the veterans are here seen as possibly having become the opposite, as parasites leeching upon postwar Iranian society. Furthermore, by taking hostages, the woman insinuates that they have become something much worse—crossing over from being disproportionately advantaged members of society into being actual traitors. Her criticism of them presents a challenge of the ideological justification that they mount for their actions. Abbas, unable to reply to her charges, ashamedly ushers her and her husband out of the agency's door and to freedom.

While several of the hostages play roles in offering coherent and legitimate challenges to the hostage takers, it is Salahshur, the negotiator, who offers the strongest criticism of their ideological project. In a climactic scene, he confronts Kazem in the center of the travel agency while surrounded by an audience of hostages:

> SALAHSHUR: Well . . . ok, I've done my research. Imagine, at one time being a sergeant, then to have to become a taxi driver, with a half-built house, a boy nearly in university . . . it must be difficult. Of course there aren't very many people like this . . . but there are some.

KAZEM: Do you think we cost anyone more than the cost of a single one of those high-rise buildings being built everywhere? Isn't it better that we be out in the open? Or, would you rather that we were sent to a museum, or put in a zoo, where you could really do some research on us?

SALAHSHUR: (*looking at the hostages for support*) Did I insult him?

KAZEM: Did you fight at the front?

SALAHSHUR: Where I've been was no less than having been at the front.

(*Kazem runs over to Salahshur and shouts various military instructions, as if to test his knowledge of them*)

SALAHSHUR: (*pauses as if to see if Kazem is finished*) Now can I ask you a question? No doubt in elementary school you were shown a map of Iran—it's shaped a bit like a cat. (*Draws a map in the air, then begins to point to the imaginary countries around it.*) Armenia, Azerbaijan, Turkmenistan, Afghanistan, Pakistan . . . the little bitty Gulf Arab countries . . . Kuwait, Saudi Arabia, Iraq, Turkey. Do you know what all of these countries think about that cat? If you did, I'm sure you'd never let a sergeant embarrass us like you're doing right now. (*Slides a rolling chair aggressively toward Kazem.*) Your decade's over, commander! If you weren't holding that gun in your hands, who would even listen to you? It's the only thing that gives you power. You spoke for a whole decade, said what you wanted to, and the rest of us shut up and listened. Whatever you did we were quiet—you took what you wanted, we stayed quiet, you gave what you wanted, we stayed quiet. But now allow us to speak for once! Do you want, ladies and gentlemen, for another one of these neighbors to attack us?

A HOSTAGE: Never!

SALAHSHUR: Would you like it if—God forbid—there was another war?

ANOTHER HOSTAGE: Never! (*Others murmur in agreement*).

SALAHSHUR: Our decade is the decade of stability! Security! When is this country going to be blessed with security? When is that son of yours going to be able to start to make plans for his own future? It's not my decade . . . it's your son's!

KAZEM: (*screams*) Get out!

This confrontation illustrates the central ideological tension within the film, between the legacy of the ideals these veterans were once fighting for and the commitments of those who now view the sacred defense values as unproductive and even destructive in the postwar context. Here, Salahshur, rather than displaying humility toward Kazem's status as a veteran or showing empathy for his grievances, instead mocks him as one whose time is over, and who is now irrelevant to the new national goals. Kazem attempts to regain his grounding by asking Salahshur if he served at the front, and by testing whether he understands certain military commands—these appear to be his only means for asserting greater legitimacy. By refusing to even respond to these means of measuring political and ideological status, Salahshur betrays the irrelevance of the old sacred defense values. Going even further, Salahshur insinuates that Kazem is acting as a traitor in jeopardizing what he asserts are the present aims of the nation: security and stability. While the veterans' previous sacrifices and ideological commitment were idealized within the sacred defense discourse, Kazem's expectation of greater social recognition of these sacrifices—signified by his sense of justification in having taken hostages to reach his goal—now transforms his ideological commitment into a treacherous act.

The Glass Agency posits a tension over the ideological legacy of the Iran-Iraq war, and in particular the social value to be accorded to the continuation of a commitment to the most extreme aspects of the justification for the war within a changing Iranian political context. While the film ends with a fairly typical melodramatic plot twist, the death of Abbas is not equivalent to the death of Sa'id in *From the Karkhe to the Rhine*. While in more paradigmatic sacred defense films the soldier's death is a transcendent moment, where his former sacrifices are redeemed by a new status as martyr, here Abbas's death is tragic but lacks any self-sacrificial charge. His wounds are not due to an act of particular heroism—in fact, his character is distinctly understated and antiheroic. Additionally, by having the doctor insist that Abbas not be exposed to undue stress or excitement, the film intimates that the cause of his death may well have been the hostage-taking and its aftermath. In this sense, Kazem and his passionate commitments themselves bear significant responsibility for Abbas' demise. The ambivalence of this ending sets out questions for the future of this legacy, even as the film itself stops short of giving priority to the view that the veterans are indeed guilty of treachery. Yet, within the confines of the sacred defense monopoly over the representation of the war, the fact that this film does give voice to characters who condemn the veterans and their actions is significant. While, in the end, the film invites identification with the veterans, the critics are also shown to be not outside the limits of reasonable discourse about the war.

The Glass Agency is one of a range of films to take on the subject of the war critically, not only by exploring the "disillusionment of veterans," but also by representing the disillusionment of a nonideological public which may no longer be willing to accept the sacred defense values as of use to postwar Iran (Ghamari-Tabrizi 2009, 121n5). The film marks a moment in developing public discourse around the war when the legacy of the war is no longer beyond question. By going as far as it does to incorporate criticism of, if not the war, then rather the continued pursuit of sacred defense aims within a postwar society, it marks a milestone in how the war is valued. At its heart the film treats the ideologically inflected characters of Kazem, Abbas, and their supporters with great sympathy—even, in a sense, mourning the dissipation of social cohesion over the centrality of the purported aims of the war. Salahshur, and his discourse of realpolitik and pragmatism, represents a retreat from these goals to those of a postwar setting, prioritizing national security and economic stability. While the film also represents Salahshur's anger and the frustrations of the hostages in very sympathetic terms, it posits the clash of these positions—of the reading of the hostage-takers as heroes or as traitors—as fundamentally tragic. The death of Abbas in the final sequence of the film is predicated on the symbolic evacuation of that which he represents from the national scene.

Counternarratives of Sacred Defense

While from an institutional perspective, the Iranian war film is rightly identified with the emergence of the sacred defense field, the cultural memory of war and postwar trauma is also explored in films that were produced outside of the sacred defense context as well. In fact, a focus upon these works provides perspectives that are often lost or sublimated within the sacred defense framework. This division in cinema, between those who emerge through sacred defense cinema and those who chose to assiduously avoid the genre and its institutional sponsors, is also a reflection of generational as well as ideological divides in Iran. The sacred defense field served as a forum for younger, ideologically committed revolutionary artists to train and gain skills, and in a sense served as an institutional base for a conflict between these filmmakers and the prior generation of the largely secular-leftist cultural and cinema elite.

While this earlier generation retained significant cultural capital both for its dissident activity before and during the revolution, as well as for the prestige it had gained for its work both nationally and internationally, it was largely viewed by the ascendant postrevolutionary political establishment as ideologically suspect. Overlaying this ideological suspicion, one may also detect class tensions, different attitudes toward cosmopolitan aspirations, and sharp differences in views on gender roles between these groups.[5] In most cases, members of this older generation either elected to work in explicitly nonideological topics, or on themes that steered clear of any form of social critique, or they faced significant barriers in production and distribution of their films. While it would have been impossible for a filmmaker within Iran to have directly challenged the pieties of the developing sacred defense cultural field, nonetheless some sought ways to elaborate an alternative cultural memory of the war.

Moves to forge a counternarrative to that which was advanced by the sacred defense field in cinema may be traced in a variety of forms and settings both during and after the war. The most exemplary case of a film that produces a counternarrative to the state's project of war memory is Bahram Beyzai's *Bashu, The Little Stranger* (*Bashu, Gharibeh-ye Kuchak*, shot in 1985 and released in 1987), which participates in an contestation, albeit indirect and nuanced, of the grounds of traumatic cultural memory as defined by the sacred defense field.[6] *Bashu* is a work that cannot but respond to the traumas of the war, even while it searches for a language and context outside the hermetic sphere of sacred defense culture. Works such as this were also a result of the crisis for the prior generation of film elites, such as Beyzai, and their uncertainty about how to engage with the experience of the war with Iraq. Motivated by nationalist sentiments, many felt obligated to support the war effort, even while they remained distant from the sacred defense discourse mobilized by the Islamic Republic. While the authorities had no choice but to recognize the support of these cultural figures, they did so in ways that expressed their dissatisfaction with their lack of adherence to the ideological aims of the war in their works.

Before making *Bashu*, Bahram Beyzai edited another iconic film made during the war period, Amir Naderi's *The Runner* (*Davandeh*, made in 1982, released in 1986). While *The Runner* makes no direct allusion to the war, there are many reasons to consider its inclusion within the current discussion. *The Runner* is set somewhere in Iran's southwestern coast, and appears to be at least partially auto-referential, as the young protagonist of the film, Amiro, is called by a diminutive form of the director Amir Naderi's first name. Naderi himself is from Abadan, a city that by 1982, the year of *The Runner's* production, was nearly completely destroyed by the fighting. *The Runner's* compelling portrait of a young orphaned boy who fends for himself through odd jobs on the margins of society begins with the formal conventions of neo-realist cinema that later became so central to the Iranian "new wave" of the 1990s–2000s. However, through unconventional editing and sound design, Naderi's film transcends realism to set his alter ego in various vignettes of competition; whether Amiro is running after a bicyclist who has stolen a block of ice from him, or beating a much larger foreign sailor who has accused him of theft, or in the various formal and informal races Amiro runs against the other poor boys in the area, the theme of competition and eventual triumph against the brutal realities of poverty finds transcendent resonances that supersede the usual social framings of neorealist cinema, particularly at the film's end. The climactic scene masterfully follows a foot race between the boys across a sweltering oil field, with the prize being a rapidly melting block of ice (figures 5.3 and 5.4).

If read with the backdrop of the war in mind, *The Runner* gives significant emotive charge to the self-perception of Iranians as being an isolated and marginalized nation struggling in a nearly cosmological conflict, one of many parentless and self-made children who live in a world where they are compelled to brutally compete against one another (the backdrop of oil fires

FIGURES 5.3–5.4 *Amiro wins the race, then offers the ice to the other boys* (The Runner)

burning in the field where the boys undertake their race only makes the link between geopolitical concerns and competition over natural resources more clear). So while the film does not overtly reference the war, one may perceive its traces on the filmmaker and the film itself—it is as if, through this portrait

of unbelievable resilience, Naderi is attempting to waylay the necessity of
mourning for the destruction of his city of origin, while also circumventing
the binaries of war discourse in his portrayal of the wretched and forgotten
boys as thrown into a desperate fight for survival that pits them against one
another in a way that is destructive to all. The triumph of Amiro is not simply that he wins the race, but that he then turns a face of compassion to his
competitors, rushing back to share the precious remaining ice with the boys
whom he had just defeated—a sentiment of ethical generosity that challenges
the binaries that defined the ethos of the wartime sacred defense culture.

If *The Runner* represents a sublimated response to the effects of the war,
Bashu may be rather understood as an attempt, shortly later, to more directly
address the subject of the war, although in a manner that would also similarly refuse its co-optation to the sacred defense project. There are similarities between the two films beyond Beyzei's central role (as editor of one, and
director of the other) in both. Both Bashu and Amiro are sons of Iran's south,
both are orphans, and both narratives are structured around the struggle of
each protagonist to overcome difficult circumstances in what may be termed
a quest for subjectivity—these are tales of *becoming*. In this correspondence
between the two films, I would argue that *The Runner* represents an early
move in the direction that *Bashu* later more firmly adopts, of attempting to
come to terms with the ravages and losses of the war, but to do so in a way
that would not be assimilable into the sacred defense project. Both filmmakers fundamentally wish to respond to the reality of the war, but facing the
constraints of the state's official discourse, seek a new cinematic language for
giving voice to the traumas of war.

Bashu begins on the front lines of the war. In the introductory scenes of the
film, a young boy, Bashu, is transported to a tranquil northern Iranian village
after escaping the war by hiding in the back of a truck, when his parents are
killed after a shell hits their simple home. After riding for hours he leaves the
truck, and finds himself in an unfamiliar landscape, surrounded by people who
speak the Gilaki dialect of Persian rather than the Arabic dialect that is his own
mother tongue. The mutually incomprehensible nature of the languages forms
the central problematic of the film and leaves Bashu an outsider in his new setting, despite being taken in by a single mother, Na'i, who has two small children
of her own. Over the course of the film, Na'i adopts Bashu, as he takes on more
and more responsibility as the putative man of the household. Overcoming
many cultural and social obstacles, Bashu eventually finds a settled place in
the family and village, but this arrangement is challenged at the end of the film
with the return of Na'i's husband to the village. Bashu's position is threatened
by this turn of events, but then it is disclosed that Na'i's husband has lost his
arm, and Bashu communes with him in their shared loss.[7] In the last scene of
the film, Bashu and Na'i's husband join together in the defense of the farm from
an unseen predatory animal that has terrorized the household for some time.

As a film driven by the narrative of an orphaned child living through the war, *Bashu* falls into a subgenre of war cinema that utilizes the "naïve perspectives" of child characters in war settings in a way that challenges the normative discourse around war (Rastegar, 2006a).[8] Yet *Bashu* goes further than most of these films, in using its protagonist to mark out a world outside the ideological impositions of wartime Iran, for in choosing a remote northern Iranian village setting, the action of the film occurs in a social context that appears to be significantly removed from of the daily violence of the war that is being waged on the country's southwestern border. This allows for the villagers to display a degree of ethnoracial prejudice toward the darker-skinned Bashu, but frees their relationship of the problematic dialectic of Persian and Arab that itself underscored the war's national divisions. Bashu, as an Arab-Iranian, falls on the fault line of war discourse, which occasionally did make use of anti-Arab Persianist chauvinism.[9] This dislocative strategy in *Bashu* (removing the young war victim from the front lines, and placing him in a setting where the war has little if any social imprint) is one significant way by which sacred defense discourse is denied any place within the film. Rather than imagining the home front as a site of committed support for soldiers sent to the battlefield, the village here is a location free of the marks of war. This allows Beyzai to set the conflict of the film in terms that exceed or at very least elude the defining terms of sacred defense. Bashu's journey is not one that brings him to a better understanding of his role within the cosmological battle that sacred defense imagines—rather, his story is one of proposing radical reconfigurations of family and belonging, despite (or through) the trauma of wartime losses. Bashu is fundamentally alienated, not only by his ethnolinguistic difference, but also by the fact that the villagers have no way to comprehend (and he has no language to narrate) his experience of trauma. These alienating factors only stoke Bashu's traumatic memory and prevent him from achieving what otherwise may be a degree of integration into the village society. Traumatic memory is woven through the fabric of the quotidian, as Bashu frequently experiences hallucinations of his dead parents, and flashbacks to the experience of war.

In representing Bashu's traumatic memory, Beyzai often layers two or more temporalities within a single cinematic space. This layering produces open-ended interpretive possibilities, a strategy that threatens the ostensible coherence of sacred defense discourse by illuminating the limits and impossibilities of commensurability between traumatic experience and its representation. In one scene, Bashu is working with Na'i, having by now been accepted by her as a member of her family. However, within the village he is still subject to harassment and ostracism by other children. The young boys of the village have gathered at the gates of Na'i's property and laugh as Bashu begins to experience what seems to be the effect of a flashback, triggered by the flames of the fire of a *tannur* clay oven. While he shouts at the family to seek cover,

the boys first mock and mimic Bashu, before storming into the yard to pick
a fight with him. Bashu attempts to fight back, and the scrum is broken up
only when Na'i throws a pail of water over the group, pulling Bashu aside.
Thrown to the ground, Bashu first reaches for a rock, as if to use it as a weapon,
but then moves over to pick up a textbook that has fallen on the soil. As Na'i
scolds the boys, Bashu begins to read the stock text of the textbook, in formal Persian: "Iran is our country, we come from one soil, one spring. We are
the children of Iran" (figure 5.5). The boys circle him and begin to ask him
questions, also in the same register of Persian, "Where are your mother and
father?" and finally, "What happened to your school?" As if in response, Bashu
picks up the rock, and throws it, hitting a small wood structure and knocking
it apart. The collapse of the structure is filmed from three angles, and replayed
three times, in slow motion. Then the children look back at Bashu, and he
looks away.

In Bashu's response the worlds of symbolic and linguistic signification collide. Bashu is able to mount the linguistic barrier between himself and the boys
in the village by displaying a knowledge of formal Persian, which is taught to
both ethnic groups as part of the national curriculum mandated within their
schools. However, when the boys press him to explain his personal history,
Bashu reverts to the symbolic communication that he had been compelled to
employ previously, representing his past experiences through a performative

FIGURE 5.5 *Bashu reads "We are the children of Iran"* (Bashu, The Little Stranger)

gesture. Throwing the rock and shattering the small wood structure, Bashu has expressed his memory of loss in the only way available to him, nonverbally. This nonlinguistic form of communication is charged with primal knowledge and ritual, and emphasized through Beyzai's staging and framing of the action.[10] Beyzai intimates that Bashu's path through trauma is one that cannot be resolved through language, much less through nationalist discourse.

While this scene is often cited in discussions of the film for its overt insertion of the nationalist recuperative statement, "We are all Iran's children," there is much more to the scene when viewed as a whole.[11] At first glance, the scene seems to intimate a resolution to Bashu's crisis, by his recourse to the use of the national language, Persian, and the nationalist discourse found in the textbook. However, a more fulsome consideration of the entire scene, from the traumatic flashback at its beginning, to Bashu looking away in the final shot, demands a reconsideration of this reading. The scene begins with the most explicit depiction of traumatic symptoms in the character of Bashu, who is portrayed as suffering a dissociative hallucination triggered by the sight of the fire of the clay oven. His traumatic reaction is, however, itself a trigger for his harassment by the village children, whose calls and laughter overlays his cries for them to take cover from what he believes to be an imminent (Iraqi) attack. While his recitation of the communal discourse of the textbook in the common national language of formal Persian promises to end his alienation from the village children, the end of the scene seems to set limits on this hopeful outcome.

When asked by the boys about the reasons for his presence in the village, Bashu is still unable to communicate his experiences linguistically. In this sense, his memory is incommensurable to the nationalist discourse he has just recited, and is still beyond linguistic representability. The gap between the composed text found in the schoolbook and the personal and cultural memory of the losses of war are too great to bridge. He resorts instead to an act that is semiotically open, lacking the ideological closure that linguistic iterations of nationalist discourse would produce. Bashu's traumatic experience has resulted in an aporia caused by the ideological fixity of the formal language taught in the schools, a crisis of meaning that cannot be resolved easily. The gaze of the children, which moves from the structure back to Bashu, is not met by his eyes. His turning away restates the line of incommensurability that exists between the official nationalist discursive realm—the only realm where he and the boys have a common language—and that of his traumatic experience. This moment fundamentally undermines attempts to create a foreclosed-upon state discourse on the war, what would become sacred defense discourse, and charts traumatic cultural memory as marked by a crisis of representability.

However, Bashu's trauma later proves productive by further opening a pathway for his full and final integration into the family. In the final sequence of the film, Na'i's husband returns to the village, potentially threatening Bashu's position in the family. Na'i and her husband argue over Bashu, with her husband critical of her decision to adopt him into the family. It is unclear if Bashu understands the discussion, but he rushes to confront Na'i's husband with a stick, shouting twice, "Who is this man?" (figure 5.6). Na'i's husband finally replies, "Father," omitting any possessive pronoun to indicate whose father he believes himself to be. Bashu then extends a hand in greeting, which Na'i's husband is unable to reciprocate, given that he has lost his arm (figure 5.7). Bashu, upon realizing this, suddenly rushes to embrace "father" and breaks out in tears (figure 5.8). Na'is husband communes with Bashu in their shared loss; it is as if they immediately perceive their commonality in trauma. Now constituting a family, in the very last scene of the film the three of them set out to chase away the wild animals that have been terrorizing the farm.

While *Bashu* may be seen to mirror sacred defense narratives that focus upon the sacrifices of the family in pursuit of the war's aims, it does so in a way that ultimately is subversive to the sacred defense. The cathartic resolution of sacred defense narratives, often coded in the sacrificial death of the father-husband, aims to expunge traumatic irresolution through a sacred valorization of his death and the redemption of the family through this loss. In *Bashu*, this redemption instead comes from a reconstitution of the family in

FIGURES 5.6–5.8 *Bashu confronts "Father," then makes peace* (Bashu, The Little Stranger)

FIGURES 5.6–5.8 (*Continued*)

terms that radically rethink the boundaries of this institution. Beyzai's refusal to explicitly associate the father's lost arm to the war can only be understood as a resistance towards sublimating his loss to the conventions of sacred defense. A young Arab-Iranian boy has arrived within this Persian-Gilaki milieu so as to compensate for the functional loss of the father's arm, yet both retain traces of their traumatic exclusions. The lack of a referent to the sacred defense themes, and indeed the visible nature of the continued traumas of both Bashu's and Na'i's family are deeply unsettling to the sacred defense discourse, constituting a profound critique of the coherence of this discourse.

Bashu adopts the narrative strategies of other home-front war films, presenting a family compelled to seek reconstitution after its losses, and resolves these losses through the overcoming of ethnic particularism in this quest. *Bashu* may be seen as participating in some of the conventional techniques that are at the heart of sacred defense narratives, particularly in its melodramatic structure and through the resolution of the narrative in terms of the reconstitution of a heteronormative family. Yet, in nearly every other possible manner, *Bashu* assiduously refuses to participate in reproducing the fundamental tropes of sacred defense, rejecting the ideologizing of memory that sacred defense themes demand. Beyzai's film sets the question of loss within the framework of ethnic and regional difference in Iran, and the need for a reformulation of national identity so as to overcome the traumas of the war.

What motivates the form of radical community imagined in *Bashu*—radical in the sense of its challenge to ethnolinguistic particularism, as well as in blurring of the role of primal masculinity between the father and Bashu, not to mention Na'i's own remarkable feminine presence that requires no subordination to a primal masculine figure—is the shared experience of loss. Bashu's adoptive family is one that has "lost" a father, and this absence is shown to be key to the boy's acceptance. This becomes most radical when the film is able to suggest the little boy as a replacement for the missing father—and later, the father's missing arm. In this way, the film achieves what so many war films set within domestic spaces attempt to do—that is, to imagine a reconstitution of the family, usually through the return of the father (although in tragic formulations, it is only his body that returns). In *Bashu*, the father does return, but he bears the indelible marks, the wounds, of the family as well as of the nation at war. He has lost an arm, and it is only through the inclusion of Bashu into the family that a sort of compensation for his lost limb is imagined. By taking on the role of compensatory object for the trauma-scarred body of the father, Bashu is again fully constituted within the national family. However, this occurs in a way that is open-ended, showing the communal relations borne through trauma to supersede those of predominant nationalist ideology. There is no valorization of sacrifice, no brotherhood of fighters, no cathartic death to pay blood to the war ideals. The traumas of the war are instead displaced within the fantasies of reconstituting the self, reconstituting the family, in ways that are fundamentally at odds with the ideologized memory discourses produced and promoted in support of the sacred defense.

Ebrahim Hatamikia's films *Minu's Watch Tower* and *The Glass Agency* exemplify in parts not only the limits that the sacred defense field places on cultural memory of the war, but also show how the field has experienced contestation and challenges from within. *Minu's Watch Tower* pushes the sacred defense field to—at least allegorically—offer broader access to the memory of the war and to its sacred charge by offering women access to the metaphysical and spiritual purity that the war and its memories are meant to represent. *The Glass Agency* goes even farther in challenging the pieties of the field through presenting urgent questions about the continued value of the war's moral and spiritual codes in a fast-evolving postwar Iran, where new challenges require national attention. The film goes so far as to imagine the death of the pious veteran as a necessary if unfortunate eventuality, as his demands are now at risk of being coded as treacherous.

Set against this internal discourse, we also find in Iranian filmmaking attempts to examine the war's social reflections in ways that are fundamentally irreconcilable to the sacred defense field. As an exemplary work in this vein, *Bashu, The Little Stranger* offers a view of the war's traumas that reflects on questions of gender roles within the family, and ethnic-racial notions of difference within the national community. Later filmmakers followed in the footsteps of Beyzai's work with *Bashu* in exploring the war's traumas first in allegorical ways (as with Abbas Kiarostami's *Life and Nothing More*) or in more direct and socially realist ways (Jafar Panahi's *Crimson Gold*). In *Life and Nothing More* (*Zendegi va digar hich*, 1991), I would argue that Kiarostami displaces the trauma of the Iran-Iraq war in his road movie that moves through the ruined landscape of a rural mountain earthquake, where the protagonist, an actor playing Kiarostami, is looking for a missing boy. The devastation and loss that the earthquake represents offers a clear analogy to the war devastation. However, given that sacred defense eschewed the representation of devastation and loss in favor of themes of sacrifice and spiritual commitment, Kiarostami's film may be viewed as exploring these same traumas through his long takes of the ruined villages of a proxy landscape. Jafar Panahi, in *Crimson Gold* (*Tala-ye sorkh*, 2003—from a script written by Kiarostami), more directly engages the troubled legacy of the Iran-Iraq war through a searing portrait of a former veteran who is now a motorcycle deliveryman, lost on the margins of Tehran society and unable to move ahead from the debilitating effects of an illness that resulted from his war service. In this film, the veteran is no longer a character invested with a sacred charge of fighting for justice until martyrdom, but rather is forgotten and downtrodden, and ready to explode in anger and frustration. Later works, such as Kiomars Purahmad's *Night Bus* (*Otobus-e Shab* 2007) go further in reconstituting sacred defense lines to offer modes of identification that view Iraqi soldiers equal status as victims of the war. Rather than imagining the trauma of the war to be productive of a consolidation of the spiritual-revolutionary ethos of the Islamic Republic, these and other films follow in the footsteps of *Bashu* in galvanizing the cultural memory of war in productively critical ways, while refusing to fall into the faltering monopoly that the sacred defense project has imposed.

Wanting to See

WARTIME WITNESSING AND POSTWAR
HAUNTING IN LEBANESE CINEMA

Near the end of Ghassan Salhab's *The Last Man* (*al-Atlal*, 2005), the film's protagonist Dr. Khalil Shams stares intently into the camera in a shot that discloses definitively that he is, in fact, a vampire (figure 6.1). After holding this head-on framing for several seconds, a reverse shot from behind him reveals that he has been staring at mirror behind the bar at which he is sitting, a mirror that does not reflect him. Vampires, of course, create no reflections. Khalil, a successful physician living in Beirut, has found that he is trapped between the living and the dead; the vampire is *un*dead. The young woman sitting beside him notices that he does not reflect in the mirror, and backs away from him slowly while cursing under her breath.

The Last Man is one of several films produced in the aftermath of the Lebanese civil war that represent the cultural memory of the war through stories with haunting ghosts, vampires, and characters caught in a liminal space between life and death. These films follow earlier generations of postwar works in which the primary framing is that of returning to the war setting and witnessing the war, often anew. In these contexts, the ghostly tropes of these later films are productive, and not simply symptomatic. More than simply a natural outcome of the trauma processes of postconflict societies, these tropes contribute to postwar cultural memory and to contestation over the narratives that codify the war experience and its memories. Social trauma is often allegorized through stories of haunting, of hallucinatory spaces between life and death, and figures of the undead, for the memories and narratives that are productive of social trauma often exist in the shadows of prevailing cultural memory, emerging in unexpected moments with shocking or frightening effect. Indeed, ghost stories and life-after-death tales may both be catalysts for the examination of these painful subjects in a mythological or allegorical frame, or they may be narrative molds into which the irresolution

FIGURE 6.1 *Khalil Shams realizes he is a vampire (*The Last Man*)*

of social trauma may be poured, and from which a particular set of meanings and interpretations may be inferred. In this sense, tropes of the haunting
specter offer themselves to the process of trauma production, and are often
socially productive vehicles for articulating social trauma.

Avery Gordon (2008, 63) cites this productivity when she argues the presence of ghosts in narratives concerning unresolved political or social conflicts
is telling: the ghost "makes itself known . . . through haunting and pulls us
affectively into the structure of feeling of a reality we come to experience as
a recognition." The affective work of haunting produces a recognition of and
active engagement with the social imperatives surrounding the ghost story.
Gordon offers us a guide in addressing these themes: "to write about invisibilities and hauntings . . . requires attention to what appears dead, but is nonetheless powerfully real" (42). Engaging with "invisibilities and hauntings"
leads us to an understanding of the undead within these contexts: undead in
the sense of being between life and death, or of showing defining symptoms
of both conditions. While we may tie these themes to the anxious pessimism
that is often found in contexts such as that of postwar Lebanon, in the bleak-
ness of this haunted landscape, there is nonetheless a small glimmer of light
that emerges from the ghost story. As Gordon further notes, "from a certain
vantage point the ghost also simultaneously represents a future possibility, a
hope" (64).

In this chapter, my discussion pursues two related threads: first, the move
from cultural memory of wartime witnessing in Lebanese documentary
works to that of exploring postconflict traumatic irresolution in imaginative fictive narratives; and second, the productivity, in a small number of
Lebanese film works, of cinematic tropes of the undead as a critical reflection
on unresolved calls for justice. These are both then addressed in relation to

the idealization of a justice that is impossible to obtain in unresolved post-conflict settings. In the case of Lebanon, I illustrate how documentary works carry out a necessary witnessing of the civil war, but lead eventually to haunting tales after the reconstruction regime's ascendancy in the late 1990s and early 2000s. Finally, as a result of the 2006 war with Israel, a new cultural formulation emerges, one that returns to questions about the necessity of witnessing, but with much greater pessimism for a linkage between witnessing and justice; a pessimism that demands a new vantage upon the act of seeing.

Undead here refers to beings or states of being that cross a line between living and dead, characteristics of the topoi of the vampire and ghost alike. Writing on the concept of the undead, Keith Jacobi (2003, 96) insists on their corporeal nature, but for the purposes of this discussion the question of materiality is not significant—what undead here indexes is the uneasy liminal status of living through death, or dying with life. Mark Westmoreland's (2010) study of postwar Lebanese visual cultures traces the presence of the undead in particular through contemporary arts practice to cinema, arguing that, "within Lebanon's catastrophic time and space, governed by selective amnesia, reproductive media has enabled the articulation of an imaginary world" (178). He argues that this world, "inhabited by phantoms and monstrous subjects," is conjured "in order to break the official silence and collective amnesia that keeps the Lebanese distracted from collectively engaging the trauma of the past" (178).

I do not depart from Westmoreland's conclusion that the interest in the undead in Lebanese cultural work of this period may be due to the fact that, "perhaps the undead thirst for resurrection because they have not been mourned . . . until the undead can be put to rest they will further compel violence" (Westmoreland 2010, 201). However, I also wish to go further in exploring how the references to a liminal world between life and death, and to specters and ghosts, may also be productive of a certain form of trauma discourse, one that inhabits unsettled domains as part of its explorations of injustice. Processes of trauma production may employ tropes of the undead to conjure the outlines of the demands for justice (which often underlie the emergence of social trauma) because the undead are emblematic of a profound threat to the social order. Where a predominant power configuration is seen to deny a just resolution to the experiences of trauma, demands for justice take a central role in the project of trauma production; the threat of undead rising is not simply a metaphor for an outbreak of war or violence, but of a deeper crisis of subjectivity that arises when the war is one that makes the enemy oneself. War crimes not addressed by postwar arrangements naturally leave unresolved the claims of victims whose response may often take the form of projects of trauma production. The unresolved claims themselves often have a haunting effect on society, rising in darkness or in dreams in reaction to the perceived threat of oblivion.[1]

Lebanon's Postwar Legacies

Thus it is not surprising that with the cessation of the cycle of violence and hostilities that are termed the Lebanese civil war, a specter rose over Lebanese cultural life—a specter representing in some measure the war itself, but also the absence of a process of accountability, as well as an accounting of the history of the war. This spirit signified many failures in the echoes and reverberations of the "last" gunshots—no accounting for the thousands of disappeared, no trials for perpetrators of massacres, no commissions to determine the cause for the war to begin with. As I have discussed in chapter 5, Sune Haugbolle (2005) has argued that the postwar environment in Lebanon was to be characterized by an "official amnesia"—conveyed for example in public school history curricula that end in the 1940s, and more generally in a lack of support for (and in some cases, repression of) acts of commemoration or public accounting. Along similar lines, miriam cooke (2002, 8) argues that the reconstruction regime's ethos demanded a "mobilizing [of] amnesia." Najib Hourani (2008, 287) rejects what he terms "the amnesia thesis" by arguing that this view "stands in marked contrast to a reality in which debates about the war implicitly or explicitly inform political struggles over the post-conflict social order"; however, he does so by recourse to the work of independent cultural producers and activists, and does not seem to dispute the issue that the war is repressed at the official level. Haugbolle (2005, 192) also notes that the years after the 1991 Taif agreements that are seen by most as marking the end of the war were characterized by confusion over how to even define the war, and "initially the war was hardly even conceived as a finite period of time." Beyond leaving individuals who had lived through a period of catastrophe and violence without a public forum for addressing these experiences, the dominant postwar agenda aimed to redirect national cultural memory to an embrace of reconstruction projects, and with it a redefinition of Lebanese national identity, by denying local culpability for any aspect of the war. In this way, the involvement of outside actors was amplified to a degree where Lebanese played the role only of victims, rather than of participants. So as to not stoke tensions, even if only by indirectly alluding to the active collaboration of local groups with these outside actors, most often even the outside forces would not be named. Due to the 2006 Israeli war on Lebanon, and the ongoing low-intensity conflicts that have erupted in Lebanon with unsettling continuity since 2005, attempts to present the civil war as a temporally discrete historical "event" have lost ground to a more pervasive sense that war has been ongoing.

While they are distinct in many ways from the post-1948 experiences of Palestinians, it is instructive to consider the ways by which the cultural memory discourse in both Lebanon and Palestine are framed by a temporal irresolution. As discussed in chapter 4, in the Palestinian case this lack of narrative closure to a historical wound is accompanied by the continuing post-1967 occupation and by state policies that have continued the experiences of loss and dispossession inaugurated by the Nakba. The Lebanese case is significantly different in that its irresolutions are caused less by the continuing policies of a powerful actor within the conflict than as a function of a highly internally fragmented and polarized political environment populated by multiple actors, none of whom has been able to assert unquestioned dominance over the others.

Thus, instead of either truth or reconciliation, the wounds of the war were cauterized by large-scale, top-down reconstruction projects, epitomized in the private-public company Solidere's massive redevelopment of Beirut's city center, and a plan to position Lebanon as an investment and financial-services hub within the circuits of neoliberal globalization, a project closely associated with the former prime minister Rafic Hariri. As miriam cooke (2002, 409) argues, "SOLIDERE promised a return, a reversion to a pre-war past. The 'return' was affected through a politics of innocence that flattened, homogenized, and aestheticized the traces of war. Agents of the destruction disappeared so that the thing itself became responsible for its own destruction. The promised return capitalizes on nostalgia for communal harmony and desire for profit without guilt or memory, in the hope that the repressed will not return." Some critics viewed this process in even more pessimistic terms. For example, Saree Makdisi (1997, 693) argues that, "What Solidere and Harirism seem to represent is precisely the withering away of the state, whatever one might have called a public sphere or civil society, and their final and decisive colonization by capital."

Along similar lines, the Lebanese theorist and videographer Jalal Toufic (2003, 72) says, "The demolition of many of the ruined buildings . . . was war by other means; the war on the traces of the war is part of the traces of the war, hence signals that the war is continuing." Much of the anxiety of those who criticized the reconstruction ideology of Solidere and Harirism was due to their sense that the collateral for such projects was paid for through a regime of silence, denial, and repression, where the subject of the war's memory was concerned. The practical political dimension also appeared difficult for many to accept: in particular that the amnesties that were agreed in an effort to end the fighting also allowed many of the most notorious figures of the war to emerge as stakeholders in the postwar reconstruction projects. Nonetheless, projects to compel a broader engagement with the question of how to remember the war began to be developed as early as the mid-1990s, largely within academic and civil society arenas. Organizations like Memory for the Future (Dhakira lil-Ghad) and UMAM Documentation and Research, among others, began in 1999 and 2004, respectively to explore memories of the war, "because 'the past doesn't want to pass,' and because it erects walls between us" as Amal Makarem, an organizing member of Memory for the

Future, intones in her introduction to published conference proceedings for the organization (Makarem 2001, 34). Artists and other cultural producers were perhaps the most active in giving voice to concerns that postwar Lebanon was not effectively confronting the legacy of the conflict. These first efforts emerged against an unsympathetic backdrop, where any discussion of the war was seen as potentially reopening the door to sectarian tensions.

During and after the war, cinema emerged as one of the primary cultural forums for engaging the experiences of the war. As Lina Khatib (2008, 169) suggests, after the war, many "seemed to choose to forget—the memory of the war was deemed too painful and guilt-inducing to be resurrected. . . . Filmmakers . . . resisted the sidelining of the memory of the war, and continued to make films about their war experiences." But this imperative has not always been viewed positively—often Lebanese filmmakers have seen the legacy of the war more as an albatross hung around their necks, preventing them from exploring other subjects. Even with such a burden, Lebanese filmmakers have served as some of the most prescient voices on the subject of the war and on its lasting legacy in postwar Lebanon. The reality of a continuing ebb and flow of conflict and violence between various sectarian groups in Lebanon often serves to drive cultural producers away from work that would address certain core issues relating to the cultural memory of the war—something that filmmakers have been more capable in doing.

The first generation of war and postwar filmmakers, from documentarians such as Mai Masri and Jean Chamoun to feature filmmakers such as Jocelyn Saab, Samir Habchi, and Maroun Baghdadi, dealt primarily with the crisis in representation of the war as lived experience. Their films, set in (and sometimes even shot during) periods of fighting, articulate the impossibility of sufficiently representing the inchoate events of civil conflict: neighbors fighting neighbors, arbitrary violence, the sudden disappearance of noncombatant loved ones, the rise and fall of hopes for an end to the conflict. The project of witnessing the war through documentary came to serve as a foremost aim for many of the filmmakers active during the war years. However, imaginative and nondocumentary approaches also emerged, often giving a more complex view of the impact of the war upon Lebanese. Joceyln Saab's *A Suspended Life* (*Ghazl al-binat*, 1985), for example, juxtaposes the backdrop of the war-torn city to the fantasies of classic Egyptian cinema through the relationship of two adolescent girls coming to terms with the adult realities of life as young women in a war-torn patriarchal context, mixing a documentary approach to location (with most of the film shot in half-destroyed buildings) with narrative fiction. Maroun Baghdadi's *Little Wars* (*Hurub saghira*, 1982) explores how the initial idealistic political commitments that drew many young Lebanese to involvement were corrupted and betrayed. It indicates that the only recourse for many who were slowly drawn into the war's logic was escaping from the country, death, or insanity. Made ten years later, and just after the end of the

war, Samir Habchi's *The Tornado* (*al-A'sar*, 1992) draws exactly the same conclusions, as its protagonist—a non-combatant who has returned to Beirut
after years away—is driven to militancy as well as madness, ending with his
shooting at the sky (to kill God), bringing on a rain of blood. These and a
small number of other narrative productions set the grounds for postwar films
that would articulate a cultural memory of the conflict, what Khatib (2008,
179) terms "a memory project giving voice to a silenced past."

Beyond the explorations of war witnessing in fictional narrative cinema works,
the most impressive catalog to offer testimony to the war's experiences comes in
the documentaries of Mai Masri (many of whose films were codirected by Jean
Chamoun). Masri and Chamoun's early work *Under the Rubble* (1982) focuses on
the consequences of the Israeli invasion of Lebanon and the siege of West Beirut in
that year. The film is an activist work, quite clearly made to demand recognition by
the international community of the devastation and war crimes carried out during
the invasion. The subjects of the film are largely socially marginalized—southern
Lebanese refugees who recount their long marches from the south to Beirut, or
Palestinian refugees in camps near Beirut whose dwellings have been bombed.
The film includes voice-over commentary, which while not exactly pedantic does
intrude upon the voices of victims of the war who are interviewed throughout the
work. However, the film's aim is to give a forum for the testimony of these people
concerning the circumstances during the Israeli invasion. In this way it serves as a
fairly paradigmatic example of cinematic witnessing-discourse.

However, in its remarkable ending sequence, the work opens an ambivalent
interpretive space, hinting at the impossibility of bearing witness, through a
collage of sometimes conflicting images. The sequence begins with images of
the evacuation of PLO fighters from Beirut, set against the soundtrack, a revolutionary song by the Egyptian singer Shaykh Imam. The images focus largely
on the actions of women who are being left behind—they are celebrating with
zagharid ululations and *dabke* dancing, but weeping as well. This sequence and
its focus on the ritual response of the Palestinian women to the departing fighters bears witness to the complexity of the traumas of this episode of the war.
Rather than simply testifying to the horrors of the war—what much film has
done up to this point—this sequence betrays the ambiguities of these experiences as well: the triumphal celebration in the face of military defeat, even as the
women and children are to be deprived of their only protection. The sequence
ends with a double-exposed image of tanks overlaying a mourning woman,
images that bleed into footage of the victims of the Sabra and Shatila massacre, carried out only shortly after the departure of the Palestine Liberation
Organization (PLO) fighters. (I will say more about the remembrance of this
massacre in chapter 7). While the film deploys witnessing-discourse to present
an urgent call for recognition of the war's most desperate victims, it also ends
ambivalently by relating scenes of defiant celebration in the face of defeat set
against the shocking images of the massacre.

The problematic of establishing a common cultural memory of the civil war may be traced back to some of the earliest works made in the postwar period. In *Suspended Dreams* (*Ahlam mu'alliqa*, 1991), Masri and Chamoun focus on the situation in Beirut just after the declaration of the end of the civil war. This documentary follows the question of how a number of individuals drawn from a broad set of social contexts deal with their memories of the war, illustrating how divergent and even irreconcilable these different memories have been and the obstacles that prevent their individual memories from coalescing into a common cultural memory. The film follows a number of characters, including a woman whose husband was kidnapped during the war and is still missing, two former fighters from opposing militia who are now friends and coworkers, and a prominent theater actor. In its portrait of each of the individuals, the film examines what it means for them to be now at the "end" of the conflict, and what social forces are acting to evoke or prohibit a new public consensus around memories of the war. For each, the question of memory is paramount—and the ties that memory brings, or the walls it establishes between individuals and groups.

The issue of memory is central in the relationship of Nabil and Rambo, the two former militiamen from opposing sides who now are friends. In one scene the two men and their families gather for a dinner. However, the topic that dominates their conversation is a car bomb that has exploded earlier in the day. Nabil, who is Muslim, begins to speak about the bombing, which had occurred in a Muslim district, and Rambo's response—he is Christian—is "hawal tinsa," "try to forget." Nabil protests, "How can I forget?" and Rambo grows uncomfortable and defensive. The question of memory—how to remember, what to remember—draws a stark line between the two, who have gone so far to overcome their prior enmity. The most self-reflective views on the role of cultural memory are offered by Rafiq, the actor, who appears in the film sitting in a bombed-out theater, its seats overturned and strewn around. He meditates on the demands being made upon victims of the trauma of the war to forget and move on. He protests against these demands, saying "it's normal to defend your memories . . . you're defending life." Later he links his wish to be able to express and retain his memory to a resolution of his trauma. In the face of a public-relations campaign to reconstruct the city of Beirut so as to erase or repress the memories of the war, Rafiq asks, "how will the destruction within me be repaired?" B-roll images of billboards of advertisements arrayed along a highway illustrate his predicament. He ends, saying that through a rising consumerism and through the destruction of the past through reconstruction projects, "they want to brainwash you."

Masri and Chamoun's film is broadly representative of the interests of Lebanese filmmakers in the postwar context, even those working on fictional narratives. In this, the cosmopolitan and largely nonsectarian milieu of cultural producers in Lebanon has been motivated to raise questions and demand an accounting of the war as a result of the lack of a coherent national accounting, an imperative imbued with urgency in the initial years after the Ta'if agreement, which signaled the end of the war. However, it is highly questionable how effective these efforts have been—one cannot help but ask what defines memory discourse among the groups that have a political stake in defining the memory of the war, for example, Hizbullah, the Lebanese Forces, or any of the other parties to the conflict who are now involved in state politics. Generally speaking, the efforts to develop a common cultural memory have shown little impact on public policy and the process of "national reconciliation" in Lebanon. In more recent years postwar trauma-production has mutated into a bitter reflection, somewhat nihilistic in its view of the possibility of achieving resolution to the problematic memory of the war.

Even until the mid-1990s, the predominant themes of Lebanese war-related cinema were mostly the scenario of the war itself, as the narratives set in those days slowly passed from vital individual memories to a more settled form of cultural memory. *West Beirut* (*Bayrut Gharbi*, 1996) represents a breaking point in this trajectory, as it successfully produced a broad and generally uncontroversial narrative of the war that invited identification across sectarian lines: the film breaks with the crisis of representation, and defiantly views the war as eminently representable. The film cleverly indexes this question of representation self-reflexively, in the cinematic aspirations of Tareq, the film's protagonist, who records his view of the war on his Super-8 camera. Even the tragic end of the film—ostensibly, his mother's death, which is signaled through the use of slow-motion Super-8 footage of her—allows for a resolution of this loss, endeavors to open the door to what Freud ([1917] 1957, 243) terms "the normal affect of mourning," and allows the audience to find a closure to the myriad tragedies of the war (figure 6.2).

FIGURE 6.2 *Tareq remembers shooting film of his mother* (West Beirut)

The release of *West Beirut* coincided with the ascendancy of the Solidere projects of rebuilding, and the nostalgic accounting of the war in the film accorded with—or at least did not significantly challenge—the representation of the war advocated by the redevelopment regime. However, the project of *West Beirut*, that of constructing a common cultural memory of the war that was based on an aesthetic of what we may term "pure representation" was one that may be said to have largely failed. Despite the popularity of the film, the broader cultural memory of the war remained fractured and irresolute, with continued reluctance on the part of the state and the commercial-mercantile elites to produce a consensus on how to remember the war. This unease bled into art practice and works of cultural production as well. As Walid Sadek (2007, 38) notes of the artists of the period, "Their inability to achieve pure representation is not a failure but rather the mark of a reluctance traceable in Beirut art starting in the mid-1990s. Some artworks exacerbate this reluctance, I argue, by dragging back onto the throne of pure representation—and consequently into public space—the instability of physical matter." One may consider the "reluctance" identified so perceptively by Sadek as a form of resistance to the ideology of reconstruction, a resistance that by effect sees pure representation as suspect and complicit.

By the early years of the new millennium, Lebanese filmmakers were engaging with war themes through a new set of concerns. More and more, films began to address the postwar context more than the experiences of the war themselves. Representation of wartime—the witnessing of violence—was replaced by representation of memory processes and by a melancholic reaction to the repression of public memorialization. This stage culminated with the assassination of former prime minister Rafic Hariri in 2005, and the outcome of the 2006 war with Israel. The period leading up to the assassination of Hariri was marked by a degree of apprehension and anxiety relating to the completion of much of the reconstruction regime and a resulting lack of ideological cohesion among Lebanon's elites as to the future direction of the country. While still the memorialization of the war would be cast as problematic, the calls for an accounting had only increased from different corners. The assassination (including its aftermath—the withdrawal of Syrian forces and popular mobilizations by Hariri's al-Mustaqbal grouping on one hand and by Hizbullah and its allies on the other) and the 2006 "Summer War" dramatically altered the cultural landscape of the country once again, opening new wounds that would result in renewed—yet not entirely separate—calls for justice that are formulated within projects of trauma production.

Postwar Hauntings

In Lebanon, despite the ambitious projects and costly investments, the specter of the war—its undead body—would rise to haunt the city in its metaphorical nights. Echoing Jalal Toufic's comment that the form of reconstruction in Lebanon ironically only "signals that the war is continuing," one may say that the continuing war, invisible on the surface but lurking in the city's corners at night, haunts the city. Westmoreland (2009, 43) has suggested that in Lebanon, "post-war mediation uncovers withdrawn subjectivities evocative of ghosts that have not been mourned and spectres that have not been tried for their crimes." The recurrent references to haunting and the undead are in fact more prevalent in literary than in cinematic representations, and a separate study—focusing on works such as Rashid al-Da'if's *Dear Mr. Kawabata* and *Passage to Dusk*, or Hoda Barakat's *The Tiller of Waters*, among others—would be needed to address these works. Nonetheless, these cinematic references are part of a broader phenomenon of explorations of the contact zone between living and dead, of which ghosts and vampires are only two popular tropes.

What, we may ask, is at stake in these evocations of the undead? Clearly, these references to the undead have little to do with the rich topoi of the vampire that lurk seductively at the margins of the enduring Gothic ethos of postindustrial Europe or in the second-millennial fantasies of pubescent North America. What the postcolonial context, here Lebanon, demands is an understanding of the grey margins between life and death—and the return to life from death (vampires and haunting) are the zones of traumatic resonance, where the productive impulses of trauma are to be found. What is at stake is what Avery Gordon (2008, 64) calls *"a concern for justice"* (emphasis in original), where that which haunts a society is a failure to achieve justice. As Bliss Cua Lim (2001, 288) argues, ghost films often serve as historical allegories—in particular those produced in the postcolonial world (she analyzes the films *Rouge* [dir. Stanley Kwan, 1987] and *Haplos* [dir. Antonio Jose "Butch" Perez, 1982]). She notes, "Ghost films that are also historical allegories make incongruous use of the vocabulary of the supernatural to articulate historical injustice, referring to 'social reality' by recourse to the undead." The repressed call for justice is animated through the figure of the undead—the haunting ghost, the vampire. The Lebanese context is one of a civil war, leading to an amnestic peace, overlaid with development and reconstruction, collapsing in the assassination of Hariri and the splintering of the postwar détente, and eventually the devastation wrought by the Israeli attacks in 2006. Put simply, these films prompt the question of "justice" through their imagining of the presence of the undead in this shifting landscape.

Declaring the Death

In *A Perfect Day* (*Yawm akhar*, 2005) a mother and her son prepare to visit a lawyer to legally declare as dead her husband, who has been missing since some time during the civil war. Both live irresolute and unresolved lives—the son, Malik, suffers a form of narcolepsy which increasingly disrupts his daily life, and the mother, Claudia, still lives in anticipation of the return of her husband, despite the many years that have passed since his disappearance. *A Perfect Day* was produced during and set in the Lebanon of the reconstruction period. In an ironic referencing of the ideals of this period, Malik's work is in property development and construction—the signature economic area of this time.

Codirectors Joana Hadjithomas and Khalil Joreige have explored the aftermath of the Lebanese civil war in other works, in particular their debut feature film, *The Pink House* (*Al-Bayt al-zahr*, 1999). *The Pink House* was one of the first Lebanese works to specifically explore the tensions that arose between those who sought to reanimate cultural memory of the civil war, and those who saw the renewal and reconstruction of the country as imperative, even when these efforts erased the traces of the war and aimed to remove it from cultural memory. As Ken Siegneurie (2011, 118) has noted, "*The Pink House* provided a nuanced vision of the conflicting imperatives of memory and change." *One Perfect Day* intimates that the ascendancy of a reconstruction ideology has in fact erased the traces of the civil war—rather, repressed perhaps, they remain in the shadows, and at times are literally unearthed in the course of the rebuilding.

One Perfect Day follows what are apparently the usual quotidian habits of the mother and son: their preparations for the day, their daily tasks, the boredom and quiet that are occasionally punctuated by action, but which seem to always return. While Malik's daytime is occupied with his work, he seems peculiarly antisocial, with few if any friends—other than Zayna, a former lover who now refuses to speak to him. Claudia is largely homebound—she spends most of her time in the small apartment they share off a relatively quiet street. At one point she offers coffee to a group of security guards who guard a notable neighbor, and at another she answers a telephone call from a friend or relative, but otherwise she also seems solitary. Before the lawyer's appointment, Malik visits a work site to oversee progress on the construction of a new apartment tower. At the site he falls asleep, until awoken to hear that workmen have discovered a corpse while digging the foundation. Malik rushes to the location, but rather than go to where the body has been found, he speaks by walkie-talkie to the men on site, asking them if the body dates from the civil war. When they reply that it seems to be much older, he is visibly disappointed. His father's missing body has ignited a quest that is inflamed by the news of unclaimed bodies found. Indeed, it would seem that bodies of victims of Beirut's various modern conflicts are scattered throughout subterranean strata below the city.

This scene finds reflections in a performance art piece by the Lebanese artist Walid Raad, under his moniker of the Atlas Group. As a purported representative of this organization, Raad performs public talks in the guise of an archivist presenting artifacts and objects collected by the fictional group; many of these directly or indirectly relate to the civil war, and comment upon memory processes and repression of memory in postwar Lebanon. At a performance at PS1's "Greater New York" show in 2005, Raad showed slides of monochromatic blue-green colors, claiming that these were digitally processed extracts of images derived from negatives discovered in the Mediterranean, off Beirut. As the audience strained to see something in the slides, Raad explained that the images were portraits of missing people whose bodies were disposed of in the sea, recovered by the Atlas Group. In the question-and-answer session after the talk, some in the audience attested to feeling as if they discerned a faint outline of faces in the images. In this performance, the haunting absence of the disappeared is evoked impressively, as is the impossibility of representing them—where so much more about the war is a subject of excess: of emotion, of violence, of incomprehensibility, the matter of the disappeared operates as a silence, an empty void, echoed in the hollow reflection of monochromatic slides that filled the screen.

The appointment with the lawyer ends without a final resolution to the matter of the missing father's status (figure 6.3). Claudia has forgotten to bring clippings of announcements that the family had placed in newspapers when her husband first disappeared. Without these, the legal dossier is incomplete. While they each sign the declaration, the lawyer tells

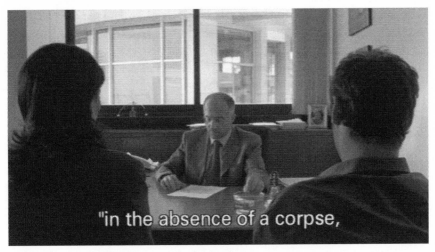

FIGURE 6.3 *Visiting the lawyer* (A Perfect Day)

them he will have to await their delivery of the clippings before the matter can proceed. It is unclear whether Claudia has purposefully forgotten the documents, or whether she has erred, but in either case she and Malik leave the office without truly resolving the matter of her husband's legal status. Even the legal route to resolving the wounds of the past is one that in fact does not produce certainty for those affected. The declaration of the father's death has now been issued, but there are still formalities and technicalities that prevent the dossier from being closed. Where Malik had apparently hoped to leave the meeting with the matter behind him, Claudia seems somehow to find further hope in these final unresolved details.

Once they arrive back home, Malik refuses to stay in the apartment with his mother, instead leaving to drive around Beirut aimlessly. As he drives, it becomes clear that he is searching for his estranged girlfriend. He visits her apartment building and, not finding her at home, then drives around looking expectantly at young women he sees on the street. Meanwhile, Claudia is left alone, and has donned the black clothes of mourning for the first time. She tries to call Malik on his cell phone, but he does not answer. Several hours later, at night, while feeling abandoned, she is visited by what seems to be the ghost of her husband. The visitation is shot as a point-of-view from the ghost's perspective. A profile shot shows Claudia sitting in the living room, when she suddenly looks up (figure 6.4). An edit cuts to her looking at the camera with an expression of both fear and recognition. The camera assumes the position of the ghost, and as it pans in a semicircle her fixed gaze follows its movement. The pan stops and she continues to look directly into the lens, eventually raising her outstretched palm toward it in a gesture that closes the sequence (figure 6.5). In this way the scene places the viewer in the position of the ghost and creates an intimate and poignant interaction between the viewer and Claudia. Her fear and desire are intensely magnified by the length of the single shot and by the simplicity of her final gesture, reaching out from the living toward the undead. The scene lacks dialogue or soundtrack music and the diegetic sound is at a minimum, which enhances the visual intensity of the moment.

While the scene marks a transitional point in the narrative, the film intimates that similar events may have occurred in the past. In an earlier scene she tells Malik, "Sometimes I see him, I feel him. You don't. You don't see him, you don't feel him" (figure 6.6). This gap in experience marks the distinction between the mother and son—and allegorizes a generational gap in the manner by which the war is remembered. Where Claudia admits to "seeing" and "feeling" the presence of her husband, Malik is unable to do so. However, he is not free from the haunting affect of the absent father—in his case, his recurrent narcolepsy, which marks his own inhabitation of a

FIGURES 6.4 AND 6.5 *Claudia sees a ghost* (A Perfect Day)

FIGURE 6.6 *Claudia and Malik in the car* (A Perfect Day)

space between life and death, is linked to the specter of his missing father. However, while Claudia may have experienced some contact with her undead husband in the past, this scene raises questions within the trajectory of the film's narrative. What effect will this visitation have upon the legal process to declare her husband dead that moves forward? If and when he is finally declared dead, will the haunting presence be removed from the lives of Claudia and Malik? While Malik, for one, views the declaration as a step that will allow him to reconcile with Zayna, and perhaps will also end his narcoleptic condition, Claudia instead views the resolution of her husband's legal state as falling short in offering her corollary resolutions to her despondency.

These two characters themselves both inhabit a liminal space separating life and death, across which the undead pass. During his narcoleptic fits, Malik is often mistaken as dead: as in one scene where he is pulled from his car by passersby concerned that he has died at the wheel, or in the opening scene of the film where his mother watches him sleep for some time before anxiously leaning over his mouth to check his breathing (figure 6.7). In this way, the film views the absence and presumed death of the father as producing not only a haunting presence, but one that also overshadows and cloaks those who are left behind. Somehow, the suspended status of his father—presumed dead but not yet legally recognized as such—has also prevented Malik or Claudia from joining the world of the living.

The lack of a resolution to the matter of Malik's father's status may symbolically overshadow his attempts to resolve the problems he has been facing. After the meeting with the lawyer, Malik once again attempts to call Zayna, but she refuses to answer his calls. He goes to the hospital to consult

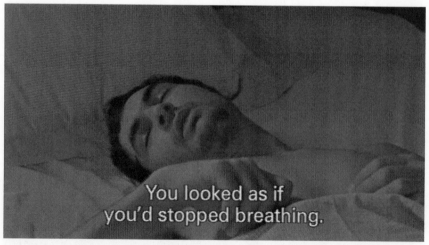

FIGURE 6.7 *Malik awakes from sleep* (A Perfect Day)

a doctor about his narcolepsy, and while in the waiting room there uses a hospital phone to call Zayna, who, not recognizing the number, answers him for the first time. Before she can hang up on him, the first thing he tells her is, "I've signed the papers about my father." Clearly it seems he views the long lack of a clear resolution to his father's situation as a cause of the problems between them, and he is hopeful that by telling her this news they may move toward reconciliation. Later, at night after Malik checks out various nightspots, he finds Zayna with a friend at a club. Approaching them, he is initially rejected by her, and her friend then tells him to leave them alone. Rather than leave the club, he retreats to a corner where he watches them from a distance. His phone rings but it is Claudia calling, so he does not answer. Eventually he slumps over, in a narcoleptic fit. Seeing him asleep, Zayna approaches him. Somehow seeing him in this repose affects her and she begins to caress his head as he slowly awakes. Shortly they leave the club together and begin to drive around Beirut, apparently reconciled. While it appears as if Malik's hopes are to be realized—and thus perhaps the process of recognition of his father's death has opened the door to their reuniting—suddenly Zayna changes her mind, as if she had been possessed, and runs away from the car to disappear into the night. Malik himself had linked the troubles between them to the status of his father, but it is unclear whether their ultimate inability to reunite relates in some way to the fact that the legal process has still not been completed, or if it is rather a sign that the hopes Malik had held were themselves ultimately false. If the latter, it would seem that his problems are due to the issue of his father less than to other unexplored complications—a matter which may allegorize other conditions in postwar Lebanon. Malik, despondent, finds that Zayna has left her contact lens' case behind in the car. He puts her lenses into his own eyes and in a POV shot we see the world as he now does, as indistinct and blurry lights and shapes. In this prosthetic attempt to see things "through her eyes," he instead sees nothing at all. The gap between his "view," framed as it is through his personal burden of familial war trauma, and that of Zayna, who is carefree young woman seeking pleasure and freedom, is signified in the visual register as Malik drives wildly down the highway while blinded by her contact lenses.

A Perfect Day engages with the historical problems of the unresolved civil war—and the claims of injustice that underlie the social trauma that haunts Lebanon—by what Gordon has called a "recourse to the undead." Here, Lebanon is haunted by the missing, the thousands who disappeared during the course of the war with no trace. The absent bodies of the disappeared serve as acute signifiers of all that is unresolved about the war. A family torn apart—missing an active father—is a potent symbol of the postwar nation. The undead lurk behind the layers of dysfunction and neurosis that paralyze both the war generation and its children, but it is unclear if the ghosts of the war hold a key to finding a way forward.

The film ends with what might be read as a qualified expression of hope. After spending the remainder of the night driving around the city, Malik goes to sleep on a bench by the corniche. He wakes the next morning at dawn, and after getting up and stretching, he limbers up and then begins to sprint along the corniche (figures 6.8 and 6.9). Shaking off his sleep, the motion of running brings to his body a sense of corporeal freedom absent from the beginning of the film. Also, for the first time, the setting and camerawork break free of the gloomy interior locations and static framings that have characterized the *mise en scène*. As Lina Khatib (2007, 106) notes, through most of the film Beirut is represented as "claustrophobic" as well as seeming like "a living nightmare: a

FIGURES 6.8 AND 6.9 *Malik runs on the corniche* (A Perfect Day)

bleak place often shot in the dark." Here the camera follows Malik as he runs, through a series of fluid takes, before settling on the last shot of the film, a sky filled with migratory birds. The open aspect of these shots—the horizon of the sea, the open sky—breaks with the prior aesthetics of framing and camera movement, to hint at a possible transformation within him or around him.

The somewhat hopeful note that ends *A Perfect Day* is one that is arrived at through traversing the line between life and death. A similar use is made of the notion of haunting, albeit in a rather more facile manner, in the film *Zozo* (2005). Joseph Fares's tale of war and emigration follows the story of a young boy whose family is killed just as they are preparing to abandon Lebanon to emigrate to Sweden. The first half of the film follows the boy, nick-named Zozo, in his attempts to survive alone in Beirut and make sense of his situation after the death of his parents, while the second half concerns his difficulties as an immigrant in Sweden, living with his grandparents. The trope of haunting is here used as an outlet for Zozo's attempts to come to terms with his fears. After the death of his parents, in a recurring sequence, Zozo imagines or dreams of himself in a house floating in space, and looking out the window he sees a bright source of light that shines in the darkness. He cries out to the light but receives no response.

Later in the film, in a climactic scene, he confronts a group of bullies on a school playground in Sweden. Just as he is about to be beaten by them, mortar shells begin to rain upon the school and the playground. Zozo stands impassively in the midst of the falling shells while the other children flee and take cover. Suddenly his mother rushes up from behind him and removes him to safety. He asks her to take him with her (thus to cross the line from life to death), but after holding him, she tells him to go back on his own. She then fades away, as do the mortar shells, and Zozo finds himself back on the playground, just as things were before the shelling began. However, instead of instigating a fight with the bullies, he simply walks away from them. The catharsis of the scene and the apparition of his mother mark the transition point from trauma to assimilation, from undead to living.

In this way, *Zozo* represents "a symptom of a culture's need to 'forget' traumatic events while representing them in an oblique form" (Kaplan and Wang 2004, 9). Released in 2005, this film largely participates in the amnestic approach that predominated during the reconstruction period, both through its own refusal to engage with specifics of the war (it is, for example, unclear who may have killed Zozo's family, what the causes of the fighting may have been, etc.) and its eagerness to portray the trauma of war as fundamentally resolvable—through immigration and assimilation. It is just as noteworthy that 2005 marked the last year of Social Democratic rule in Sweden, and so the film was to be released only months before the ascendance of the right-wing anti-immigrant coalition that assumed office in the 2006 elections. *Zozo* thus fits a cultural context in Sweden, where debates around immigration were highly politicized, and by representing the traumas of both war and emigration in a resolvable form, the film avoids taking on more difficult discussions around the limitations of assimilation and the experience of marginality among immigrants in Sweden.

Vampire-Healing in the City

The Last Man was also made in the months leading up to the assassination of Rafic Hariri, after which the specter of the civil war once again arose, overshadowing the claims that the wounds of the war had been healed through the projects of reconstruction. The specter would again and more clearly materialize in the form of clashes between Hizbullah and its supporters and militias affiliated with the March 14th coalition in May 2008. The specter also haunted Lebanon during the Israeli war on Lebanon in the summer of 2006, with destruction again spread across the country, with hundreds of thousands of refugees, and thousands of wounded and dead, and ethnic and sectarian tensions again in the foreground of national politics. Presaging these events, in *The Last Man*, Dr. Khalil Shams works at a hospital in Beirut. The film initially outlines a series of vignettes following Khalil through his daily life, beginning with a long series of POV underwater shots coming to reveal the protagonist as he climbs out of the Mediterranean Sea in scuba gear. Khalil is respected by his patients and colleagues, has a girlfriend whom he rarely sees but with whom he communicates regularly by text message, and is part of a group of friends who dine together regularly. However, he nonetheless seems a paradigm of solitude and alienation from his surroundings. In the first sequence of the film, after he has been scuba diving, Zayna, his mostly unseen lover, sends him an SMS: "Always under water?" To which he replies, "Yes, always under water." In this introduction, we encounter a protagonist defined by his social disconnectedness. Intercut with these scenes of Khalil underwater, shots show police removing a body from an apartment. Later it is revealed that the body is of a young man, bearing a bite mark on his neck, the victim of an apparent vampire attack. The editing is not causal, there is no explicit link between the actions, but as a form of dialectical montage, a mode of relation is set out that links Khalil's distracted, "under water" state to the discovery of victims of vampires around the city.

A variety of cinematic techniques are employed to explore Khalil's condition—in particular the use of double exposure. Also, Khalil often is shot through windows that reflect the world outside (figure 6.10), as in one scene where the camera is set outside his car's windshield and his face is only barely seen through the reflection on the glass. Differing from the alienated framing and screening techniques of Elia Suleiman, discussed in chapter 4, these techniques produce layers that cover Khalil's face, producing a ghostly effect (figure 6.11). The explicit artifice of the double exposures and layered

FIGURES 6.10 AND 6.11 *Double exposures over Khalil's face* (The Last Man)

shots—which increase and intensify over the course of the film—visually drain Khalil of detail and texture, and mark his progress toward becoming a vampire. The overlaid images signify a loss of identity and intimate the move from the world of the living to that of the undead. The use of this technique for other worldly effect is not new: double exposure has been associated with the supernatural from before the inception of cinema. As Lisa Starks (2002, 185) notes in discussing an early cinematic rendition of Hamlet, the use of "the cinematic technique of using a double-exposure Ghost tapped into a nineteenth-century myth that photographs were thought to record the ghostly remains or spirit of their subjects." Additionally, early *Dracula* adaptations such as Murnau's *Nosferatu* (1922), made copious use of double exposure in attempting to represent the undead as living-but-not.

More victims are found. Khalil crosses paths with these bodies in his work at the hospital. But as with other issues in his life, the mounting number of victims seems not to affect him. Similarly, as he drives through the city after scuba diving in the Mediterranean, the radio intones news of Palestinian civilian casualties of a recent Israeli military operation—again, he displays little emotion or response. In the hospital, a television reports clashes on the border with Israel. He treats his patients and colleagues at the hospital with the same quiet distance, often distracted or lost in thought. In the gap that grows between Khalil and the rest of his world, we begin to sense a link to the vampire attacks—his inability to live among others, to live a life of the living, begin to direct him toward a liminal space, that of the dead.

The film also makes frequent use of reverse POV shots in which Khalil stares into the camera (figure 6.12). While in the ghost scene in *A Perfect Day*, this technique places the audience in the position of the haunting ghost, the shots of Khalil staring into the camera have a different implication. The final employment of this technique—the scene described at the beginning of this chapter—reveals the subject of his gaze to be a mirror, one which does not reflect him. In prior shots there is no reverse shot to also observe what it is toward which Khalil's gaze is directed. Taking the final iteration of this visual motif as a key, the prior uses of this technique also place the audience in a mirroring position, as if complicit with Khalil. The blank quality of his gaze—so different from *A Perfect Day*'s staging of Claudia's gaze that signifies desire and terror—indicts the viewer with its lack of provocation or emotion.

While Khalil continues his daily activities, various indications mount to signal his being implicated in the vampire attacks. At a dinner gathering with friends, he slowly grows distracted. As the conversation continues, the

FIGURE 6.12 *Khalil stares (*The Last Man)

rainstorm outside ends and a sunbeam shines upon his face. He raises his hand and swears angrily. (His growing hatred of the sunlight bears irony, given that his own last name means "sun.") From this point, Khalil is unable to go outside without wearing dark sunglasses. He stops going to his office, and refuses to answer urgent calls from the hospital, sleeping in his dark room at day and going out only after dusk. The film ends with a long sequence following Khalil at night as he wanders the streets of Beirut, eventually discovering another vampire whom he follows. When Khalil finally does strike, it appears more as initiation than as habit, as he steps in to suck the blood of a person who has already been killed by the other vampire. In the last shot of the film Khalil follows the other vampire into what may be a larger world of the undead, as he disappears into a desolate and shadowy urban landscape.

The Last Man resists a simple allegorical reading more than *A Perfect Day*. Lacking any coherent signifier for the fragmented nation, the film posits Beirut as a space of dislocation, perhaps no less haunted than other cities. In the one panoramic shot of the city in the film, Beirut is overcast with what seems like an apocalyptic storm (one that resonates with Suleiman's apocalyptic storm that begins *The Time that Remains*, as discussed in chapter 4). However, Khalil's slow transformation takes him from being an alienated bourgeois doctor to becoming a man driven by indeterminate needs or impulses, to wandering the streets of Beirut, to eventually accepting his new identity as a vampire. Where *A Perfect Day* intimates, however tentatively, the possibility of a rebirth—a new day—where Malik is able to live a life free of the haunting of his father, *The Last Man* instead closes in the depths of an endless and sleepless night, with Khalil wandering lost into the devastated landscape of a city infested by vampires. *A Perfect Day* envisions a generational shift where the issues of both responsibility and trauma—marked by the ghost of Malik's father—are left behind. While the move toward a legal recognition of the father's death results in the appearance of the ghost in Claudia's presence, Malik moves from the category of undead, signified by his narcolepsy, toward that of the living. Conversely, Khalil's descent into vampirism at the end of *The Last Man* suggests an unresolved question of complicity and responsibility that draws him from the realm of the living into that of the undead. His disappearance into the night landscape of Beirut is in a mirror distinction to Malik's dawn awakening on the corniche of the city.

Returning to Witnessing

Just months after the 2006 war, Ghassan Salhab released an experimental video called *Posthume*, a twenty-minute-long meditation on the aftermath of the conflict. The work largely comprises double- or multiply exposed images, often including a face (or back of the head) of an actor overlaid by moving shots of a camera driving through the war-affected areas of Beirut, or television broadcasts about the war. Nondiegetic voices intone a script of meditative statements that appear to address the question of life from the view of the dead. In the use of double exposure and the attention to the spaces of the city, both evoke *The Last Man*. However, the question of complicity is no longer at the center of the work; this is a work of mourning, of seeking to imagine a venue for the dead to speak.

While the 2006 war must be viewed as fundamentally a different form of violence than much of what characterized the Lebanese civil war (even during the Israeli invasion of 1982), for many in Lebanon the onset of the war brought about a return of traumatic memories of the earlier conflict. Despite ending in just over one month, the hostilities in 2006 unleashed widespread destruction of infrastructure, mass displacements of people, as well as widespread injury and loss of life. As Laura Marks (2000, 22) observes, "The 2006 war did not just irritate the surface of forgetting and distraction so necessary for survival. It viciously tore it away and opened up an abyss that no story can render meaningful." Given the overall development of Lebanese videography and cinema since the time of the civil war, and given the significant experience that many filmmakers had by now gained in exploring war themes in their narratives, it is not surprising that during and in the immediate aftermath of the 2006 war a plethora of video and film works were produced. Kaelen Wilson-Goldie (2007, 69–70) describes the scene in the months after the war:

> In the three months that followed the August 14 ceasefire, more than fifty short films and videos made during or in response to the war were screened publicly at film festivals and in gallery exhibitions in Beirut. . . . Some of the works were shot abroad; others were composed from footage collected in Lebanon during the siege. Some of the authors were artists, while others were amateurs, students, or hobbyists with adequate camera equipment and access to editing software. Hundreds more films were made than shown. Some were projected casually among friends, in homes, and in coffee shops. Untold numbers are still being raked through and refined.

This abundance of visual materials, which spanned from documentary works to art projects that aimed at protesting the war or conveying its horrors to the world beyond Lebanon, to fully fictive works that were staged in the devastated landscapes before the new reconstruction wiped them away, signified Lebanon's entry into the world of hypermediated cultural memory, and the definitive shift from literary to visual cultural production as the favored representational realm for the formation of cultural memory. Two feature narrative films that were made in the immediate aftermath of the war were *Under the Bombs* (*Taht al-qusuf*, 2007) by Philippe Aractingi, and *I Want to See* (*Biddi ashuf*, 2006) made by Hadjithomas and Joreige, (the codirectors of *A Perfect Day*). The two films are fairly distinct in their film language and aesthetics, but are both road films that take place with characters who are touring the war-afflicted areas. Since both films were shot in the immediate aftermath of the war, they are in a sense both semidocumentary, in that they include significant material that is documentary footage of the actual devastation brought by the war and they place their actors in settings and scenarios that involve nonactors who are residents or refugees living in the locations that were used for the film.

In *Under the Bombs*, Zayna, a wealthy Lebanese expatriate, returns from Dubai just days after the end of the war, to search for her son and sister who have gone missing during the bombing. She employs a taxi driver, Tony, at the Beirut port to take her south, to the areas most badly hit during the war. At first her relationship with Tony is initially somewhat contentious, as they drive toward the south. They stop at a refugee shelter in Sidon where she looks for her son Karim, and her sister Maha. In the shelter she speaks to refugees who tell her of their experiences in the war and their losses. The refugees in the film are nonactors, their dialog is not scripted. Zayna listens to their stories and watches as volunteers organize activities for the refugee children. The scenes are staged within the actual setting of a refugee shelter, with soundtrack music that adds emotive overtones to the already tragic accounts and scenes. In this way the film develops a film language that is close to melodrama, but whose artifice is undermined by the placement of this drama within a live setting, with nonactors representing their own experiences.

Eventually Zayna and Tony begin to develop a more friendly rapport. At first the subtext of the tension may not seem clear, but to a Lebanese audience there would be little doubt that in part their sectarian identities (she is apparently a Shi'i Muslim while he is Christian—this is never explicitly stated but implied in various ways) may have a role in the tension between them, as well as differences in gender and class. However, the film imputes that through common cultural referents and aspirations—Tony wishes to emigrate as well, for example—they begin to find more of a common ground. Tony breaks the tension between them more than once by mockingly playing a teach-yourself-German cassette tape that he has listened to for years in anticipation of immigrating to Germany. Other national cultural referents, including shared tastes in music and food, also allow for the two to build a tenuous friendship as they continue to search for Karim.

When they arrive at Zayna's ancestral village they find her sister's house completely destroyed—the neighbors tell her that Maha was killed in the bombing, but that Karim was taken away by journalists who were at the scene. Tony speaks to a boy who had been with Karim, who describes the bombings. As he tells his story of hiding in a shelter with Karim, and of how they saw a third friend killed in the attack, his account is edited against a documentary clip of a building collapsing under a bomb. At another point, more documentary footage shows workers exhuming bodies from a mass grave for reburial by their families. Zayna and Tony circumambulate the coffins as the workers remove them from the earth searching frantically for Maha's body, which is eventually found. Through the trauma of finding and burying her sister, Zayna and Tony tenuously grow closer, as he relates her loss to one experienced by his family. His brother, who was a collaborator with Israel during its occupation of the south until 2000, fled from Lebanon when the Israelis withdrew, and now resides in Israel along with his family, being considered a traitor in Lebanon. Tony's sense of loss has no political space for expression, even as he seems to disavow his brother's political choices. Even though Tony's brother collaborated with the forces that have now killed her sister, the film imagines a sort of reconciliation through her recognition of a shared traumatic past. In the final scenes of the film, their search eventually leads them to a monastery where they have been told Karim was left by the journalists who had rescued him from the village. Once there, they find a boy who is wearing Karim's jacket, but who is not Karim. As Zayna begins to cry, the boy tells them that Karim "stayed under the bombs."

Under the Bombs utilizes an emotive narrative arc that places the two protagonists of the film in a dramatic point of reconciliation through the recognition of their respective traumas. Arguably, their losses are not easily comparable; her sister is a civilian casualty of war, while his brother is neither dead nor in any real sense a victim, as he was a military fighter who chose to support an occupation. Beyond the problematic of this equivalence, the film's melodramatic staging of a scripted narrative over the documentary setting has the unintended result of draining the "real" footage of its affective power, subordinating the scenes of destruction and of rubble to the continuing drama between the protagonists.

By contrast, Hadjithomas and Joreige's *I Want to See* employs a less dramatic and narrative-driven approach, while still adopting a very similar story framework. Here again, the film's protagonists are two individuals who are driving to and around the south of Lebanon, a woman who is a passenger and a man who is her driver, in the aftermath of the war. *I Want to See* is a self-reflexive work, where the protagonists, Catherine Deneuve and Rabih Mroue, are played by actors of the same name, and where the filmmakers occasionally appear before the cameras as they direct the action or make decisions about the trajectory of the film. The film begins with Deneuve in a hotel in Beirut, accompanied by the filmmakers, as they argue with her hosts over her wish to participate in the film by going on a day trip to the south of the country. The camera is stationary and poorly framed, as if shooting discretely from the hip. The handler who objects to her trip is concerned that she will be exposed to danger, or that she may return too late for a gala dinner to which she has been invited. Deneuve replies, "I want to see." The handler asks, "I don't understand. What do you want to see?" Deneuve simply replies again "I want to see. I want to see." After convincing her hosts to allow her

FIGURE 6.13 *Deneuve and Mroue drive toward the south (*I Want to See*)*

to leave, she sets out on the shoot with her companion-driver, Rabih Mroue, a noted Lebanese artist and actor (figure 6.13). During their initial conversation, she again says, "I want to see." To which Mroue answers, "Me too, I want to see." And Deneuve replies again, "You want to see again, I imagine." Through this repetition in the dialogue, the film asserts the primacy of visual representation in coming to terms with the effects of war, and gives voice to a desire for comprehending these effects visually, on the part of both characters. This dialogue of visual desire is offset by the footage in much of the film which is most often made up of a static shot of the two actors in the front seats of the car. At one point, when the crew exits their cars to shoot footage in the southern suburbs of Beirut, they are prevented from doing so, presumably by security men working for Hizbullah, whose headquarters are in that area. When in the south, the two characters look for Mroue's ancestral home, but given the destruction are unable to finally find it. In these and other ways, the film suggests that seeing is not always possible, or that even when seeing, one is not necessarily brought closer to understanding.

When, near the end of the film, they arrive at a huge rubble heap where tons of debris have been gathered, Mroue's voice carries out a sort of epistolary monologue, while the camera tracks slowly, deliberately, over the rubble (figures 6.14 and 6.15):

> Do you see? We can't recognize anything. We can't distinguish the hall from the dining room, the kitchen from the entrance, the bedrooms from the bathroom. Just stones, all mixed up. It's like a town that had to be discarded, hidden, buried under the sea. It's strange. It reminds me of an image. . . . A town washed up on the seashore, like a whale. A dismantled monster that can no longer move, a body decaying, far from the eyes of people.

In the sequence, the camera finally allows the viewer to assume the position of the spectator represented by Deneuve, as if to allow her to finally see.

FIGURES 6.14 AND 6.15 *Viewing the rubble* (I Want to See)

Where before, seeing was difficult if not impossible, here she is allowed to
see, but there are "just stones, mixed up," with no recognizable referents or
traces of human spaces remaining. The sight of the debris is monstrous; the
town that it once had been is now like the rotting corpse of a beached whale.
Most importantly, it is "far from the eyes of people." This monologue and its
end on an abject image, a "dismantled monster" that is decaying, conjures a
liminal space between human and nonhuman, or humanity and inhumanity.
But it is, again, difficult to view, set away from sight, hidden from the eyes.
Here again Hadjithomas and Joreige raise the monstrous figure of the war's
destruction as a form of liminal experience, to unsettle the function of viewing and to reorient it toward a position of justice-seeking.

Both *Under the Bombs* and *I Want to See* use the documentary setting of
postwar Lebanon as a staging area for narrative explorations. One presumes
in this gesture that the scripting of narrative action somehow presents a com-
plementary or additional depth to the documentary "reality" of the war-torn
landscape that both explore. What distinguishes the two films from each
other is how they imagine the fictive and documentary working together as
a whole. In this way, both works endeavor to position themselves as works of

witnessing—but they present the act of witnessing in significantly different ways. *Under the Bombs* allows the victims of the war to speak for themselves, but circumscribes their testimony and seeks closure for their trauma through its melodramatic framing. *I Want to See*, however, is a work that opens the subject of witnessing to a more critical treatment, hinting that perhaps that which cannot be seen, which is out of eyesight, being monstrous and liminal, affords a truer understanding of the war's traumas.

This discussion has hinted at the reading of these several films as particular reflections of the historical circumstances that separate them, even if only several months separate them. The years 2005–2006 were tumultuous even in the unsettled context of Lebanon's postwar identity. The transition from the reconstruction era, defined by the Solidere project, to a fragmentation of what had been developed of a national consensus that resulted in the Hariri assassination and its aftermath, may be traced in the outlines of these two works, which were then quickly followed by the 2006 summer war and the various representational challenges this new crisis augured. However, it would be too deterministic to limit our readings to such details, for all of these works more broadly should be viewed apart from their immediate historical contexts—none are works of reportage, and all have a tenuous relationship with the use of realism, even when evoking the real. These works, taken as a whole, are representative of the much larger question of how trauma production intervenes in and produces meaning for postconflict Lebanon. Where official discourse on war has been muted or "amnestic," cultural producers have taken a central role in the projects of producing social trauma in defiance of the irresolute memory of war.

We return to the concern for justice that began this chapter, by returning to the argument that the ghostly, the undead, and the monstrous act upon the witnessed reality and charge them with an unsettled place within the broader framework of trauma production. In conjuring the liminal, these works ask questions about the nature of justice and the impossibility of a just world or the hope of its achievement. During and shortly after the civil war, filmmakers such as Mai Masri endeavored to present first works of witnessing as a form of testimonial to the losses of the war, before shifting to offer works that engaged critically with the cultural memory of the war as it was affected by the reconstruction regime. Where *A Perfect Day*'s hopeful ending fits well within the troubled-but-optimistic air of the reconstruction period at its ascendance before Hariri's assassination, *The Last Man*—made about one year later—seems prescient in predicting the return of the haunting effects of the war in the shape of a vampire or vampires who cannot be distinguished from society at large. *A Perfect Day* sets the question of justice in the hands of a new generation, hoping for a new day when the past is finally set to rest. *The Last Man* is more pessimistic, and provokes us to envision a world lacking justice, where complicity and guilt are shared, and where Khalil's hollow gaze into the camera provokes the viewer to act before sliding into a similar torpor, caught in limbo on the fine line between life and death. The context for such evocations of trauma changed, however, in the year after the production of these films, when the 2006 war demanded a return to a position of witnessing. In this setting, where a film such as *Under the Bombs* sought to subordinate the scenes of destruction and to relegate them to a backdrop function against which an allegorical drama of Lebanese reconciliation was to be staged, other works such as *Posthume* and *I Want to See* positioned the liminal and monstrous at the center of their acts of viewing, and through them synthesized the role of testimony-offering with that of justice-seeking in a single work.

"Sawwaru Waynkum?"

HUMAN RIGHTS AND SOCIAL TRAUMA
IN *WALTZ WITH BASHIR*

There is talk . . . that many Vietnam films are antiwar, that the
message is that war is inhumane. But actually, Vietnam films are
all pro-war, no matter what the supposed message, what Kubrick or
Coppola or Stone intended.

—ANTHONY SWOFFORD, *in Weschler (2005, 65)*

Human Rights, Social Trauma, and Cinema

In chapter 6, I examined how Lebanese cultural memory concerning the civil
war and its aftermath has remained deeply irresolute by virtue of an absence
of social consensus on how the war is to be memorialized, as well as a prioritization of stability over justice, however imperfect, in national and intercom-
munal discourse. Any mention of justice must raise the question of the law,
and by extension the areas of law that are most often central to war and postwar settings: the laws of war and human rights law. The institutionalization
of human rights discourse over the course of the twentieth century follows
the parallel development of psychoanalytic conceptions of traumatic cultural
memory. Coincidentally, the emergence of both human rights discourse and
conceptions of social trauma also maps closely on to the rise of the cinematic
medium and its centrality in the development of cultural memory of historical events—one aspect of "cinema memory" (Kuhn 2004). This chapter presents an overview of the intersection of these three concepts—cinema, trauma,
human rights—by examining how the critically acclaimed Israeli film *Waltz
with Bashir* (*Valz im Bashir*, dir. Ari Folman, 2008) recast postwar memory as
framed by trauma. *Bashir* is an exemplary subject for observing the increasing turn to memory and trauma discourse in postwar Israeli texts, a turn
that, as others have noted, has led to increasingly narrow attention being

given to "perpetrator traumas," which diminish the ethical charge of both human rights and social trauma as categories (Morag 2013).

First, it may be useful to here dwell briefly on the common grounds that have come to link social trauma and human rights. Social trauma often emerges with cases of human rights violations, as a sort of specter, where the war crime is followed by the collective trauma of the survivors. One may argue that it becomes ultimately necessary to consider the degree to which the categories of "social trauma" and "human rights crimes" reflect one another, interrelate, and coalesce. Among activists, theorists, and mental health practitioners alike, the link between individual trauma and human rights is of increasing interest. Elizabeth Kornfeld (1995, 128), writing on human rights crimes in Pinochet-era Chile, argues, "The concept of *trauma* has been the basis for understanding the subjective impact and the consequences of human rights violations." Similarly, mental health theorists may note a possible resonance between psychological diagnosis and international law when arguing that, "trauma occurs because of human rights violations such as physical and/or psychological torture. International civil and human rights movements have cast trauma survivorship as a global movement. . . . For example, protection from traumatic events and the rehabilitation of survivors aligns with the United Nations' (1966) International Covenant on Civil and Political Rights" (Johnson et al. 2012, 104). While there is no doubt that crimes of torture may often result in psychological damage to their individual victims, what has been less often considered is how the phenomenon of *social* trauma relates to the discourse of human rights. The tension resulting from the problematic slip between individual and social trauma is not fully recognized by those who find the category *trauma* to be a useful portal by which to explore questions of human-rights violations. What is necessary is to recognize that human rights operates as an ideological construct emerging from the social imaginary in a way that roughly mirrors the social production of collective trauma. This critical view is meant neither to invalidate the ethical claims that adhere to social trauma nor to diminish the personal experiences of trauma, and the therapeutic apparatuses that are developed to address them, any more than it aims to undermine the project of human rights. However, as I have already discussed, social trauma is primarily a social phenomenon, and thus must be attributed not to "natural" causes in the same way as individual trauma, but must be regarded as a form of social production.

Perpetrator Memories: *Waltz with Bashir*

A group of Israeli soldiers accompany an armored personnel carrier through a Lebanese orchard, as Bach's Harpsichord Concerto No. 5 in F Minor lends a soothing ambience to the pastoral scene. Two near-adolescent boys emerge from

FIGURE 7.1 *A boy fighter shoots a rocket-propelled grenade* (Waltz with Bashir)

behind a tree. One crouches at a distance, raising a rocket-propelled grenade launcher, which he fires [figure 7.1]. *The grenade impacts the vehicle, and the soldiers throw themselves to the ground, firing in the direction of the second boy who is about to fire another grenade. He is killed, and the camera pans back from his bloody body.*

This short scene illustrates a range of motives and strategies employed in the Israeli animated feature film *Waltz with Bashir*, a film that explores the troubled memories of veterans of the 1982 invasion of Lebanon, in particular the director's own memories surrounding the Sabra and Shatila massacre. The scene begins first by framing the action of the soldiers, but then employs a reverse point of view to show the action from the perspective of the Palestinian boy, compelling the audience to inhabit his position as he is shot at by the troops. The scene ends with the camera positioned again from the soldiers' point of view, as they look at the dead boy and the weapon fallen at his side. In a subsequent scene, Folman tells his self-described therapist that he cannot remember having been in the orchard, although other former soldiers have placed him at the scene of the action. The exploration of a reverse position offers a degree of identification with the Palestinian and Lebanese side of the war, even if only momentarily. The later disclosure reveals, however, that this scene is not an actual recollection but a reconstructed or falsified memory, and the ethical content of the scene—the confrontation between the boys and the soldiers and the violence that frames it—fades to the background as questions about memory come to the fore.

Formally, *Waltz with Bashir* is an innovative synthesis of documentary and animation, meaning that frame-animated documentary footage is combined with imaginative animation, giving the text an overall texture of animation while including "authentic" interview materials. The film explores the troubled memories of the director, Ari Folman, about his service as a young man in the Israeli army in 1982. Seeking a context for his own absent memory, he speaks to a range of other former soldiers as well as his therapist and experts, exploring questions of repressed memory. As his investigations develop, Folman becomes fixated on the Sabra and Shatila massacre, in which between several hundred and over 2000 Palestinian refugees (and a number of Lebanese civilians as well) were subject to rape, maiming, and/or slaughter by Lebanese militiamen allied with, and by most interpretations acting with the blessings of, the Israeli military. The film ends with Folman resolving to some extent his confusion about his own role in the invasion and its aftermath.

On one hand driven by a need to reposition the Israeli cultural memory of the war, *Waltz with Bashir* nonetheless gives priority to exploring the problematic realm of memory-discourse over other forms of representation, which results in the film avoiding the starker political and ethical issues that are raised within the experiences of the director, as well as those of other Israeli soldiers in the war. What happens when the claim of trauma is adduced by those who acted as instruments of the same violence that produced this social trauma? Does trauma's potential toward presenting an ethical framework, or articulating a cause, through its recognition of the suffering of the traumatized subject or society, counteract the collapsing of the perpetrator and victim into mirroring molds as casualties of trauma? LaCapra (1999, 723) offers a succinct comment on this problem: "There is the possibility of perpetrator trauma that must itself be acknowledged and in some sense worked through if perpetrators are to distance themselves from an earlier implication in deadly ideologies and practices. Such trauma does not, however, entail the equation or identification of the perpetrator and the victim." In his psychiatric practice, Frantz Fanon encountered and critically empathized with the traumatic repercussions of French colonial police and of soldiers following orders to torture and abuse Algerians who supported independence, but even when reporting these, he insisted upon a clear ethical distinction between those whose role it is to carry out policies that are the primary causes of the conditions of trauma (in Algeria, the colonial forces) and those who are primarily the victims of these policies (who, for Fanon, would include the nationalist resistance to colonialism). Fanon ([1963] 2007, 249) observes that "in this war psychiatric phenomena entailing disorders affecting behavior and thought have taken on importance where those who carry out the 'pacification' are concerned," but reminds his reader that "these same disorders are notable among the 'pacified' population." For Fanon the ethical approach is one that elucidates the "mental disorders" that arise from colonial war, while focusing not on the "pacifiers" (the perpetrators) but on those subject to pacification (the victims).

While establishing a distinction between perpetrator and victim must be held out as an ideal, one may argue that, more broadly speaking, the category of social trauma is too easily stripped of its ethical catalytic energies, leading instead to open competition between groups for the presumed cultural and political capital that the mantle of trauma may offer. We may borrow from John Mowitt (2000) the term "trauma envy," to denote the idea that trauma may give access to a socially desirable status rather than being a conduit for establishing justice. Similarly, Elizabeth and Hester Baer (2003) speak of "postmemory envy" as a way of understanding the desire of children of those who have experienced trauma (e.g., children of Holocaust survivors) to in fact share in claiming this experience. While "postmemory" articulates a secondary (often second-generation) relationship to the initial trauma, the Baers view the magnetism of trauma as a desire for accessing what is seen as authentic in the experience of trauma: "What does it mean, then, to have postmemory envy? Do we truly desire the authenticity, the access, the legitimacy that that entails?" (Baer and Baer 2003, 89). The "authenticity," "access," and "legitimacy" that are sought (whether as "postmemory" or as a more direct claim on experiencing trauma) bring with them a degree of cultural capital that makes accessing the experience of trauma socially valuable. The challenge of aligning trauma with the political, ethical, and legal demands of social justice is nowhere better illuminated than in the phenomenon of texts exploring cultural memory and trauma in wartime experiences of soldiers who are participants in offensive warfare, anti-insurgency, and occupation.

The question of perpetrator trauma and the problem of ethical responsibility define many, perhaps most, American films on the Vietnam War. Not surprisingly, in the body of films on this conflict we may find a wide range of responses, perhaps reflecting the shifting nature of a national consensus on the war. Broadly speaking, the war's end left the project of a national memorialization of the conflict very fraught, with significant opposition to the war predominating many of the narratives that found public accord. By the 1980s, however, the predominant view of the war can be said to have undergone a fairly significant shift, with the figure of the returning Vietnam soldier coming to take a more central role in defining the narratives on the war, and public discourse moved from a focus on the horrors of the war for Vietnamese civilians to one that expressed guilt for the unacknowledged sacrifices of the veterans by representing them as the subject of the war's horrors. In this, prior fixation on spectacular violence such as the My Lai Massacre—which served as only a tiny projection of the more sanitized or "sanctioned" violence of the American war machine—diminished, and instead the trauma of the Tet Offensive, as a definitive moment of military defeat for US forces, came to predominate as the determinative event through which the war was interpreted. In contextualizing *Waltz with Bashir*'s adoption of a framing of cultural trauma, it is instructive to look comparatively at the trends that emerged in US Vietnam War cinema, where we may find a similar problematic of a focus upon trauma-stricken war veterans.

Broadly speaking, the earliest American films on the Vietnam War followed a propagandizing agenda. By the early 1970s, documentary remained the predominant genre for exploring the war's experience, often through individual portraits of soldiers either in Vietnam or back in the United States after their tour of duty. However, more politically oriented films such as *Hearts and Minds* (1974) were significant in consolidating the opposition to the war, through highlighting the racism underlying the views of Vietnamese among policymakers and military leaders, and illustrating widespread antipathy among the soldiers and veterans. This and other similar documentaries took on the political and historical dimensions of the war and gave them a name and face in interviews with officials as well as fighters. Later, *Apocalypse Now* (1978) gave the war a more epic, even mythic, narrative treatment, tinged with traumatic resonance as well. While adapting to the Vietnam experience a key psychologically inflected text on colonialism in Africa, Joseph Conrad's *Heart of Darkness*, the film evacuates the materiality of colonialism and imperialism that the novel acknowledges, and turns the war into a transcendent struggle for the very soul of the United States, the loss of which in Asia constitutes a form of national trauma.

Somewhat counterintuitively, the screenwriter of *Apocalypse Now*, John Milius, cites the Israeli victory in the 1967 as providing him inspiration in scripting the film, reminiscing that after that war, "I was beside myself, transfixed, I couldn't stop imagining the exhilaration of being in a tank racing through burning Arab villages, like a descendant of King David himself. . . . Ariel Sharon became one of my greatest heroes" (Weschler 2005, 72–73). In this, the idea that *Apocalypse Now* is simply antiwar is one that misunderstands the broader ideological landscape from which it emerges, as through the work overlaid visions of burning Vietnamese hamlets and an idolization of military prowess (summarized in the oft-cited line, "I love the smell of Napalm in the morning") find echoes with the figure of General Sharon destroying Arab villages. Margot Norris (1998, 730) argues that, instead of exploring the historical and geopolitical responsibility that lay behind the war, director Francis Ford Coppola made "a film about the Vietnam War that eschews historical verisimilitude and reference in favor of what T. S. Eliot called 'the mythical method.'" This mythical approach, by the very virtue of its avoidance of historical context or specificity, denudes *Apocalypse Now* of an understanding of either the colonial genealogies behind the US war or the neocolonial impetus behind American imperialism in the region. It is noteworthy that while Coppola did shoot one sequence that references Vietnam's colonial legacy, a scene of a dinner party Captain Willard joins in the home of an isolated French colonial settler family, it was not included in the released film. Even if this scene were included (it does appear in the reedited *Apocalypse Now Redux*, released in 2001), the film's mythical charge displaces the political context and replaces it with allegories of binaries such as humanity and animalism, or barbarity and civilization.

Despite the critical impetus behind *Apocalypse Now*, the film's fundamental framing of the narrative as a struggle between barbarity and civilization is by the end deeply racialized; when he finally finds Kurtz, Willard sees that he has gone native and taken on the role of a deity among the jungle tribesmen. In its final narrative point, Willard comes to the realization that he too has become a mirror to Kurtz, and inhabits his new barbaric role by sublimating his American identity for one of a native. Willard, who is shown as already deeply traumatized by his wartime experiences at the beginning of the film, drinking himself into a stupor and destroying his hotel room in the first scene, comes to be even more affected by the "horror" he observes throughout his journey. In the very final scenes of the film, Willard escapes the temple as it is bombed, and presumably reverts back to the identity of an American soldier, even if one imprinted with the traumatizing mark of having briefly shared in the identity of the barbarian. In this turn, the American experience in Vietnam is elevated from a war of specific geopolitical and ideological aims to an existential civilizational crisis which remains fundamentally based upon an ontological distinction between an advanced and humanist West and a primitive and possibly inhuman Other. While *Apocalypse Now* offers a cathartic rejection of the shallow anticommunist propagandizing of the war, and directs its critical questions to essential aspects of American popular and national culture, it nonetheless avoids a historically grounded examination of the specific nature of American involvement in the war, and it does not militate for determining ethical responsibility for the crimes that American forces were to carry out in its course.

As John Carlos Rowe argues about the changes in American public discourse on the Vietnam War, by the mid-1980s the prevalent view had been

> shaped significantly by a "revisionary" desire that aims to redeem the War and thus absolve us of responsibility. One of the strategies of this revisionary desire is to employ the presumably cathartic value of personal confession, anecdote, and relived experience. Ostensibly "realistic," each of these modes of dealing with the War presumes that the contact it offers is equivalent to knowledge and understanding, even when such direct contact yields only clichés or baffled incomprehension. Certainly the best antidote for this tendency to confuse personal accounts and direct impressions with understanding and informed knowledge is careful study of the historical and political forces informing any particular impression or experience.
>
> (ROWE *1986, 127*)

These processes present the war as a stage upon which a "Vietnam" appears that is framed as essentially consumable for American audiences. The presumption of comprehension of this Vietnam is given legitimacy through the audiences' engagement with the modes of confession and anecdote that focus upon the experiences of Vietnam veterans, modes that present themselves as authentic and legitimate due to their link to the lived experiences of those who were there. We see this in numerous later Vietnam narrative films, many of which made claims of being biographical, and all of which made claims of verisimilitude, including *The Deer Hunter* (1978), *Platoon* (1986), *Born on the Fourth of July* (1989), *Jacob's Ladder* (1990), and even *First Blood: Rambo* (1982). In Stanley Kubrick's *Full Metal Jacket* (1987), the claim of true experience is somewhat tempered but replaced by a dystopian view of the war as a venue for psychological damage; nonetheless, once again, "Vietnam" is a stage upon which these purportedly humanistic questions are played out.

A similar dynamic is well illustrated in the representational activity in Israel regarding the country's 1982 invasion of Lebanon and subsequent occupation. The war in 1982 quickly became deeply unpopular and was the first significant national conflict to which a vocal and prominent proportion of Israelis were opposed. And yet, this invasion also led to the long Israeli occupation of the south of Lebanon, which lasted from 1982 until 2000. The occupation, over time also faced significant public opposition, largely due to the steady stream of casualties that resulted from an increasingly effective military resistance movement inside Lebanon. The sense of an intractable war facing a determined and able foe only allowed such criticism to continue to take hold. In this sense, the invasion and subsequent occupation came to be termed by many Israelis "Israel's Vietnam," in the sense of being a misguided war that went on for too long, with reasons that were by the end far too obscure to enjoy continued public support.

Waltz with Bashir fits within particular trends in Israeli cinematic works on the Lebanon war, and belongs to a group of Israeli films produced within a year of one another, all of which address questions of memory and trauma as relating to the experiences of Israeli soldiers—these also include Joseph Cedar's *Beaufort* (2007) and Samuel Moaz's *Lebanon* (2009). These are not the first films Israelis have made about the war—earlier, in the 1980s and early 1990s, other works (e.g., *Ricochets* [*Shtei Etzbaot Mitzidon*], 1986; *Cup Final* [*Gmar Gav'ia*] 1991; *The Cherry Season* [*Onat Haduvdevanim*], 1991) were produced that examined the same war by what Raz Yosef (2011b, 67) terms representing the Israeli soldier as an "'enlightened occupier' who 'shoots and weeps.'" However, what differentiates the later set of films from those of the earlier period is the introduction of a new frame of narration, one that is infused by the discourse of cultural memory and social trauma, in reflecting upon the memory of the war. *Lebanon* participates in a similar framing of the "fighter as witness," a framing that is even more effective than *Waltz with Bashir* through the aesthetic conceit of staging the film's entire action within an Israeli tank, or as seen through the tank's scopic devices. The film is structured as a road movie, beginning with an Israeli tank entering Lebanon as part of the 1982 invasion, and follows the actions of the invasion through the experiences of the tank crew. In turns the film gives the tank crew a range of roles allegorizing responses to the war: the paralyzing fear of one, the brash machismo of another, and so on. Eventually the tank takes on as a prisoner of war a Syrian soldier, who allows for the film to present points of crossing perspective and identification. Through the trip taken by the tank crew, the film presents the experiences of the soldiers as bewildering, traumatizing, and at times surreally beyond comprehension.

In *Lebanon* the war is presented as a conflict that is not essentially Israel's, and the Israeli fighters are presented as ethically uninvolved observers in a fight that is being carried out barbarically between other parties with whom they have no particular affiliation. The Syrian soldier is taken by the Israelis because he has been taken prisoner by an Israeli-allied Lebanese militia, and the Israelis come to realize that he is likely to be brutalized or killed by the Lebanese, so they protect him. *Lebanon* does nothing to explain the nature of the alliances that Israel maintained in the Lebanese civil war, nor does it explore the long history of previous Israeli involvement and military intervention in that war. Instead of relying upon memory discourse and themes of personal trauma, *Lebanon* situates its frame upon an aestheticized "pure" experience of the war. As a result it circumvents any critical assessment of the war's conduct or rationale, much less examining the manner of its prosecution. If the war is now charged with a degree of moral ambiguity, this ambiguity is linked more to the experience of the war by the soldiers than by the political, ideological, or ethical questions that surround it.

Where *Lebanon* remembers the war through a limited and fragmentary set of storylines framed through the necessarily constrained visual register afforded by the interior of a tank, Joseph Cedar's *Beaufort* presents a similarly boundaried view of the war—set claustrophobically within the walls of a military base—as a setting for carrying out a character study of the qualities of an ideal soldier. *Beaufort* takes as a setting the Israeli outpost established on the strategic bluff where the ruins of Beaufort Castle, a remnant of the Crusader kingdoms in the region, still stand. The ancient fort was a key Israeli base that served as a military center in the administration of the Israel occupation of southern Lebanon between 1982 and 2000. The film is set in the last days of this occupation regime, just before Israel all but fully withdrew from Lebanon, after a long war of attrition and a mounting daily roster of Israeli dead and wounded at the hands of Lebanese resistance groups who fought against the occupation. At heart, the film is a work of mourning for the lost purpose of the Israeli military role in the occupation of Lebanon, as well as a search to recuperate a sense of honor for the conduct if not the mission of this occupation.

The film trains a tight focus upon the soldiers who man the base, allowing a few of the ensemble to take more leading roles in the action leading to the withdrawal. At the center of the story is the base commander,
Liraz, an aggressive young officer who is admired by some of the soldiers
but kept at a distance by others. Liraz acts as a cipher for a certain set of
ideals in what is presented as the Israeli military ethos. Other soldiers
in the film remark on his personal history; as an enlistee he had wanted
badly to join the officer corps but was passed over, and when he took the
entrance exam he failed to gain a place in the academy. However, his personal perseverance impressed his superiors enough to grant him a place
nonetheless, and eventually he achieved the top marks in his class. In
this way he reflects a trope of outcasts who must prove themselves with
instinctual prowess rather than intellect—the scrappy underdog who
must constantly substantiate himself against great odds. As a result, however, Liraz is burdened by a sense of *ressentiment* that is first evinced as
resulting from the orders he is given to assume a defensive posture in
response to attacks on the base by the Lebanese resistance. Several times
he begs his superiors to allow him to aggressively engage these adversar-
ies, and at one point declares in a strategy meeting that, "We have become
an army of pussies. We're getting shafted. They're wasting our men. And
your answer is protection—one more layer of concrete? Let's go to [the
Lebanese village of] Arnoon, we'll show them. If we are staying—and
I don't see us leaving—then let us do the job." While the other officers are
visibly annoyed by his impetuous interjection, the commander chairing
the meeting shows no little empathy for him and says, "In principle, you're
right." Liraz's brooding later conflicts with the order for withdrawal, as he
repeatedly announces that he will refuse to accept the decision and will
not begin to dismantle the base. At one point he angrily complains about
the fact that he will have to live forever with being remembered as the
commander who oversaw the retreat from Beaufort. At another point he
physically removes a bomb-sniffing dog from the truck that is to evacuate
his trainer, as if unable to face the fact that the base is indeed being closed
down. However, at the end, Liraz has a change of heart and accedes to the
finality of the command. He dutifully if forlornly oversees the withdrawal
and the demolition of the base. In the final scene he joins the other soldiers in rejoicing emotionally once they have crossed over the border back
into Israel.

Beaufort largely works to reinforce nationalist mythologies around the
Israeli army, mourning the realpolitik that limited its role in Lebanon during the occupation. While the film explores with some nuance the emotional
responses of the ensemble of soldiers who are fated to spend long periods in
the isolated fortress, it lacks any substantive engagement with the political or
ideological context that has led to their deployment in that place. Through

the film, director Joseph Cedar gives voice to criticism of tactical decisions made by absent and at times incompetent commanding officers; however, he does so in a way that again avoids any substantive self-criticism concerning the rationale for the Israeli presence in Lebanon. Instead, *Beaufort* enacts a celebration of the sacrifices of individual soldiers, idealizing an individualist and rebellious spirit embodied in Liraz's character as the ideal type for the national warrior. As a memory text of the Lebanese war, the film enacts a much more severe erasure of the broader repercussions of the war, aestheticizing the military ethos and mourning its constraint by national and international political considerations.

As Raz Yosef (2011a, 141) has argued, "*Lebanon* and *Beaufort* seek to release the Israeli psyche—and especially that of the Israeli soldier—from the trauma of guilt and responsibility." Both films posit the experience of war as transformative; however, neither gives voice to any sentiment of guilt or raises questions of responsibility for the war. Yosef views these films as "releasing the Israeli psyche" of these burdens primarily as a consequence of their lack of any reference to these concerns—elsewhere he has suggested that the Israeli cinema of the this (early twenty-first century) period "highlights a radical discontinuity between history and memory" and that this cinema "is thus a melancholic cinema that bears witness to the crises of historical national memory in Israel" (Yosef 2011a, 5). While the aforementioned films on Lebanon are explicitly or implicitly framed by questions of cultural memory, *Waltz with Bashir* instead employs social trauma as a productive discourse for interpreting the war. I will examine how this move attempts a cross-affiliating identification with the war's victims, but ultimately masks or sidesteps a serious discussion of the ethics of or responsibility for the war and the subsequent military occupation. I share with Raya Morag the view that this film is an exemplary representation of perpetrator trauma, of which she argues (2013, 216), "the perpetrator complex is determined by the irresolvable relationship between the perpetrator and society; the unpredictable ecology of perpetrator trauma; instability in relation to guilt, and the propensity to remain on the periphery of collective moral responsibility." In this sense, the rise of perpetrator trauma in Israeli cultural memory can be considered alongside other more unsettling aspects of the broader turn to social trauma—as with American memory discourse on Vietnam, perpetrator trauma emerges as the paradigmatic framework for discussing the 1982 invasion and reflects a broader trend in public discourse about the war inside Israel, as commentators increasingly made use of the discourse of social trauma in discussing the war. For example, Raz Yosef (2011b, 66, 68) describes this as a war that "has been denied entry into a shared national past," and having "left searing marks on Israeli national memory," making it "one of the most traumatic wars in the history of the State of Israel." These references to "national memory" and a "national past" are only broadly and commonly in evidence in the years following the war's initial prosecution. The notion of the war as being "traumatic" is itself novel, especially when one remembers that in comparison with the other major Israeli wars of 1948, 1967, and 1973, the invasion of Lebanon involved little if any threat to Israeli national territory and caused the least disruption to daily life inside Israel. The fact that this conflict is articulated as being "one of the most traumatic" of Israel's wars invites our attention—what specifically undergirds the claim of trauma, and why is it productive to speak of trauma in relation to this war?

Waltz with Bashir uses the personal memory of the filmmaker Ari Folman as a prism through which problematics of Israeli cultural memory of the 1982 invasion are explored. The film moves between present-day discussions between Folman and other former soldiers who served in 1982, as well as discussions with his personal therapist and a specialist on the psychology of trauma, and scenes that illustrate some of the war memories of the former fighters. The recurring theme of repressed memory—or as it is put more than once in the film, of memories "not stored in my system" (figure 7.2)— comes to allegorize broader tensions between memory and forgetfulness as they relate to the events of that war. The experiences in Lebanon, the film intimates, lack a social context or value, and thus have been pushed into the recesses of a repressed national consciousness. But these memories present problems for the veterans, and Israel more broadly, as signified by nightmares and other eruptions into their daily lives. The film's title sequence depicts one such nightmare: a pack of feral dogs run through the streets of central Tel Aviv, terrifying the city's residents before gathering beneath the window of the former soldier whose dream it is (figure 7.3). The man explains that the dream is drawn from his war experience of shooting Lebanese village dogs

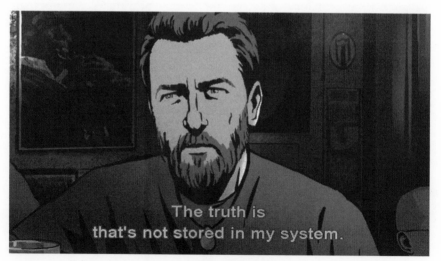

FIGURE 7.2 *Folman can't remember* (Waltz with Bashir)

FIGURE 7.3 *Dogs terrorize Tel Aviv* (Waltz with Bashir)

as the Israeli army entered villages. Although the number of dogs in the dream—twenty-six—matches the number of dogs that he shot, the scene is more than simply an exercise in illustrating a repressed guilt over the killing of the dogs, the dream operates as a metaphor for the repression of cultural memory of the war: dead yet revived, this memory runs wild through society, terrifying those with whom it comes into contact.

The film's prioritization of cultural memory over other frameworks for reflecting upon the experiences of Folman, or for more broadly addressing the national trauma that the Lebanon war represented for Israel, in part feels intrinsic to the chosen form of the work: not only the animated-documentary hybrid on a broader level, but also in terms of the color scheme, the grain of the image, the electronic music soundtrack and so on. In some ways the film echoes another experimental animation work, Richard Linklater's *Waking Life* (2001), and although they use different animation techniques, visually the two works have much in common. Linklater's film, a meandering follow-up to his first feature, *Slackers* (1991), is also an animated work based largely on dialogues and interviews. The two films share in their focus upon a series of discussions with epistemologically unstable narrators whose imaginations are visually represented through the animation. What this cinematic technique affords is an intensive visual foregrounding of imaginative and memory processes that itself produces a critique of stable and objective narration. The outcome is one where memories may fill the screen, but what is viewed is fundamentally subject to doubt, since the film itself is predicated upon the fragility and unreliability of memory as a psychic process and as an index of the truth.

As the filmmaker Folman interviews former comrades and attempts to piece together a narrative of his own memories of the invasion, his position shifts from being at first a witness to the putative effects of trauma on his friends, to realizing a degree of traumatic resonance in his own unstable memories of the war. The film's internal metadiscourse, which includes "expert" views on the nature of traumatic memory, treats memory as a burden. Folman and his former comrades bear the undesirable weight of their war memory, which seeps into their lives, despite having been repressed. As Folman slowly regains memories of his time in Beirut, the film intimates that he comes closer to establishing an objective truth, which is affirmed through the testimony of others. More conventional approaches to the role of memory and truth—such as those found in many if not most crime, detective, or courtroom dramas—link the restoration of memory and its contribution to establishing the truth as being fundamental to the pursuit of justice. How many films end with a memory disclosure in a courtroom that serves the cause of exonerating the innocent or convicting the guilty? By comparison, in perpetrator trauma narratives, memory is often seen as both a problem and a solution for the troubled or unstable psyche of the protagonist, who suffers the burden of his repressed memories until finally being released from their hold by a cathartic rupture. *Waltz with Bashir* adopts just such a framing, setting the restoration of memory not as a precondition to establishing justice for the victims of Sabra and Shatila, but rather as a problem to be solved for Folman and his comrades.

In comparison with *Beaufort*'s hermeticism (which lacks any referent outside of the community of Israeli soldiers), in *Waltz with Bashir* there are powerful moments of empathy and cross-identification with Lebanese and Palestinian counterparts throughout the film. For example, the journalist Ben Yishai notes that inside the camp he saw the body of a little girl who was "like my own daughter," and also relates images of the massacre to those of the Warsaw Ghetto rebellion. At another point, Folman's therapist notes that his sensation of guilt over the invasion of 1982 may be rooted in the fact that his parents were Holocaust survivors, and that his "interest in those [Palestinian] camps is actually in the 'other' camps." Folman is by no means the first to allow for such inversions—in 1982, Primo Levi famously responded to a reporter's question about Sabra and Shatila with the comment, "Everybody is somebody's Jew" (Perugini and Zucconi 2012). This rearticulation of how victim and perpetrator are arranged, and the ethical charge behind the realization of the potential of such inversions, opens a possible reversal of view that is profound as it may be unsettling to some viewers. However, while Folman includes and certainly highlights the possibilities of such reversals, the continual return to the veteran's traumatic memories forecloses on the opportunity to more richly develop them. Folman's question is: Where was I when the Sabra and Shatila massacre took place? The question reflects on the Israeli military endeavor as a whole and by implication on Israeli society more broadly. His unresolved memories produce guilt for him.

He retains only one image that is associated with the massacre, a scene that replays itself several times—he and other soldiers are bathing in the sea off of Beirut, he walks out of the sea; the final version of this hallucination has him walking up a street and coming face to face with a crowd of Arab women who rush toward him and pass him, leaving him standing alone in an alleyway.

The image, as he finds out, is likely false—he comes to discover that his actual position during the massacre was on a building's roof nearby, while none of his comrades recall having swum in the sea off of Beirut. The false memory is one that places him within the action, and which seems to implicate him in the violence in some way. The uncertain memory has placed a sense of unresolved responsibility upon him, one that he knows not how to shoulder. A painful question haunts his memory: Am I, too, ethically implicated in the massacre? Folman, assisted by the overview of experts and the memories of the other soldiers, learns that on that night he and other soldiers were given orders to shoot illuminating flares over the camp, but that he was not in the camp itself. His memory problems are due to the fact that he has condemned himself without knowing quite why. In the assessment of his therapist, "you can't remember the massacre because in your opinion, the murderers and those around them are the same circle . . . unwillingly you took on the role of a Nazi." Yosef (2011a, 153) compelling has argued that this indexing of the Holocaust "equates the victimizer and victim by linking the massacre at Sabra and Shatila to the Jewish trauma of the Holocaust." What is fascinating here is that this problematic but powerful allegorical relationship between Palestinian and Jewish trauma is not mobilized in order to give identity to the victims of Sabra and Shatila. Rather, this link allows Folman to occupy the space of the victim even while acting as a perpetrator. Again, Yosef notes, "Folman's position as victim does not allow for the possibility that Israeli-Jews are themselves responsible for creating non-Jewish victims" (153).

With this disclosure, Folman's friend Ori Sivan (who is described in the film's press materials as the former's "personal shrink, what one may call his ready-made therapist") then assuages him: "You were there firing flares, but you didn't carry out the massacre" (figure 7.4) (www.waltzwithbashir.com). In this, the final scene pertaining to Folman's quest for understanding his personal role, the film offers us a form of resolution. The self-identified therapist has diagnosed his patient, and discovered the kernel of his neurosis—the patient has taken on an excessive sense of responsibility, and will only be at peace when he realizes that he was wrong to view himself "in the same circle" as the Phalange who carried out the massacre. This scene posits Folman as an unfortunate and perhaps unnecessary victim of his own memory; a sort of collateral damage or a casualty of friendly fire—Yosef (2011a, 153) critically views the film as constructing his character as an "'innocent victim' of history." Morag (2013, 132) follows this view in terming Folman's character a "complicit indirect perpetrator." However, it is worth noting that the claim

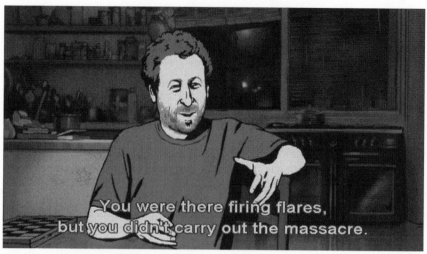

FIGURE 7.4 *A therapeutic diagnosis* (Waltz with Bashir)

of poor memory is one that was mobilized by Israeli soldiers much earlier. The British reporter Robert Fisk, in his history of the Lebanese war, *Pity the Nation*, describes his colleague Loren Jenkins confronting an Israeli soldier in a stadium near the camp, where survivors of the massacre are being interrogated the day after, by Israeli officers who suspect them of being "terrorists." The reporter urgently asks the soldier, "Why don't you tell us what's happened?" The soldier replies, "*I don't remember*. I have no idea what's been happening here" (Fisk 1992, 368; emphasis added). This exchange is recounted to illustrate the manner in which Israeli soldiers—who in Fisk's determination certainly "*knew*" about the massacre as it happened—employed evasive memory claims when questioned about it afterwards. Faulty memory, either as conceit or as symptom, has allowed for an evasion of the question of responsibility. What the film shows is that the reconstruction of memory may be done in a way that still evades such difficult questions.

In the film, one hint at addressing Israeli responsibility comes in the grotesque caricature of Ariel Sharon eating an immense breakfast. This and other indications in the film place primary Israeli guilt the shoulders of only a small circle of over-ambitious leaders. This view has its merits, as the responsibility held by Sharon and others among the Israeli leadership was recognized even at the time. Seth Anziska reports that the US Middle East envoy, Morris Draper, broke with rules of diplomatic decorum in confronting the Israeli defense minister Ariel Sharon just after the massacre, shouting, "You should be ashamed. The situation is absolutely appalling. They're killing children! You have the field completely under your control and are therefore responsible for that area" (Anziska 2012). Beyond Sabra and Shatila, the widespread violence carried out by the Israeli military against civilians across Lebanon

is telescoped within two black-humor musical montages, where little indica-
tion of the scale of civilian suffering is offered. Paradoxically, the massacre
at Sabra and Shatila counterintuitively results in the obfuscation of a discussion of the broader destruction the invasion wrought, and the focus on the
violence of the Phalange serves to offset the representation of the violence
carried out by the Israeli forces.

At the end, the cause of the suffering of the Israeli soldiers is tied first to
a hazy set of decisions made by the upper leadership, and to the capricious
violence of the Phalange, who are coded as falling beyond the pale of rational
politics. Rather than explore in any way the political and ideological basis of
the Phalange, and avoiding any substantive linking of the rise of the Phalange
to Israeli policy toward Lebanon, the film instead relies only on painting the
group as irrational, fanatical devotees of Bashir (Gemayel, president-elect of
Lebanon and senior member of the Phalange), driven mad by his assassination. The film's sole analysis of the Phalange's motivations occurs when one
character says, "they even felt an eroticism for [Bashir], totally erotic . . . it
was as if their wife was murdered, this was about family honor, which runs
deep." The interpretation offered sets the violence into a realm of irrational,
primitive cultural traits, tendencies for which the Israeli soldiers are not to
be condemned in a substantive manner. The Orientalist frame of the analysis
is not problematized, either in the sexualization of love for a leader, or in the
reference to honor and violence, both of which are tired cultural clichés that
are conjured to rationalize a view of Arab societies as fundamentally irrational; as if honor has no analogous value in the military culture of the Israeli
armed forces.

Returning again to the therapist's final comments, reassuring Folman
that he was situated outside of the circle of responsibility for the massacre,
it is revealing that just as it is raised, the question of why Folman and other
troops were commanded to shoot flares is abandoned and not explored further. Instead, almost immediately, the film makes a sharp aesthetic turn with
the unforgettable ending sequence—comprising about two minutes of raw
video footage from 1982 of mourning Palestinian women returning to the
camps, crying out while surrounded by bodies of those killed. The effect of
the video footage obliterates the thread of investigation that could have led to
an exploration of the question of responsibility, and spectacularizes the crime
of the massacre and the suffering of those who survived. While viscerally
powerful, the ending intimates a peculiar catharsis—is the video the unlock-
ing of Folman's memories? Divested of direct responsibility, is Folman only
now able to view the stark brutality of what happened there? It is true that the
choice of ending acts as an amplified revision of the orchard scene, where the
audience is drawn into a new mode of relation and even identification with
the victims. However, the catharsis triggered by this sequence overwhelms
the unsettled and troubling memories that the film discloses. Even while

including this scene, Folman objectifies the victims rather than engaging with them as the haunted subjects of the film's search for truth. In this, it is noteworthy that Folman neglects what the Palestinians in the footage—who speak for the first time in the film—are themselves saying.

As the news videographer walks through the camp, littered as it is with bodies, one woman looks directly into the camera and cries out, "Sawwaru, sawwaru, sawwaru, waynkum?" (figure 7.5). A contextual translation of her call would be: "Photograph all you want, but where were you when it happened?" However, the film does not subtitle the Arabic spoken by the woman; she uses the imperative, demanding that the videographer shoot, photograph, document, but also confronts her or him with the fact that the world was not able to prevent the event from occurring. Although the woman later addresses this to "al-'Arab," meaning the Arab world, her demand challenges the videographer, and by extension Folman the filmmaker, and no less the audience, to themselves take responsibility. It is a challenge to which Folman seems unable to rise. While the ending is somewhat open to interpretation, the view that it exonerates the Israeli soldiers is not uncommon: for example, Garrett Stewart (2010, 61) reads the final sequence as affirming that Folman (and the other Israeli troops) were not themselves responsible but rather indicates how he was at "the truer remove of his disengaged complicity: that of an emotionally detached onlooker forced finally to see." In this reading, Folman positions himself as a witness and even victim, rather than as a perpetrator, a move that is justified by approaching memory as a traumatic burden when narrating the war's experience, rather than using memory in pursuit of justice for the victims.[1]

FIGURE 7.5 *A massacre survivor shouts at the videographer* (Waltz with Bashir)

Meg McLagan (2008, 191) suggests that cinema and other visual media play an increasingly significant role in framing human rights matters: "In today's globally mediated world, visual images play a central role in determining which violences are redeemed and which remain unrecognized." In McLagan's formulation, "northern human rights activists . . . have built a formidable transnational communications infrastructure through which 'local' actors' claims (often, although not always, from the global South) are formatted into human rights 'issues'" (191). Thus, human rights violations are often framed as problems endemically situated within non-Western societies, and justice presumably demands their being made visible for audiences located in the metropolitan West. McLagan's critical perspective on the relationship of northern activists and organizations to subjects located within the global South offers a postcolonial framing that situates the representation of human rights issues within a globalized context divided along developmental and historical lines. At the other extreme, cinematic productions on war in the region have come to exemplify the way in which social trauma discourse and human rights discourse may overlap, and how a humanist reversal of perspective offers some possibility of an ethical acceptance of responsibility, but also betrays the manner in which the discourse of social trauma may also serve to obscure engagement with questions of human rights violations. *Waltz with Bashir* intrudes upon this setting by occupying a prominent space through which the metropole has constituted memory discourse on the 1982 invasion of Lebanon. Rather than fitting the instrumental aims of northern solidarity activists who seek to generate metropolitan support for victims of human rights abuses, the film diminishes the unfulfilled human rights claims of Palestinian and Lebanese victims through its focus on the trauma of the perpetrator.

Returning to the Vietnam context, American cinematic responses to the war often contributed to refining the cultural memory of the conflict along lines that replaced historical specificity and understanding with mythologization, and which often gave priority to the victimization of American soldiers with only passing recognition of the broader impact of the war on Vietnamese or other Southeast Asian victims. In response to this, John Carlos Rowe insists that a turn away from such practices is necessary, insisting that,

> this is not to say that "Vietnam" is undecidable or unrepresentable. Quite the contrary, "Vietnam" has in many ways already been decided in this culture and is endlessly represented in very familiar and recognizable ways. What is needed, however, is a better understanding of the social arts by which these versions of Vietnam are designed and then accepted by Americans anxious to substitute myth for knowledge, understanding for responsibility.
>
> (ROWE *1986, 150*)

Similarly, in *Waltz with Bashir*, despite Folman's exploration of a reversal of perspective, which is woven into the visual language of the film but which also enters into the film's elaboration of a cultural memory of the war, the film's use of personal and cultural memory comes to act as a screen that fore-closes on the question of responsibility. The narrative of the film is deeply predicated upon a search for resolution that releases the characters from the ethical burden of memory, without directing the investigation into difficult questions of the broader, more structural responsibility of Israel in the war. Folman quite poetically reflects the fragility of memory and the threat of oblivion, while also intimating the lingering irresolutions that such repres-sion of memory may bring. In so doing, the film participates in a broader tendency in Israeli public discourse to remove any question of ideology or historical relationships in setting out an understanding of the prosecution of the war. The aesthetic conceits of both *Beaufort* and *Lebanon* frame the Israeli perspective as isolated and separated from the broader effects of the war, and even more, the regional context and its history. By emphasizing a memory- and trauma-based framing of the war, *Waltz with Bashir* projects an ascendant view that Israeli soldiers, and indirectly, Israeli society, were in a fundamental sense victims of the war themselves, not willful participants whose ideological and political interests were often served by the invasion and what proceeded from it. By avoiding an ethical consideration of the war's crimes, *Waltz with Bashir* produces a false correspondence, even a degree of equivalence, between the victims of the war and its perpetrators—betraying what is perhaps most dangerous about trauma production and the spread of social trauma discourse: a loss of ethical clarity and political purpose.

{ Conclusion }

Multitudinous Memory

REVOLUTIONS AND POSTCINEMATIC
CULTURAL MEMORY

Within and against this infernal machine, which globalizes culture
at the very same time that it ravages and perverts its values, there is
always a ghost, an insurgent spirit. Yet while the circuit of cultural
communication is perfect and self-sufficient, this spirit can only
proceed by nourishing itself on things extraneous and other: bodily
desire, the freedom of the multitudes, the power of languages.

—ANTONIO NEGRI, *(Negri and Henninger 2007)*

The golden age of cinema, and perhaps with it the age of the predominance of
cinema memory, is fading, and the definitive role of cinema in developing cultural memory is no longer unchallenged. Nonetheless, the continuing impact
of cinematic work on the constitution of cultural memory may yet remain
significant, as culture industries mutate the art form to include new genres
and aesthetic experiences—it may well be far too premature to speak of the
death of cinema. However, what is more significant in understanding what
has been termed the *postcinematic* is the range of competitors that cinema
now faces in remaining the determinative form of visual representation that
produces cultural memory. As Shaviro (2010, 2) argues, "We are now witnessing the emergence of a different media regime, and indeed of a different mode
of production, than those which dominated the twentieth century. Digital
technologies, together with neoliberal economic relations, have given birth
to radically new ways of manufacturing and articulating lived experience."

This transformation is fundamentally a technological one, in the same
way that cinema itself dismantled the hierarchies defined by prior technologies, and through its own innovations produced a new language for comprehending and representing the changing visual-emotive sphere of human
social experience in the early twentieth century. In the current postcinematic

landscape, the technological is married to other fundamental—even if largely coincidental—shifts: particularly in the areas of political and social mobilization, and the rise of new circuits of transnational cultural circulation. Even more significant has been the emergence of new expectations on the part of viewing publics, producing unprecedented links between areas of the world, from those under the deadening blanket of paternalistic authoritarianism, to those in areas termed "free," but which have found their avenues of cultural expression delimited by conformist consumerism, hypercapitalism, and the oligarchical consolidation of political power.

The convulsions of an ever more crisis-ridden global capitalist economy, along with eruptions of persistent popular resistance movements and aspirant revolutionary constellations, especially since the first years of this century, raise questions about the continued stability of a world system that has come to define global economic, cultural and social relationships over the course of the last two centuries or more. The environmental crisis that beckons on our planetary horizon raises even more urgent questions about the presumed stability of this world order. When the transformative shifts do come, which following Foucault (1970, 168) we may imagine as *epistemic* (in that they are part of a system that organizes "the conditions of possibility of all knowledge"), they will have both temporal and spatial dimensions. This epistemic configuration is already transmuting, bringing with it new representational strategies that serve to archive, catalog, and interpret the increasingly complex formations that are emerging on the historical horizon. Already, recent uprisings and social struggles arising in both the advanced metropolitan centers of this world system, as well as those in certain more "peripheral" settings (whether termed as Green Movements or an Arab Spring) have demanded new manners of representing, and hence remembering, these events, which have already been appropriated within the new conditions for memory and trauma discourse. While cinema continues to play a role in developing cultural memory—as with Jehane Noujaim's *The Square* (*Al-Maydan*, 2013) does with the Egyptian uprising of 2011—it does so alongside of, and informed by, the forms of cultural memory articulated by these newer media.

Putting paid to the conventions of sacred defense cinema, in the course of the mass demonstrations in Iran after the 2009 presidential elections, mobile-phone video recordings came to play a defining role in producing narratives of the events on the ground, especially in the absence of more traditional modes of news reporting. Discrete acts of defiance and repression were captured by cameras discreetly angled by street-level passersby, or held furtively out of apartment windows. These scenes, when uploaded for viewing across the globe, acted as powerful gestures of witnessing, despite appearing to be lacking in analysis or context. The videos were used for various ends; some fed into a genre of web activity that may be termed "prosecutorial," in that anonymous activists published screen shots of acts of violence that allowed for the identification of police or military agents; their names would be then listed along with other information. Some of these individuals were charged publicly with having committed various crimes against protestors. While these investigatory activities adopted the language of legal proceedings, the justice-seeking aims of them were limited to serving as a symbolic call for action. Some works were elegiac, others romantically nationalist, while many further works confounded genre expectations and were circulated as testaments to the seeming impossibility of reliance upon former genres and conventions as interpretive frameworks for the events.

Beyond the witnessing and testimonial use of these videos, another set of representational activities aimed to intervene on the development of cultural memory around the events. Circulating online, the short "witnessing" videos that were posted daily were then often subject to editing and recirculation in the form of montages, often set to music, which aimed to play upon the emotive dimensions of the events. Rather than follow the immediacy of the raw footage that emerged on a daily basis, these videos instead tended to take a broader view of the materials, crafting from them a canvas of themes and narratives that set out to define the way the events would be remembered. In the face of the defeat of the activists, in subsequent anniversaries and commemorations of the 2009 protests, new videos have been produced, often with higher production values and original music, that continue to refine the manner in which these original images contribute to the cultural memory of the demonstrations. From these materials cinematic works such as Bani Khoshnudi's *The Silent Majority Speaks* (2010) have appeared, which draw upon this catalog of visual materials in an attempt to curate them towards a more definitive statement on how to remember these events. Iran's 2009 uprising is thus one of the first major national political movements the cultural memory of which will be defined by the use of not only new media but also new forms of distribution, dissemination, and commentary. The same broad constellation of actors and media have come to define events in other contexts—the uprisings in Tunisia, Libya, and Egypt, in the long civil war in Syria, and in the 2014 Israeli war on Gaza.

While it is still early to summarize the role of postcinematic media in the development in cultural memory of conflicts such as these, what appears to be certain is that in the face of these developments, the role of cinema in refining and elaborating upon the discursive parameters for remembering social conflicts is fundamentally changing. Viewers had these images seared to memory long before any cinematic production could do so—cinematic works can only emerge in the aftermath of these visual imprints. Cinema memory has been displaced by these new forms of visually mediated memories; or at very least, cinema memory must now share a place within the social imaginary where once it was uncontested. The phenomenon of social trauma, linked as it has been to the mass mediations of cinema memory, is no less defined by these new forms of representation and signification; indeed they may serve only to increase the intense competition over supremacy in the field of social trauma. Whether in the cycle of representations that emerge from the rubble of another Israeli attack on Gaza, or in the confusion of claims and counterclaims that emerge from a massacre on the streets of Cairo, the discourse of social trauma appears only to be more powerful as enunciated in the stream of mediated images that result from the traumatic event, and circulate in the aftermath.

The postcinematic has been defined in a variety of ways, but it most often relates to the emergence of forms of new, often digital, visual representational media that in some sense undermine or transform the primacy of what may be termed the cinematic. In some instances, postcinema has been treated as a form of intervention into the cinema form by technologies that are not "native" to the original film-based technologies of the medium. For example, Beatriz Sarlo (2003, 304) has argued that "the best works of postcinema are commercials and video-clips [music videos]"; in her framing, postcinema related primarily to the revolutionary forms of editing and montage that these genres introduced in the 1980s. In other readings of the term, in the 1980s the introduction of computer-generated sets into which the live action of cinematic works was sutured or still earlier incarnations of computer-generated effects within the medium came to be viewed as representing forms of postcinema. As these and much more advanced digital or computer-generated elements have been increasingly assimilated into the cinematic form, the term has come to take a different application. As digital media begin to fundamentally deviate from the classical narrative forms associated with cinema (for example in narrative-driven computer games), as well as exploring more and more unfamiliar visual aesthetics and techniques that have no relation to the film-based cinematic form (for example, with pixelation effects), we may begin to envision a postcinematic visual cultural field that is no longer dominated by the values of the narrative cinematic form. In its most stark elaboration, postcinema is used to proclaim the imminent death of cinema as it has been known—for example, Jeffrey Pence (2003, 238) states unambiguously that, "In terms of cultural and institutional dominance, cinema faces a future that is lesser than its past. In Hegelian terms, we have reached the End of Cinema."

It is now commonplace to remind ourselves of the degree to which these new digital media offer alternatives to the economic models that defined the cinematic age—the capital-heavy motion-picture industry that employs dozens of specialists in the production of a single work, the limited and highly commercialized distribution networks that often defined the degree to which a film work would be accessible to broad publics, whether in the cinema or on television. Yet, as I have already argued, any prediction of the death of cinema either as a culturally relevant form or even as a commercially successful venture would be far too premature at the time of this writing. Instead, by speaking of postcinema, what we come to better appreciate is the manner in which the cultural capital that was commanded by the cinema form is shifting and the extent to which often younger global audiences find their consumption of cinema works to be framed by their access to other media—computer games, mobile phone videos posted on the internet, and so on. "We are now at the end(s) of the cinematic. This is being registered within cinema, even as cinema remains strongly influential across all of cineman's inheritors. (Hence, the times are 'post-cinematic' and not 'anti-' or 'non-cinematic'.) Thus, gaming, all things interactive, the music video, and so forth, all remain hugely informed by cinematography, but they move away from its technological limitations" (Bowman [2014]). Meanwhile, cinema attempts to incorporate the new technological advancements within itself; for example, Brian De Palma's *Redacted* (2007) uses the conceit of appearing to be a compilation of amateur video footage, shot by US soldiers in the lead up to and aftermath of the rape of an Iraqi girl and the resulting massacre of an extended family of Iraqi civilians—an account of an actual atrocity formally masquerading as mediated postcinematically. But in efforts such as these, one discerns a lack of authenticity and thus failure when compared to the more visceral experience afforded by viewing non-cinematic "real" footage, such as the video shot from a US Apache helicopter of the deliberate targeting of a number of Iraqis (including two journalists) in a series of attacks in July 2007, which was released by the Internet activist group Wikileaks. The Wikileaks video, in its own global circulations, has had an impact that far outweighs that of De Palma's film, and even for those who have seen both works, the images of the former video set a much more indelible imprint upon the memory.

The rise of a postcinematic cultural ethos coincides with new constellations of global capital accumulation, as well as new forms of resistance to it. Just as the rise of cinema coincided with the heights of the colonial period, drawing the early stages of the narrative film form into an intimate relation with ideologies of imperialism and colonialism, so too does the postcinematic period reflect the complexities of the new economic and ideological formations that coincide with the technological innovations that are at the heart of these new representational regimes. As Jeffrey Pence (2003, 238) suggests, "postcinema/postmemory may be read both as a symptom of, and as an indispensible strategy for, our new historical epoch of globalization." For Pence, the question is not how postcinematic visual culture will contribute to the management of memory, but rather how postcinematic media themselves align with what he is terming postmemory: "If film's felt ability to model and remake the world seemed to deliver reality to our collective control, newer technologies like video seem to deliver reality to our individual control. This possibility destabilises our notions of what memory might be by privatising its collective form and totalising its subjective form" (237–238). Pence argues provocatively that new visual media that will augur the end of the era of cinema coincide with transformations in the ways cultural memory is formed and how such collective memory works in a social context.

The new processes of global capital accumulation, the challenges of a globalized neoliberal order to the old concepts of national sovereignty and citizenship, and the effect of the changes here predicted all results in new visual and affective forms that will more and more assume the role that cinematic representation has played in producing cultural memory. The constituency for this new form of cultural memory is perhaps not unrelated to what Negri and Hardt (2004, 100) have termed "the multitude"—which they define in as "an internally different, multiple social subject whose constitution and action is based not on an identity or unity (or, much less, indifference) but on what it has in common." As a phenomenon, cinematic memory remains a powerful cultural force in indexing an archive of images for the development of cultural memory. For the purposes of the present discussion, what is at stake is how cultural memory will be affected by the emergence of a form of social subjectivity that may be termed "the multitude," coinciding with the diversification of visual representational media away from cinematic technique to other, perhaps as yet undeveloped forms. The shifting dynamics are becoming clearer, and the trajectories lead from the unfulfilled revolutions of Iran, Tunisia, Egypt, Yemen, and Syria through to new forms of resistance and new forms of representation that the future may bring.

Best perhaps to end with the words of Syrian filmmaker Ossama Mohammad, remarking on the Syrian revolution and subsequent civil war: "Since the first moment this was a revolution of images . . . it was Syria screening itself each day" (*Agence France Press* 2014).

{ NOTES }

Introduction

1. The attribution of this quote to Wilson has been challenged, although it seems uncontroversial that he was among those who admired *Birth of a Nation* upon viewing it. However, in his study of the origins of the quote, Mark Benbow (2010, 527) sees Wilson's authorship of the phrase to be supported by the evidence, although it is more likely that he said the film was "like *teaching* history with lightning," which works just as well in the present discussion.

2. See, for example: Joshua Hirsch, *Afterimage: Film, Trauma and the Holocaust* (Philadelphia: Temple University Press, 2004), Janet Walker, *Trauma Cinema: Documenting Incest and the Holocaust* (Berkeley: University of California Press, 2005), Adam Lowenstein, *Shocking Representation: Historical Trauma, National Cinema, and the Modern Horror Film* (New York: Columbia University Press, 2005), or the uses of cinema in Cathy Caruth, *Unclaimed Experience: Trauma, Narrative, and History* (Baltimore: Johns Hopkins University Press, 1996), or in Kaja Silverman's treatments of trauma themes in cinema in her two works, *The Threshold of the Visible World* (New York: Routledge, 1996) and *Male Subjectivity at the Margins* (New York: Routledge, 1992).

Chapter 1

1. The film is similar in aspiration to Spike Lee's *Miracle at St Anna* (2008), about African American soldiers who served in the Italian theater of the Second World War, as well as George Lucas's *Red Tails* (2012). Both films expressly aimed to draw public recognition of the largely forgotten contributions of African Americans to the military efforts in the war. Neither, however, enjoyed success at the American box office, especially when compared to *Days of Glory*'s record as was one of the top grossing works French of 2006–2007. The two films by Lee and Lucas both closed at theaters after only short runs.

2. These adventuring personae are enduringly popular, as is obvious simply from reviewing the titles of biographies of some of the pioneering figures of Hollywood, such as Vaz (2005) and Moss (2011).

3. See for example, Ryan (1997) or Edwards (1991).

4. Solanas and Getino (1970–1971). Also see Gabriel (1982).

5. Rothberg (2009) offers a conceptual grounding for transcending the typically "competitive" forms of cultural memory that distinguish not only colonizer from colonized, but which increasingly divide social groups who may in different ways and from different historical circumstances be defined by their traumatic memory. While Rothberg's work focuses upon the cultural memory of the Holocaust in France during the period of the Algerian War of Independence, his paradigm of multidirectionality may find useful application in other contexts—for example the Israeli-Palestinian conflict. Other scholars

have similarly begun to address colonial histories through the paradigms of trauma studies, for example in Craps and Buelens (2008), Craps (2013), and Ifowodo (2013).

6. The terms "social trauma" and "cultural trauma" are broadly equivalent, although they arise through somewhat different genealogies. Here I use "social trauma" in part to give a greater grounding to the form of trauma I describe—one that has social implications and uses—while relying on "cultural memory" to articulate the somewhat more ephemeral processes by which a cultural notion of the past may accumulate through sedimentary textual and other influences.

7. Cultural theorists have long resisted assimilating empiricist findings in these areas. While efforts have been made to find new links between the two areas, the most often cited cultural theorists appear to be those who are most reluctant to engage with the current thinking among practitioners and clinicians in the field. Genetic and neurobiological research has introduced new questions where the clinical diagnosis of trauma (most often as part of post-traumatic stress disorder, PTSD) is concerned. For example, the author of a recent epidemiological study on PTSD, Sandro Galea (2010, 56), reports that, "our findings suggest a new biological model of PTSD, in which alteration of genes, induced by a traumatic event, changes a person's stress response and leads to the disorder."

8. For example, in his discussion of Daniel Goldhagen's *Hitler's Willing Executioners*, most of LaCapra's criticism comes only in the margins of his discussion or as voiced through intermediary critics. See LaCapra (2001), 114–141.

9. LaCapra rarely has addressed other, arguably more contested traumas—for example, the Palestinian Nakba or the Armenian genocide. His work usefully explores tensions in what may be seen as the core terrains of trauma studies—in particular the Holocaust—but by avoiding what may be more controversial he tends to treat as normative questions concerning the production of trauma discourse that fall outside of the parameters of discussions of the Holocaust, such as those of colonial or postcolonial contexts.

Chapter 2

1. "Too Late!" *Pall Mall Gazette*, February 5, 1885, p. 8.

2. "Fall of Khartoum," *The Times* (London), February 6, 1885, p. 5.

3. "London's Saturday Night," *New York Times*, February 8, 1885, p. 1.

4. "Fall of Khartoum," *Belfast News-Letter*, February 6, 1885, p. 5.

5. "Fall of Khartoum," *Lloyds Weekly Newspaper*, February 15, 1885, p. 1.

6. "The Four Feathers," *Academy and Literature*, 63, November 1, 1902, p. 468.

7. "The Four Feathers," *Academy and Literature*, 63, November 22, 1902, p. 551.

8. The term is used in both "The Four Feathers," *Athenaeum* (London) (3916), November 15, 1902, p. 647; "The Four Feathers," *Spectator*, 89 (3880), November 8, 1902, p. 708.

9. "The Four Feathers," *Saturday Review of Politics, Literature, Science and Art* 94 (2457), November 29, 1902, p. 681.

10. The romantic turn in British cultural circles far predated the setting of *The Four Feathers*, and summarizing romantic idealizations of masculinity requires a nuance and breadth beyond the immediate purview of this discussion. Nonetheless, given the contextual descriptions of Harry, I will use "romantic masculinity" as a shorthand description of the masculinity attributed to him in the book and film.

11. Speaking of his partner, Cooper (1925, xii) writes, "I cannot speak too highly of his technical ability, resourcefulness, and pluck. The chief credit of the actual making of the motion picture [*Grass*] is, without question, his."

12. This dispute is well chronicled in Raymond Schwab's monumental work *The Oriental Renaissance* (1984), in particular in his study of the image of Iran in the work of Friedrich Nietzsche.

13. Among the various alterations the film performs in adapting the novel is the change of the name Feversham to Faversham. The reason for this is mysterious, but to remain faithful to each text I use both spellings here, depending on how the name is spelled in the text I am discussing.

Chapter 4

1. See, for example, Shohat (1988).

2. See "al-Milif: al-Nakba mujaddadan" (2012).

3. For a critical assessment of the New Israeli Historians, see Beinin (2005).

4. For more on the gendering of Nakba memory, see Hammami (2003).

5. While Hawl is Iraqi by nationality, given the film's production context and topic, the film is often cited as a work of Palestinian cinema. See for example the film's inclusion on the Palestine Film Foundation website http://www.palestinefilm.org. I offer a similar rationale for selecting the film for my filmography of Palestinian cinema (Rastegar 2006, 180).

6. For a more detailed examination of the function of space and locality in Suleiman's first two feature films, see Gertz and Khleifi (2008, 171–189).

Chapter 5

1. Bourdieu's field of cultural production serves an understanding of the state-led definitions of the culture of sacred defense in a way that is more useful than comparable theoretical models, by viewing culture as series of interrelating "fields" that may be subject to legitimation by either the state or by other actors, but which are also subject to forms of contestation and resistance in struggles that involve accumulation of cultural capital by the competing actors (Bourdieu 1993, 29–73).

2. This council was later renamed Anjoman-e Sinama-ye Enqelab va Defa'-i Moqaddas (the Council on Revolutionary and Sacred Defense Cinema); Alireza Sajadpour, "Sepah ulgu-ye sarmaye gozari-ye salem dar sinama," *Chehrehha-ye Aftab*, [Mehr 1382] 2003, 52.

3. The work of Seyyed Morteza Avini remains the paradigmatic example of the marriage of documentary technique and ideological aims in line with state policy, and is definitive of sacred defense culture in its highly committed phase. Avini's documentaries—collectively called "Revayate Fath" (Tales of Victory)—present witnessing discourse through footage of front-line sacrifices set against commentary by Avini, framing the quotidian struggles of the soldiers within a discourse of metaphysical collisions between good and evil, and the search for martyrdom as a path toward God. Avini's films rarely speak of the enemy in terms of national identity, but rather posit the battle as a transcendent field of conflict where the lessons of past Shi'i martyrs are put into practice by young Iranian soldiers in an abstracted, and cosmologically dense, battlefield which

operates both as a literal front line and as an allegorical stage for performing the codes of commitment to revolutionary ideals. For more on Revayat-e Fath, see Varzi (2006), chapter 3, and Karimabadi (2011).

4. As Westmoreland (2002, 47–48) comments, "Some Lebanese filmmakers also critique the predominance of Western funding for feature films, believing that this dependence negatively dictates what gets made and how it gets made. . . . Some also critique the West's fascination with watching the Arab world at war, saying funding for films that probe into the 'civil' war is easier to come by than other themes."

5. The tension between these generations is often self-consciously acknowledged by the filmmakers themselves. In *The Glass Agency*, Hatamikia has included the character of an "artist" who is made a hostage in the travel agency, who is planning to travel to attend a festival. The character is physically and in terms of his dress very similar in appearance to the Iranian director Abbas Kiarostami, who is sharply parodied. Kiarostami perhaps represents the epitome of the prior generation of filmmakers who were pitted against younger filmmakers such as Hatamikia.

6. It is worth noting that scholars differ on the dating of *Bashu*, primarily due to the fact that the film was not released for some two or so years after its completion: Zeydabadi-Nejad (2009, 109) cites 1985, Dabashi (2001, 91) 1986, and Mottahedeh (2008, 20) 1987. The problem leads to different dates being cited in the same edited volume. In Tapper (2002), Tapper himself suggests 1988 in the introduction, but then in her chapter in the same volume, Azadeh Farahmand (2002, 105) cites a date of 1986 for the film, while in her contribution to the same work, Nasrin Rahimieh (2002, 238) cites 1985. As both Rahimieh and Mottahedeh confirm, the film was in fact completed in 1985 but was withheld from release until later due to political problems faced by Beyzai in those years. Mottahedeh cites the date of 1987 for its release, while Rahimieh cites 1988 (a distinction perhaps presented by the ambiguity that accompanies converting Iranian Hijri Shamsi dates to Gregorian ones). After reviewing a wide range of materials on the film, I have found 1987 to be the most likely date for its release. It is also worth noting that *Bashu*, while not a product of sacred defense institutions, and initially viewed skeptically by the arbiters of sacred defense culture, does feature on some subsequent lists of sacred defense filmmaking, such as in Mo'azzi Nia's study of the genre (2001, 27).

7. It is unclear if this is due to the war, or to some workplace injury; the only hint comes when Na'i asks him, "couldn't you find any other kind of work?" This statement seems to indicate the injury was not war related. However, the image of a man who has lost an arm cannot but conjure, for an Iranian audience in that period, associations with war injuries.

8. Within Lebanese cinema, for example, the genre has several entries, including *West Beirut* (1996), *In the Battlefields* (2004), and, in particular, *Zozo* (2005). Each of these films fundamentally depends upon the naïveté of its protagonist for the developments within its narrative, for it is only his or her inability to comprehend the ideological rationales of the war that is ongoing that allows for the story's development. In Hollywood, a fine example of this framing is to be found in Steven Spielberg's *Empire of the Sun* (1987), while in British cinema, John Boorman's *Hope and Glory* (1987) uses a very similar narrative approach. I have written more on the use of children in narratives of war trauma (2006a).

9. Rahimieh's (2002) analysis of the film focuses on this question. Anecdotally, as a child growing up in Shiraz during the war, I observed fairly common anti-Arab racism toward internally displaced war refugees in my school and elsewhere, often paradoxically

on the presumption that they shared an ethnic link with the "enemy." However, sacred defense rhetoric rarely made use of such prejudice, given that it made use of transcendent religious claims and not ones based upon national or ethnic difference.

10. Dabashi's (2001) discussion of the film emphasizes the ritual and mythical elements present in the work.

11. Both Rahimieh (2002) and Mottahedeh (2008, 20–48) discuss the scene at length, using rather different but not incongruent approaches. Mottahedeh's reading focuses on semiological dimensions of the work, arguing that the film must be read against "ta'ziyeh's spatial tropes."

Chapter 6

1. While not directly related to the concerns of this chapter, Jacques Derrida also relates the question of justice to his interest in the haunting effect of Marxism in the late twentieth century. As he writes in *Specters of Marx* (Derrida 1994, xix), "If I am getting ready to speak at length about ghosts, inheritance, and generations, generations of ghosts, which is to say about certain *others* who are not present, nor presently living, either to us, in us, or outside us, it is in the name of *justice*."

Chapter 7

1. Yosef (2011a, 154) also argues that the film's conclusion posits that Folman "became a bystander at traumatic events," and that the film "seeks a redemption that will release him from his moral responsibility." He joins Raya Morag in arguing that this ambition masks a more troubling question of social culpability for the Israeli role in the war generally and in the massacre of Sabra and Shatila more specifically. Morag (2013, 131) suggests that "the redemptive narrative structure . . . prevents the circumstances around the massacre to be dealt with."

{ BIBLIOGRAPHY }

"Fall of Khartoum." 1885. *Lloyds Weekly Newspaper*, February 15, 1.

"Fall of Khartoum." 1885. *Belfast News-Letter*, February 6, 5.

"Fall of Khartoum." 1885. *Times* (London), February 6, 5.

"The Four Feathers." 1902. *Academy and Literature*, 63, November 1, 468.

"The Four Feathers." 1902. *Academy and Literature*, 63, November 22, 551.

"The Four Feathers." 1902. *Athenaeum*, 3916, November 15, 647.

"The Four Feathers." 1902. *Saturday Review of Politics, Literature, Science and Art* 94 (2457), November 29, 681.

"The Four Feathers." 1902. *Spectator*, 89 (3880), November 8, 708.

"London's Saturday Night." 1885. *New York Times*, February 8, 1.

"Too Late!" *Pall Mall Gazette*, February 5, 1885. 8.

Abecassis, Michaël. 2011. "Iranian War Cinema: Between Reality and Fiction." *Iranian Studies* 44 (3): 387–394.

Abu-Remaileh, Refqa. 2008. "Palestinian Anti-Narratives in the Films of Elia Suleiman." *Arab Media & Society* 5: 1–28.

Abu Sayf, Salah. 1996. *Salah Abu Sayf: Muhawarat Hashim al-Nahhas*. Cairo: Al-Hay'a al-Misriyya al-'amma lil-kitab.

Acocella, Joan. 2002. "A Hard Case: The Life and Death of Primo Levi." *New Yorker*, June 17. http://www.newyorker.com/magazine/2002/06/17/a-hard-case.

Agence France Press. 2014. "Syrian Woman's Siege of Homs Film Gets Standing Ovation at Cannes." May 16. https://now.mmedia.me/lb/en/nowsyrialatestnews/547627-syrian-womans-siege-of- homs-film-gets-standing-ovation-at-cannes.

Alessandrini, Anthony C., ed. 1999. *Frantz Fanon: Critical Perspectives*. London: Routledge.

Alexander, Jeffrey C. 2004. "Toward a Theory of Cultural Trauma." In *Cultural Trauma and Collective Identity*, edited by Jeffrey C. Alexander, Ron Eyerman, Bernhard Giesen, Neil J. Smelser, and Piotr Sztompka, 1–30. Berkeley: University of California Press.

Alexander, Livia. 2002. "Let Me in, Let Me out, Going Places and Going Back." *Framework* 43 (2): 157–177.

Allan, Diana. 2005. "Mythologizing al-Nakba: Narratives, Collective Identity and Cultural Practice among Palestinian Refugees in Lebanon." *Oral History* 33 (1): 47–56.

"al-Milif: al-Nakba mujaddadan." 2012. *Al-Dirassat al-Filistiniyya* 89 (Winter), 37–119.

Amireh, Amal. 2003. "Between Complicity and Subversion: Body Politics in Palestinian National Narrative," *South Atlantic Quarterly* 102 (4), 747–766.

Anziska, Seth. 2012. "A Preventable Massacre." *New York Times*, September 16, A23. http://www.nytimes.com/2012/09/17/opinion/a-preventable-massacre.html? pagewanted=all&_r=0.

Armbrust, Walter. 1995. "New Cinema, Commercial Cinema, and the Modernist Tradition in Egypt." *Alif: Journal of Comparative Poetics* 15: 81–129.

Armes, Roy. 2005. *Postcolonial Images: Studies in North African Film*. Bloomington: Indiana University Press.

Armes, Roy. 2009. "Cinemas of the Maghreb," *Black Camera* 1 (1): 5–29.

Austin, Guy. 2009. "Trauma, Cinema and the Algerian War." *New Readings* 10: 18–25.

Baer, Elizabeth R., and Hester Baer. 2003. "Postmemory Envy?" *Women in German Yearbook*, 19: 75–98.

Bal, Mieke, Jonathan V. Crewe, and Leo Spitzer, eds. 1999. *Acts of Memory: Cultural Recall in the Present*. Hanover, NH: University Press of New England.

Bannerjee, Himani, Shahrzad Mojab, and Judith Whitehead. 2010. "Of Property and Propriety: The Role of Gender and Class in Imperialism and Nationalism: A Decade Later." *Comparative Studies of South Asia, Africa and the Middle East* 30 (2): 262–271.

Baron, Beth. 2005. *Egypt as a Woman: Nationalism, Gender, and Politics*. Berkeley: University of California Press.

"Bayan al-Sinima al-Jadida fi Misr (1968)." 1994. *Al-Sinima wa al-Tarikh* 3 (11): 71–76.

Beinin, Joel. 2005. "Forgetfulness for Memory: The Limits of the New Israeli History," *Journal of Palestine Studies* 34 (2): 6–23.

Benbow, Mark E. 2010. "Birth of a Quotation: Woodrow Wilson and 'Like Writing History with Lightning.'" *Journal of the Gilded Age and the Progressive Era* 9 (4): 509–533.

Bliss Cua Lim. 2001. "Spectral Times: The Ghost Film as Historical Allegory." *Positions: East Asia Cultures Critique* 9 (2): 287–329.

Booth, Marilyn. 2002. "Translator's Introduction." In *The Open Door*, edited by Latifa al-Zayyat. Cairo: American University in Cairo Press, ix–xxxi.

Bourdieu, Pierre. 1993. *The Field of Cultural Production: Essays on Art and Literature*. New York: Columbia University Press.

Bouzid, Nouri. 1995. "New Realism in Arab Cinema: The Defeat-Conscious Cinema." *Alif: Journal of Comparative Poetics* 15: 242–250.

Bowman, Paul. 2011] "Post-Cinematic Effects." *In Media Res*. August 30, 2011. http://medi-acommons.futureofthebook.org/imr/2011/08/30/post-cinematic-effects.

Bresheeth, Haim. 2007. "The Continuity of Trauma and Struggle: Recent Cinematic Representations of the Nakba." In *Nakba: Palestine, 1948, and the Claims of Memory*, edited by Ahmad Sa'di and Lila Abu Lughod, 161–190. New York: Columbia University Press.

Campbell, Ian. 2001. "Blindness to Blindness: Trauma, Vision and Political Consciousness in Ghassân Kanafânî's *Returning to Haifa*." *Journal of Arabic Literature* 32 (1): 53–73.

Caruth, Cathy. 1996. *Unclaimed Experience: Trauma, Narrative, and History*. Baltimore: Johns Hopkins University Press.

Chapman, James, and Nicholas J. Cull. 2009. *Projecting Empire: Imperialism and Popular Cinema*. London and New York: I. B. Tauris.

Chaudhuri, Shohini. 2005. *Contemporary World Cinema: Europe, the Middle East, East Asia and South Asia*. Edinburgh: Edinburgh University Press.

Chelkowski, Peter. 2002. "The Art of Revolution and War: The Role of the Graphic Arts in Iran." In *Picturing Iran: Art, Society and Revolution*, edited by Shiva Balaghi and Lynn Gumpert, 127–141. New York: I. B. Tauris.

Coly, Ayo. 2008. "Memory, History, Forgetting." *Transition* 98: 150–155.

Cooke, Miriam. 2002. "Beirut Reborn: The Political Aesthetics of Auto-Destruction." *Yale Journal of Criticism* 5 (1): 393–424.

Cooper, Merian C. 1925. *Grass*. New York: J. Putnam & Sons.

Craps, Stef, and Gert Buelens. 2008. "Postcolonial Trauma Novels." *Studies in the Novel* 40 (1–2) [special issue].

Craps, Stef. 2013. *Postcolonial Witnessing: Trauma Culture Out of Bounds.* New York: Palgrave.

Curiel, Jonathan. 2002. "Romance Meets Empire in *The Four Feathers*: Kapur Questions Britain's Imperialist Past." *San Francisco Chronicle*, September 15, 42.

Dabashi, Hamid. 2001. *Close Up Iranian Cinema: Past, Present and Future.* New York: Verso.

Dabashi, Hamid. 2006. "In Praise of Frivolity: The Cinema of Elia Suleiman." In *Dreams of a Nation: On Palestinian Cinema*, edited by Hamid Dabashi, 131–161. New York: Verso.

Dabashi, Hamid. 2007. *Masters & Masterpieces of Iranian Cinema.* Los Angeles: Mage.

Dasgupta, Susmita. 2003. "Commercial Cinema and Sociology." In *Encyclopaedia of Hindi Cinema*, edited by Gulzar, Govind Nihalani, and Saibal Chatterjee, 367–382. New Delhi: Encyclopaedia Britannica.

Davidson, John E. 1999. *Deterritorializing the New German Cinema.* Minneapolis: University of Minnesota Press.

Derrida, Jacques. 1993. *Aporias.* Translated by Thomas Dutoit. Stanford: Stanford University Press.

Derrida, Jacques. 1994. *Specters of Marx.* Translated by Peggy Kamuf. New York: Routledge.

Donadey, Anne. 2011. "Representing Gender and Sexual Trauma: Moufida Tlatli's *Silences of the Palace*." *South Central Review* 28 (1): 36–51.

Drazin, Charles. 2011. *Korda, Britain's Movie Mogul.* New York: I. B. Tauris.

Edkins, Jenny. 2003. *Trauma and the Memory of Politics.* Cambridge: Cambridge University Press.

Edwards, Elizabeth, ed. 1991. *Anthropology and Photography, 1860–1920.* New Haven: Yale University Press.

Enjelvin, Géraldine, and Nada Korac-Kakabadse. 2012. "France and the Memories of 'Others': The Case of the Harkis." *History & Memory* 24 (1): 152–177.

Esmeir, Samera. 2003. "1948: Law, History, Memory." *Social Text* 21 (2): 25–48.

Fanon, Frantz. (1963) 2007. *The Wretched of the Earth.* New York: Grove.

Farahmand, Azadeh. 2002. "Perspectives on Recent (International Acclaim for) Iranian Cinema." In *The New Iranian Cinema: Politics, Representation and Identity*, edited by Richard Tapper, 86–108. New York: I. B. Tauris.

Fisk, Robert. 1992. *Pity the Nation: Lebanon at War.* Oxford: Oxford University Press.

Foucault, Michel. 1970. *The Order of Things: An Archaeology of the Human Sciences.* New York: Pantheon.

Freud, Sigmund. (1899) 1962. "Screen Memories." In *The Standard Edition of the Complete Psychological Works of Sigmund Freud.* Vol. 3, *Early Psycho-Analytic Publications*, translated and edited by James Strachey, 301–322. London: Hogarth.

Freud, Sigmund. (1917) 1957. "Mourning and Melancholia." In *The Standard Edition of the Complete Psychological Works of Sigmund Freud.* Vol. 14, *On the History of the Psycho-Analytic Movement, Papers on Metapsychology and Other Works*, translated and edited by James Strachey, 237–258. London: Hogarth.

Gabriel, Tehsome. 1982. *Third Cinema in the Third World: The Aesthetics of Liberation.* Ann Arbor: University of Michigan Press.

Galea, Sandro. 2010. "Wired for Trauma: Altered Genes May Trigger Post-Traumatic Stress." *Columbia Magazine* (Summer): 56.

Gertz, Nurith. 2002. "Space and Gender in the New Israeli and Palestinian Cinema." *Prooftexts* 22 (1–2): 157–185.

Gertz, Nurith, and George Khleifi. 2008. *Palestinian Cinema: Landscape, Trauma and Memory.* Edinburgh: Edinburgh University Press.

Gertz, Nurith, and George Khleifi. 2011. "A Chronicle of Palestinian Cinema." In *Film in the Middle East and North Africa: Creative Dissidence*, edited by Josef Gugler, 187–197. Austin: University of Texas Press.

Ghamari-Tabrizi, Behrooz. 2009. "Memory, Mourning, Memorializing: On the Victims of the Iran-Iraq War, 1980–Present." *Radical History Review* 105: 106–121.

Giesen, Bernhard. 2004. "The Trauma of Perpetrators: The Holocaust as the Traumatic Reference of German National Identity." In *Cultural Trauma and Collective Identity*, edited by Jeffrey C. Alexander, Ron Eyerman, Bernhard Giesen, Neil J. Smelser, and Piotr Sztompka, 112–154. Berkeley: University of California Press.

Gilroy, Paul. 2004. *After Empire: Melancholia or Convivial Culture?* Abingdon, UK: Routledge.

Ginsberg, Terri, and Chris Lippard. 2010. *Historical Dictionary of Middle Eastern Cinema.* Lanham, MD: Rowman and Littlefield.

Gordon, Avery. 2008. *Ghostly Matters: Haunting and the Sociological Imagination.* 2nd ed. Minneapolis: University of Minnesota Press.

Greenberg, Jonathan D. 2005. "Generations of Memory: Remembering Partition in India/Pakistan and Israel/Palestine." *Comparative Studies of South Asia, Africa and the Middle East* 25 (1): 89–110.

Grosfoguel, Ramón. 2002. "Colonial Difference, Geopolitics of Knowledge, and Global Coloniality in the Modern/Colonial Capitalist World-System." *Review* (Fernand Braudel Center), 25 (3): 203–224.

Gulzar, Govind Nihalani, and Saibal Chatterjee, eds., 2003. *Encyclopaedia of Hindi Cinema.* New Delhi, India: Encyclopædia Britannica.

Hall, Vince. 1939. "The Four Feathers." *North American Review* 248 (1): 190–197.

Hammami, Rema. 2003. "Gender, Nakba and Nation: Palestinian Women's Presence and Absence in the Narration of 1948 Memories." *Annual Review of Women's and Gender Studies* 2: 26–41.

Haugbolle, Sune. 2005. "Public and Private Memory of the Lebanese Civil War." *Comparative Studies of South Asia, Africa and the Middle East* 25 (1): 191–203.

Herbert, Christopher. 2008. *War of No Pity: The Indian Mutiny and Victorian Trauma.* Princeton: Princeton University Press.

Herr, Ranjoo Seodu. 2003. "The Possibility of Nationalist Feminism." *Hypatia* 18 (3): 135–160.

Hill, Tom. 2011. "Staging the Sublimation of Cliché: Elia Suleiman's Silences in *The Time That Remains* (2009)." *Jerusalem Quarterly* 48: 78–90.

Hirsch, Joshua. 2004. *Afterimage: Film, Trauma and the Holocaust.* Philadelphia: Temple University Press.

Hourani, Najib. 2008. "The Militiaman Icon: Cinema, Memory, and the Lebanese Civil Wars." *CR: The New Centennial Review* 8 (2): 297–307.

Hoyle, Ben. 2010. "Thousands Protest at Cannes over Algerian Film *Hors La Loi.*" *The Times* [London], May 21.

Ifowodo, Ogaga. 2013. *History, Trauma and Healing in Postcolonial Narratives: Reconstructing Identities.* New York: Palgrave.

Jacobi, Keith. 2003. "The Malevolent 'Undead': Cross-Cultural Perspectives." In *Handbook of Death and Dying*, edited by Clifton D. Bryant, vol. 1, 96–109. Thousand Oaks, CA: Sage.

Jaher, Frederic Cople, and Blair B. Kling. 2008. "Hollywood's India: The Meaning of RKO's *Gunga Din.*" *Film & History* 38 (2): 33–44.

Jaysh, Muhammad. 2006. *Bayn Salah Abu Sayf wa Yusuf Shahin: al-ru'ya al-fikriyya al-sinama'iyya.* Al-Qahira: Markaz al-hadhara al-masriyya.

Johnson, Eboneé T., et al. 2012. "Trauma Survivorship and Disability." In *Trauma Counseling: Theories and Interventions*, edited by Lisa Lopez Levers, 116–131. New York: Springer.

Journal of Palestine Studies. 1972. "The Killing of Kanafani," 2 (1): 149.

Kanafani, Ghassan. 2000. *Palestine's Children: "Returning to Haifa" and Other Stories.* Translated by Barbara Harlow and Karen E. Riley. Boulder, CO: Lynne Rienner.

Kandiyoti, Deniz. 2003. "End of Empire: Islam, Nationalism and Women in Turkey." In *Feminist Postcolonial Theory: A Reader*, edited by Reina Lewis and Sara Mills, 263–284. New York: Routledge.

Kansteiner, Wulf. 2002. "Finding Meaning in Memory: A Methodological Critique of Collective Memory Studies." *History and Theory* 41 (2): 179–197.

Kaplan, E. Ann. 1999. "Fanon, Trauma and Cinema." In *Frantz Fanon: Critical Perspectives*, edited by Anthony C. Alessandrini, 146–158. London: Routledge.

Kaplan, E. Ann. 2005. *Trauma Culture: The Politics of Terror and Loss in Media and Literature.* New Brunswick, NJ: Rutgers University Press.

Kaplan, E. Ann, and Ban Wang. 2004. "From Traumatic Paralysis to the Force Field of Modernity." *Trauma and Cinema: Cross-Cultural Explorations*, edited by E. Ann Kaplan and Ban Wang, 1–22. Hong Kong: Hong Kong University Press.

Karimabadi, Mehrzad. 2011. "Manifesto of Martyrdom: Similarities and Differences between Avini's *Ravaayat-e Fath* [Chronicles of Victory] and more Traditional Manifestoes." *Iranian Studies* 44 (3): 381–386.

Khatib, Lina. 2007. "The Contested City: Beirut in Lebanese War Cinema." In *Visualizing the City*, edited by Alan Marcus and Dietrich Neumann, 97–110. London: Routledge.

Khatib, Lina. 2008. *Lebanese Cinema: Imagining the Civil War and Beyond.* New York: I. B. Tauris.

Khaza'i, Mohammad. [1389] 2011. "58 Film az 36 keshvar jahan dar jashnvareh film defa'-e moghaddas." *Bani Film* [26 Tir] November 26.11.

Khosronejad, Pedram, ed. 2013. *Unburied Memories: The Politics of Bodies of Sacred Defense Martyrs in Iran.* Abingdon, UK: Routledge.

Khoury, Elias. 2012. "Rethinking the Nakba." *Critical Inquiry* 38 (2): 250–266.

Kornfeld, Elizabeth Lira. 1995. "The Development of Treatment Approaches for Victims of Human Rights Violations in Chile." In *Beyond Trauma: Cultural and Societal Dynamics*, edited by Rolf J. Kleber, Charles R. Figley, and Berthold P. R. Gersons, 115–132. New York: Plenum.

Kuhn, Annette. 2002. *An Everyday Magic: Cinema and Cultural Memory.* London: I. B. Tauris.

Kuhn, Annette. 2004. "Heterotopia, Heterochronia: Place and Time in Cinema Memory." *Screen* 45 (2): 106–114.

LaCapra, Dominic. 1999. "Trauma, Absence, Loss." *Critical Inquiry* 25 (4): 696–727.

LaCapra, Dominic. 2001. *Writing History, Writing Trauma.* Baltimore: Johns Hopkins University Press.

Lang, Robert. 2014. *New Tunisian Cinema: Allegories of Resistance.* New York: Columbia University Press.

Leys, Ruth. 1994. "Traumatic Cures: Shell Shock, Janet, and the Question of Memory." *Critical Inquiry* 20 (4): 623–662.

Leys, Ruth. 2000. *Trauma: A Genealogy.* Chicago: University of Chicago Press.

Limbrick, Peter. 2009. "Playing Empire: Settler Masculinities, Adventure, and Merian C. Cooper's *The Four Feathers* (US 1929)." *Screening the Past.* http://tlweb.latrobe.edu.au/humanities/screeningthepast/26/the-four-feathers.html.

Livingston, David. 2008–2009. "Lebanese Cinema." *Film Quarterly* 62 (2): 34–43.

Lotfalian, Mazyar. 2009. "Islamic Revolution and the Circulation of Visual Culture." *Radical History Review* 105: 163–167.

Lowenstein, Adam. 2005. *Shocking Representation: Historical Trauma, National Cinema, and the Modern Horror Film.* New York: Columbia University Press.

MacKenzie, John M. 1999. "The Popular Culture of Empire in Britain." In *The Oxford History of the British Empire,* edited by Judith M. Brown and William Roger Louis, vol. 4, *The Twentieth Century,* 212–232. Oxford: Oxford University Press.

MacKenzie, Scott, ed. 2014. *Film Manifestoes and Global Cinema Cultures.* Berkeley: University of California Press.

Makarem, Amal. 2002. "Introduction" in *Dhakira lil-Ghad: Memoire pour l'avenir,* n.a., 34–43. Beirut: Editions Dar An-Nahar.

Makdisi, Saree. 1997. "Laying Claim to Beirut: Urban Narrative and Spatial Identity in the Age of Solidere." *Critical Inquiry* 23 (3): 661–705.

Makdisi, Ussama, and Paul A. Silverstein, eds. 2006. *Memory and Violence in the Middle East and North Africa.* Bloomington: Indiana University Press.

Malek, Amy. "'If You're Going to Educate 'em, You've Got to Entertain 'em Too': An Examination of Representation and Ethnography in *Grass* and *People of the Wind.*" *Iranian Studies* 44 (3): 313–325.

Marks, Laura. 2000. *The Skin of the Film: Intercultural Cinema, Embodiment and the Senses.* Durham, NC: Duke University Press.

Marks, Laura, and Lamia Joriege. 2007. "Objects of War." *Art Journal* 66 (2): 21–33.

Marquand, Robert. 2010. "Cannes Film Festival's 'Hors la Loi': How Well Does France Face Its Past in Algeria?" *Christian Science Monitor,* June 1. http://www.csmonitor.com/World/Europe/2010/0601/Cannes-Film-Festival-s-Hors-la-Loi-How-well-does-France-face-its-past-in-Algeria.

Masalha, Nur. 2008. "Remembering the Palestinian Nakba: Commemoration, Oral History and Narratives of Memory." *Holy Land Studies: A Multidisciplinary Journal* 7 (2): 123–156.

Massad, Joseph. 2006. "The Weapon of Culture: Cinema in the Palestinian National Liberation Struggle." In *Dreams of a Nation: On Palestinian Cinema,* edited by Hamid Dabashi, 32–44. New York: Verso.

Matz, Jesse. 2007. "Masculinity Amalgamated: Colonialism, Homosexuality, and Forster's Kipling." *Journal of Modern Literature* 30 (3): 31–51.

McLagan, Meg. 2008. "Introduction: Making Human Rights Claims Public." *American Anthropologist* 108 (1): 191–220.

Mehrez, Samia. 2008. *Egypt's Culture Wars: Politics and Practice*. Cairo: American University in Cairo Press.

Meisami, Julie Scott, and Paul Starkey, eds. 1998. *Encyclopedia of Arabic Literature*. 2 volumes. London: Routledge.

Mitchell, W. J. Thomas. 1994. *Picture Theory: Essays on Verbal and Visual Representation*. Chicago: University of Chicago Press.

Mirzoeff, Nicholas. 2011. *The Right to Look: A Counterhistory of Visuality*. Durham, NC: Duke University Press.

Mo'azzi-Nia, Hossein. 2011. "Chand nokte dar morede hamzisti-ye sinama-ye Iran va sinama-ye defa'-i moghaddas." *Mahname-ye naghd-e film* 7: Shahrivar 1380 [August 2001] 27–29.

Morag, Raya. 2013. *Waltzing With Bashir: Perpetrator Trauma and Cinema*. New York: I. B. Tauris.

Moss, Marilyn Ann. 2011. *Raoul Walsh: The True Adventures of Hollywood's Legendary Director*. Kensington: University Press of Kentucky.

Mosteghasi, Sa'id. 1380 [2001]. "Janr-e sinama-ye defa'-i moghaddas dar Iran." *Farabi* 11 (42–43): 147–155.

Mottahedeh, Negar. 2008. *Displaced Allegories: Post-Revolutionary Iranian Cinema*. Durham, NC: Duke University Press.

Mowitt, John. 2000. "Trauma Envy." *Cultural Critique* 46: 272–297.

Musa, Saleh. 1963. "Al-Bab al-maftuh." *Sabah al-Khayr*, October 17 (1406): 38–39.

Nagel, Joane. 1998. "Masculinity and Nationalism: Gender and Sexuality in the Making of Nations." *Ethnic and Racial Studies* 21 (2): 242–269.

Negri, Antonio, and Michael Hart. 2004. *Multitude: War and Democracy in the Age of Empire*. New York: Penguin.

Negri, Antonio, and Max Henninger. 2007. "Art and Culture in the Age of Empire and the Time of the Multitudes." *SubStance* 36 (1): 47–55.

Nicoll, Fergus. 2004. *The Mahdi of Sudan and the Death of General Gordon*. Stroud, UK: Sutton.

Norindr, Panivong. 2009. "Incorporating Indigenous Soldiers in the Space of the French Nation: Rachid Bouchareb's *Indigènes*." *Yale French Studies* 115: 126–140.

Norris, Margot. 1998. "Modernism and Vietnam: Francis Ford Coppola's *Apocalypse Now*." *Modern Fiction Studies* 44 (3): 730–766.

Pappé, Ilan. 2011. *The Forgotten Palestinians: A History of the Palestinians in Israel*. New Haven: Yale University Press.

Partovi, Pedram. 2008. "Martyrdom and the 'Good Life' in the Iranian Cinema of Sacred Defense." *Comparative Studies of South Asia, Africa and the Middle East* 28 (3): 513–532.

Pence, Jeffrey. 2003. "Postcinema/Postmemory." In *Memory and Popular Film*, edited by Paul Grainge, 237–254. Manchester, UK: Manchester University Press.

Perugini, Nicola, and Francesco Zucconi. 2012. "False Syllogisms, Troublesome Combinations and Primo Levi's Political Positioning on Israel and Palestine." *Open Democracy*,

August 23. https://www.opendemocracy.net/nicola-perugini-francesco-zucconi/false-syllogisms-troublesome-combinations- and-primo-levi's- politic.

Prime, Rebecca. 2006. "Living Dangerously: The Adventures of Merian C. Cooper, Creator of *King Kong*." *Film Quarterly* 60 (2): 63–64.

Radstone, Susannah. 2007. "Trauma Theory: Contexts, Politics, Ethics." *Paragraph* 30 (1): 9–29.

Rahimieh, Nasrin. 2002. "Marking Gender and Difference in the Myth of the Nation: A Post-Revolutionary Iranian Film." In *The New Iranian Cinema: Politics, Representation and Identity*, edited by Richard Tapper, 238–253. New York: I. B. Tauris.

Rahmani, Zabihollah. 2008 [Azar 1387]. "Filmsazi baraye defa'-e moghaddas tofigh ast: Goft o gou ba Abolqasem Talebi, filmsaz va rooznameh negar." *Soureh* 40: 42–51.

Ramachandran, Naman. 2003. "The Four Feathers," *Sight and Sound* 13 (9): 48, 50.

Rastegar, Kamran. 2006a. "Trauma and Maturation in Women's War Narratives: The Eye of the Mirror and Cracking India." *Journal of Middle East Women's Studies*. 2 (3): 22–47.

Rastegar, Kamran. 2006b. "Filmography." In *Dreams of a Nation: On Palestinian Cinema*, edited by Hamid Dabashi, 179–200. New York: Verso.

Rastegar, Kamran. 2010. "The Glass Agency: Iranian War Veterans As Heroes or Traitors?" In *Traitors: Suspicion, Intimacy, and the Ethics of State-Building*, edited by Sharika Thirangama and Tobias Kelly, 188–199. Philadelphia: University of Pennsylvania Press.

Rastegar, Kamran. 2013. "Sawwaru, Waynkum? Human Rights and Social Trauma in Waltz With Bashir." *College Literature* 40 (3): 60–80.

Reid, Donald. 2005. "Re-viewing *The Battle of Algiers* with Germaine Tillion." *History Workshop Journal* 60, 93–115.

Ricoeur, Paul. 2004. *History, Memory, Forgetting*. Chicago: University of Chicago Press.

Rose, Jacqueline. 2011. *Proust among the Nations: From Dreyfus to the Middle East*. Chicago: University of Chicago Press.

Rothberg, Michael. 2009. *Multidirectional Memory: Remembering the Holocaust in the Age of Decolonization*. Stanford: Stanford University Press.

Rowe, John Carlos. 1986. "Eye-witness: Documentary Styles in the American Representations of Vietnam." *Cultural Critique* 3: 126–150.

Ryan, James R. 1997. *Picturing Empire: Photography and the Visualization of the British Empire*. Chicago: Chicago University Press.

Sadek, Walid. 2007. "Place at Last." *Art Journal* 66 (2): 34–47.

Sa'di, Ahmad H., and Lila Abu-Lughod. 2007. *Nakba: Palestine, 1948, and the Claims of Memory*. New York: Columbia University Press.

Sa'id, Ehsan. 2002. *Surat al-mar'a al-misriya fi sinima al-tis'iniyat*. Alexandra: Maktabat al-Iskandariyya.

Said, Edward. 1993. *Culture and Imperialism*. New York: Vintage.

Said, Edward. 2000. "Invention, Memory, and Place." *Critical Inquiry* 26 (2): 175–192.

Said, Edward. 2001. *Reflections on Exile*. Cambridge, MA: Harvard University Press.

Sajadpour, Alireza. 2003. "Sepah ulgu-ye sarmaye gozari-ye salem dar sinama." *Chehrehha-ye Aftab*, [Mehr 1382] 52.

Sandford, Alasdair. "French Film Aims to Unite Nation," *BBC News*, 27 September, 2006. Web. 11 June 2010.

Sarlo, Beatriz. 2003. "Post-Benjaminian." In *Mapping Benjamin: The Work of Art in the Digital Age*, edited by Hans Ulrich Gumbrecht and Michael Marrinan, 301–310. Stanford: Stanford University Press.

Schivelbusch, Wolfgang. 2003. *Culture of Defeat: On National Trauma, Mourning, and Recovery*. New York: Metropolitan.

Schochat, Ella. 1983. "Egypt: Cinema and Revolution." *Critical Arts: South-North Cultural and Media Studies* 2 (4): 22–32.

Shafik, Viola. 2007. *Arab Cinema: History and Cultural Identity*. Revised edition. Cairo: American University in Cairo Press.

Shah, Meerah. 2007. "'A Different Kind of Memory': An Interview with Zochrot." *Middle East Report* 244: 34–38.

Shail, Robert. 2007. *British Film Directors: A Critical Guide*. Edinburgh: Edinburgh University Press.

Sharpe, Jenny. 1994. "The Unspeakable Limits of Rape: Colonial Violence and Counter-Insurgency." In *Colonial Discourse and Post-Colonial Theory: A Reader*, edited by Patrick Williams and Laura Chrisman, 221–243. New York: Columbia University Press.

Shaviro, Steven. 2010. *Post Cinematic Affect*, London: Zero.

Sherzer, Dina. 2000. "Remembrance of Things Past: *Les Silences du palais* by Moufida Tlatli." *South Central Review* 17 (3): 50–59.

Shohat, Ella. 1988. "Sephardim in Israel: Zionism from the Standpoint of its Jewish Victims." *Social Text* 19–20: 1–35.

Siegneurie, Ken. 2011. *Standing by the Ruins: Elegiac Humanism in Wartime and Postwar Lebanon*. New York: Fordham University Press.

Silverman, Kaja. 1992. *Male Subjectivity at the Margins*. New York: Routledge.

Silverman, Kaja. 1996. *The Threshold of the Visible World*. New York: Routledge.

Slavin, David Henry. 1997."French Cinema's Other First Wave: Political and Racial Economies of "Cinéma colonial," 1918 to 1934." *Cinema Journal* 37 (1): 23–46.

Slavin, David Henry. 2001. *Colonial Cinema and Imperial France, 1919–1939: White Blind Spots, Male Fantasies, Settler Myths*. Baltimore: Johns Hopkins University Press.

Slawy-Sutton, Catherine. 2002. "*Outremer* and *The Silences of the Palace*: Feminist Allegories of Two Countries in Transition." *Pacific Coast Philology* 37: 85–104.

Solanas, Fernando, and James Roy MacBean. 1970–1971. "Fernando Solanas: An Interview." *Film Quarterly* 24 (1): 37–43.

Solanas, Fernando, and Octavio Getino. 1970–1971. "Toward a Third Cinema." *Cineaste* 4 (3): 1–10.

Starks, Lisa S. 2002. "'Remember Me': Psychoanalysis, Cinema, and the Crisis of Modernity." *Shakespeare Quarterly* 53 (2): 181–200.

Stewart, Garrett. 2010. "Screen Memory in *Waltz with Bashir*." *Film Quarterly* 63 (3): 58–62.

Suleiman, Elia. 2000. "A Cinema of Nowhere." *Journal of Palestine Studies* 29 (2): 95–101.

Sztompka, Piotr. 2000. "Cultural Trauma: The Other Face of Social Change." *European Journal of Social Theory* 3 (4): 449–466.

Tabori, Paul. 1959. *Alexander Korda*.

Talebi, Shahla. 2013. "From the Light of the Eyes to the Eyes of the Power: State and Dissident Martyrs in Post-Revolutionary Iran." In *Unburied Memories: The Politics of Bodies of Sacred Defense Martyrs in Iran*, edited by Pedram Khosronejad, 120–147. Abingdon, UK: Routledge.

Tapper, Richard, ed. 2002. *The New Iranian Cinema: Politics, Representation and Identity*. New York: I. B. Tauris.

Telmissany, May. 2010. "Displacement and Memory: Visual Narratives of *al-Shatat* in Michel Khleifi's Films." *Comparative Studies of South Asia, Africa and the Middle East* 30 (1): 69–84.

Thénault, Sylvie. 2007. "Indigènes, un film contre l'oubli." *Vingtième Siècle: Revue d'histoire* 93: 205–219.

Thompson, Elizabeth. 2003. "Public and Private in Middle Eastern Women's History." *Journal of Women's History* 15 (1): 52–69.

Toufic, Jalal. 2003. *Vampires: An Uneasy Essay on the Undead in Film*. Sausalito, CA: Post-Apollo.

Van de Peer, Stefanie. 2010. "Selma Baccar's *Fatma 1975*: At the Crossroads between Third Cinema and New Arab Cinema." *French Forum* 35 (2–3): 17–35.

Varzi, Roxanne. 2006. *Warring Souls: Youth, Media, and Martyrdom in Post-Revolution Iran*. Durham, NC: Duke University Press.

Vaz, Mark. 2005. *Living Dangerously: The Adventures of Merian C. Cooper, Creator of King Kong*. New York: Villard.

Walker, Janet. 2005. *Trauma Cinema: Documenting Incest and the Holocaust*. Berkeley: University of California Press.

Wehrey, Frederic, et al. 2009. *The Rise of the Pasdaran: Assessing the Domestic Role of Iran's Islamic Revolutionary Guards Corps*. Santa Monica, CA: Rand.

Weissbrod, Rachel. 1999. "*Exodus* as a Zionist Melodrama." *Israel Studies* 4 (1): 129–152.

Weschler, Lawrence. 2005. "Valkyries over Iraq: The Trouble with War Movies." *Harpers Magazine*, November, 65–77.

Westmoreland, Mark. 2002. "Cinematic Dreaming: On Phantom Poetics and the Longing for a Lebanese National Cinema." *Text, Practice, Performance* 4: 33–50.

Westmoreland, Mark. 2009. "Post-Orientalist Aesthetics: Experimental Film and Video in Lebanon." *Invisible Culture* 13: 37–57. https://www.rochester.edu/in_visible_culture/Issue_13_/pdf/mwestmoreland.pdf.

Westmoreland, Mark. 2010. "Catastrophic Subjectivity: Representing Lebanon's Undead." *Alif: Journal of Comparative Poetics* 30: 176–210.

Wilson-Goldie, Kaelen. 2007. "The War Works: Videos under Siege, Online and in the Aftermath, Again." *Art Journal* 66 (2): 68–82.

Woodhall, Winifred. 2003. "Unveiling Algeria." In *Feminist Postcolonial Theory: A Reader*, edited by Reina Lewis and Sara Mills, 567–585. New York: Routledge.

Yosef, Raz. 2011a. *The Politics of Loss and Trauma in Contemporary Israeli Cinema*. New York: Routledge.

Yosef, Raz. 2011b. "Traces of War: Memory, Trauma and the Archive in Joseph Cedar's *Beaufort*." *Cinema Journal* 50 (2): 61–83.

Zayzafoon, Lamia Ben Youssef. 2007. "Memory as Allegory: The Spectre of Incest and the (Re)naming of the Father in Moufida Tlatli's *The Silences of the Palace* (1994)." *Critical Arts* 21 (1): 47–67.

Zeydabadi-Nejad, Saeed. 2009. *The Politics of Iranian Cinema: Film and Society in the Islamic Republic*. London: Routledge.

Žižek, Slavoj. 2000. "Melancholy and the Act," *Critical Inquiry* 26 (4): 657–681.

al-Zubaydi, Qays. 2006. *Filastin fi al-Sinama*. Beirut: Mu'assisat al-Dirasat al-Filistiniyya.

INDEX

77122619R00150

Made in the USA
Columbia, SC
29 September 2019